For the Sake
OF
HEAVEN
AND
EARTH

The publication of this book
was made possible
by a grant from the
Harold Grinspoon Foundation
lovingly dedicated
in the memory of
J. J. Greenberg
who was
an incredible human being
whose life
was lost prematurely

For the Sake OF HEAVEN AND EARTH

The New Encounter between Judaism and Christianity

IRVING GREENBERG

5764 · 2004
The Jewish Publication Society
Philadelphia

The Jewish Publication Society
2100 Arch Street
Philadelphia, PA 19103

Design and Composition by Book Design Studio

Manufactured in the United States of America

04 05 06 07 08 09 10   10 9 8 7 6 5 4 3 2 1

Library of Congress Cataloging-in-Publication Data
Greenberg, Irving, 1933-
  For the sake of heaven and earth : the new encounter between Judaism and Christianity /
Irving Greenberg.— 1st ed.
    p. cm.
  Includes index.
  ISBN 0-8276-0807-1
  1. Judaism—Relations—Christianity—1945- 2. Christianity and other religions—Judaism—
1945- 3. Covenants—Religious aspects—Judaism. I. Title.
  BM535.G73 2004
  296.3'96—dc22
                            2004006651

To the Memory of our beloved Son
Jonathan Joseph (J. J.) Greenberg, (ז״ל)
Who taught us every day how to respect every person as
the image of God and to accept and affirm all people
in their distinctive religious places

Contents

vii

Preface

This volume began as a collection of my past essays on a variety of topics; it morphed into a book on the new encounter between Judaism and Christianity. For this I owe a great debt of gratitude to Dr. Ellen Frankel, editor-in-chief of The Jewish Publication Society, who virtually midwifed this book. Not only did she initiate a volume of selected essays, but she also identified, midcourse, the presence of a work focused solely on the subject of Jewish-Christian relations, embedded within the larger collection. Further, through her creativity and imagination, she conceived of this book consisting of three new writings on the subject along with the previously published essays gathered in this volume. She also skillfully edited the new essays.

The collected essays were written over the course of four decades. They are published in chronological order so as to give the reader a picture of the evolution of my thinking. I must confess that in reading them all together, the shifts are striking even to me. To preserve the record accurately, the essays have been edited slightly, and then only to eliminate duplication or confusion as to meaning. The single exception is the essay "Covenants of Redemption" (2000), to which I added a new section regarding a Jewish perspective on Jesus as a messiah.

I am also grateful to Carol Hupping, who was a partner to Ellen in much of the process, and whose strong editorial skills have helped to shape the book further. I also thank Emily Law for her skillful copyediting. Since most of the original essays were scattered over the course of four decades in a variety of publications, some obscure, I welcome the opportunity to bring them together in the hope that in tandem with the new material they will be read and critiqued by a wider audience.

I want to express my gratitude to many others, particularly those who worked directly on this project. Daniel Septimus volunteered to edit the collected essays, and pressed me to rescue them from oblivion by getting them republished. He also edited the major new essay, "Covenantal Partners in a Postmodern World," and prepared the fine study guide for this book. I thank Rachel Levine, my invaluable program assistant at Jewish Life Network, who carried out countless services, from research to enabling, always intelligently and diligently; Susan Weinblatt, who makes possible all my work, tirelessly and graciously; Seth Skolnick, who typed endless versions, accurately deciphering my illegible hieroglyphics; and Stacy Merkel, who began this same task several years ago. Erica Coleman backed all these efforts with good judgment and discretion.

My gratitude goes to others who have enabled my efforts over the years. Michael Steinhardt has been a true partner, inspiring and goading all that I do professionally; at the same time, Michael and his wife, Judy, have become dear friends in our family's life. My colleagues at Jewish Life Network—first and foremost my loving, devoted, exemplary son, J. J., of blessed memory; David Gedzelman; Felicia Herman; Shira Hutt; Bill Robinson; Leah Strigler; and, not least, Eli Valley—have been a helpful, discriminating audience and an important source of feedback. Several philanthropic partners—I want to single out Harold Grinspoon and Diane Troderman, and Lynn Schusterman in particular, and their professional representatives Sandy Cardin, Joanna Ballantine, Galina Vromen, and Jeremy Pava—have become sustaining friends. They have made my life easier and more fruitful, giving me the opportunity and a clearer mind to work on theological and ideological issues. This is true as well for Shimshon Shoshani and Gidi Mark of birthright israel, and Joshua Elkin and Naava Frank of the Partnership for Excellence in Jewish Education. The professional excellence and personal friendship of all of these colleagues inspire me with the possibilities of Jewish renaissance; in turn, these developments have lifted my conception of what Judaism can do theologically. Harold and Diane, whose friendship has been a special blessing of the past decade, further expressed their caring in underwriting this volume for The Jewish Publication Society. I thank them for all that they do for Blu and me.

Over the course of 40 years, there have been many who have inspired me and influenced my thinking on the subject at hand. My gratitude to each of them has not lessened with time. In the opening essay, I acknowledge their individual contributions; here I offer general thanks to all of them. I offer special thanks to James Carroll and to Professors Mary Boys, David Novak, Michael Novak, and Krister Stendahl, who graciously made time to write reflections for inclusion in this book despite their enormous workloads and responsibilities. I also thank Dr. Steven Bayme, director of the Department of Contemporary Jewish Life of the American Jewish Committee, for a most insightful reading and critique of the manuscript.

My wife, Blu, is, as always, my confidante, my first and last reader, my critic and editor, as well as my rock and refuge. Our children and their spouses, Moshe and Abbie, David and Mindy, Deborah and Jonathan, and Goody and Eric, have been unfailing in their love, solidarity, and encouragement throughout the years, and never more so than during this darkest period of our lives together.

In all candor, I feel some trepidation in publishing this book. It is no small responsibility to go beyond the established consensus of the traditional Jewish views on Christianity, and I do not take the step lightly. However, awareness of the extraordinary Christian efforts at self-purification vis-à-vis Judaism after the Holocaust and encounter with the religious power and ethical contributions of Christianity have evoked in me the recognition that Christians seek to worship the same God and to perfect the same world that Jews do. Furthermore, acts of love and repentance deserve to be reciprocated. While I acknowledge and respect the inherited traditional views as justified in their context, I am convinced that moving forward in a reimagined relationship is this generation's *shlichut* (mission). This is what God wants and humnity needs of us now. Still I fear that people pursuing the path of assimilation may exploit the closeness and partnership between the two religions, which I advocate, to justify religious syncretism or even intermarriage. Lower religious standards will only damage Judaism's (and Christianity's) capacity to function in an open society. Similarly, I fear that traditionalists who oppose my views on Jewish religious development may again exploit the avant-garde positions in this book to inflame opposition and damage the credibility of my teaching.

Nevertheless, I proceed, trusting in the goodwill of most Jews and Christians who yearn for a better world and who will deal with my thinking with integrity and compassion. And should my views have negative fallout, I throw myself on the mercies of the divine court and of the God whose kingdom I seek to bring closer. The world so much needs healing. I hope that in some small way this book will help those who labor to overcome past enmity between the two faiths and thus open the door to cooperation and partnership for the sake of perfecting the world—the original and unfinished mission of both faiths.

Irving Greenberg
Summer 2004

Acknowledgments

I thank these publishers for their kind permission to reprint the following essays in this book:

"The New Encounter of Judaism and Christianity," reprinted from *Barat Review*, vol. 3, no. 2 (June 1967), pp. 113–125.

"New Revelations and New Patterns in the Relationship of Judaism and Christianity," reprinted from *Journal of Ecumenical Studies*, vol. 16, no. 2 (Spring 1979), pp. 249–267.

"The Relationship of Judaism and Christianity: Toward a New Organic Model," reprinted from *Twenty Years of Jewish/Catholic Relations*, eds. Eugene Fisher, James Rudin, and Marc Tanenbaum, (NY: Paulist Press, 1986), pp. 191–211.

"Judaism and Christianity: Their Respective Roles in the Divine Strategy of Redemption," reprinted from *Visions Of The Other: Jewish and Christian Theologians Assess the Dialogue*, ed. Eugene J. Fisher (NY: Paulist Press, 1994), pp. 7–27.

"Covenantal Pluralism," reprinted from *Journal of Ecumenical Studies*, vol. 34, no. 3 (Summer 1997), pp. 425–436.

"Pluralism and Partnership," reprinted from *Unity without Uniformity: The Challenge of Pluralism*, Martin Buber House Publication Number 26 (International Council of Christians and Jews, Spring 1999), pp. 68–81.

ACKNOWLEDGMENTS

"Judaism and Christianity: Covenants of Redemption," reprinted from *Christianity in Jewish Terms*, eds. Tikva Frymer-Kensky, David Novak, Peter Ochs, David Fox Sandmel and Michael A. Signer (Boulder, CO: Westview Press, 2000), pp. 141–158.

Part One

LOOKING FORWARD

On the Road to a New Encounter between Judaism and Christianity: A Personal Journey

Almost 2000 years ago, Judaism and nascent Christianity separated from each other. The two communities set out on very different journeys through history, guided by the star of a parallel policy: hear no good, see no good, and speak no good of each other. Important Christian canonical texts portrayed Judaism as a religion that had no right to exist; Jewish faith was a once valid, now spiritually bankrupt creed, repudiated by God. Great Jewish rabbis defined Christianity as a faith founded on folly, whose dogmas violently twisted classical Jewish concepts into a not-to-be-recognized form of idolatry.* The church was viewed as a bastard offspring (a medieval polemicist would say: the offspring of a bastard) that grew up and became big and violent enough to abuse its parent unmercifully.

Yet in the past century, both religions have begun a new encounter with each other. Every passing decade reveals that this process is offering both faiths a true historical rarity: a second chance to connect and thus an opportunity to re-vision themselves. I believe that by responding openly with honesty, both communities will discover that God has given them an opportunity to renew the purpose of their sacred existence on earth. The current cultural

---

* In the medieval period, Rabbi Menachem HaMeiri, a leading Talmudist in Provence, France, defined Christians (and Muslims) as "nations guided [or restricted–IG] by the ways of religion" who "recognize the Godhead." Therefore, they are *not* idolaters. He also wrote that "they believe in God's existence, unity, and power, although they misconceive some points according to our belief." *Beth HaBehira on Avodah Zarah*, A. Schreiber edition, p. 46, and *Beth HaBehira on Gittin*, K. Schlesinger edition, p. 246, cited in Jacob Katz, *Exclusiveness and Tolerance* (New York: Oxford University Press, 1961), pp. 115, 121. However, Meiri's views remained a distinctively minority view down to this day.

situation is no less than a call to re-imagine the mission of the people Israel to be "a holy nation" and to reconfigure two faith communities' respective roles as the people of God.

The new encounter was set in motion by the interacting influences of three major spiritual currents: the magnetism of modern culture with its strong liberalizing and universalist elements; the stunning impact of the Holocaust, which has shattered religious paradigms and re-fused them; and the galvanizing rebirth of the State of Israel. The reestablishment of sovereignty brings the Jewish people full circle, back into making history as a nation, and tests Israelite faith in relation to others. The newborn state brings Christians to direct encounter with the ongoing life of the Jewish people; the renaissance of the earthly Jerusalem compels Christianity to confront a living, alternative fulfillment to the prophetic promises in Hebrew Scriptures. The dominant Christian theological interpretation of Scriptures of the past two millennia cannot account for this development and must be replaced. But in the past century, the classic Rabbinic tradition's explanation of the operation of history has also come up short in the face of unprecedented destruction and a redemption of biblical scope. Rethinking the logic of both faiths opens the door to new mutual relationships.

A PERSONAL JOURNEY

My personal journey into a reconsideration of the connection of Judaism and Christianity began in 1961, with a year in Israel that changed my life forever. I had grown up in an American Jewish immigrant home, tinged with my parents' memories of the tensions between Jews and Christians in the old country. The potential alienation from Christians, however, was tempered by my parents' natural liberality of spirit, their more positive experiences with American non-Jews, and the all-pervasive spirit of tolerance and respect for others, which we identified with the longed-for imprimatur of Americanization.

Perhaps I unthinkingly absorbed an even more positive foundation. I went to a secular college after 12 years of intensive Jewish religious education and a lifetime cocooned within a learned, observant family environment. At Brooklyn College, my Orthodoxy ran into a series of intellectual/cultural challenges: in science and religion (the clash between geology and evolution and my early training in literalist faith), in history and tradition (the conflict of critical methods with the claims of absolute authority and eternal truths taught in advanced yeshivah studies), and so on. I was simultaneously attending a rabbinical seminary whose teachers and students were refugees and/or survivors of the *Shoah*. The fire of their living tradition warmed me and sustained me in my crises of faith, but they had no cultural clue as to how to deal with the philosophical challenges.

As I searched for religious answers, it seemed to me that many of the liberal Christian writings that I encountered solved the problems by accepting the conclusions of the modern positions. But that way undermined many claims of the tradition, whereas I found my tradition still emotionally compelling and religiously moving. However, I found numerous Protestant neo-Orthodox writers who yielded up fundamentalist literalism but restated the central claims of the faith with greater sweep and evocative power than before. I soon learned to read their books "Jewishly." Mostly, in my theological neediness and naïveté, I simply translated the frequently appearing word "Christ" as God. Ninety percent of the time, this stratagem worked. Their sophisticated approach gave the tools and vocabulary to articulate an intellectually credible version of Jewish Orthodoxy for myself.

Of those Protestant neo-Orthodox thinkers, none was personally more powerful and more influential than Reinhold Niebuhr, whose dialectical thinking was eye-opening. His approaches illuminated and broadened religious consciousness and launched a thousand insights into Jewish texts. A few years later, I would meet Rabbi Joseph B. Soloveitchik and be profoundly stimulated by his dialectical readings of Judaism. As I reflect back now, the realization dawns that Niebuhr prepared me for Soloveitchik even as Soloveitchik was shaped by his encounter with the neo-Protestant thinkers whose names and writings fill the footnotes of his classic theological masterwork, *Halakhic Man*. Still, while in college, I did not reflect on my attitude toward Christianity as a religion; on the whole, I remained mildly dismissive of the faith as practiced and remembered that its practitioners had not treated Jews well historically.

CONFRONTING THE HOLOCAUST

In 1961, all my religious positions blew up in the course of an explosive confrontation with the Holocaust. I went to Israel with my wife, Blu, and our newly born first child, Moshe, to serve as a Fulbright visiting lecturer in American history at Tel Aviv University. Blu and I decided to live in Jerusalem because, like other diaspora Orthodox Jews, we were uniquely engaged with that city. Jerusalem was the place toward which we prayed daily. Jerusalem was the embodiment of the religious, history-suffused contemporary land of Israel that we fantasized from afar. The week we arrived in the capital was the last week of the Eichmann trial, and an acquaintance offered to help me gain admission to the trial. I declined because we were not settled in yet. Honestly, such a direct encounter with the *Shoah* was not my highest priority.

Without talking about the Holocaust openly, my parents had communicated in muffled—but deep—ways that something terrible had happened. My mother had lost five of her seven brothers; all five had stayed behind in Poland, together with their entire families, just as my father had lost one sister and her family who did not come to this country. I have dim memories, from World War II and after, of my mother crying in her room, away from the children—but we did not talk about the catastrophe openly. As a Zionist teenager, I was haunted by the abandonment of the Jews and stirred by the desire of the survivors to come to Israel, but those feelings were never translated into a force in my religious life.

Within a few weeks after passing up a chance to attend the Eichmann trial, I was caught up in a reading frenzy about the Holocaust. Soon the encounter with the *Shoah* took over my days and nights. I went to Tel Aviv two days a week for my American history seminars; other than the hours in which I prepared for classes, I spent all my time reading about the Holocaust. At first, the reading was done at the Hebrew University library; then, increasingly, my time was spent at Yad Vashem. Yad Vashem was dowdy, neglected, and poorly organized. Books were frequently missing or off the shelves. In the winter, the building was cold; but the chill in my soul was icier. The grip of death and destruction penetrated and froze me to the bone. Shock followed shock. Outrage, humiliation, and fear took over, and soon my religious life was invaded by tormenting doubts and moral revulsion. How could God have allowed this to happen? Where was God? The events seemed to make a mockery of the prayers I had mouthed all of my life—and of all the hopes, expectations, and norms in which I had always been so firmly and happily ensconced. I was drowning religiously. By the late 1960s, with the publication of such works as Arthur Morse's *While Six Million Died*, it became obvious that the United States had abandoned and betrayed the European Jews. As for Americanization, I recoiled from my infatuation with American history and culture and with Franklin D. Roosevelt, the great liberal revered in my childhood home.

I had always been a good boy and dutiful son. Whatever adolescent rebellion my brother and I expressed toward my parents, I was careful not to fail to deliver A grades and good report cards. In this same spirit, in the encounter with the *Shoah*, I continued to observe *halakhah*, although the religious questions now took over my life. There were mornings when I would put on my tefillin and then sit there, overwhelmed by horrifying sights and disturbing sounds from *Shoah* sources that flashed through my mind, unable to recite the words of the siddur. The only relief from desolation was to go home nightly to my wife. The streets of Jerusalem, teeming with life, were a stunning, almost surreal contradiction to the death that reigned at Yad Vashem. Then I would encounter our newborn son, Moshe. Every day, he grew; he responded more; he crawled. He was happy to see me, to smile and play and giggle at my tickling.

This unbelievable contrast of limitless death and burgeoning life was burned into my mind daily. Days of helpless despair sequenced into nights of joy. Hours of sitting, enveloped by consuming, all-pervasive anxiety and fear of what the next moment would bring, were followed by walks through the peaceful, secure, unafraid streets of Jerusalem. In the end, my wife's loving presence preserved me from madness, and a living Israel saved me from death of the soul. Although I since have moved on to other stages of Holocaust consciousness and religious response, there is a piece of my soul that is permanently fixed in this relentless, locked embrace of the life force and the death force. In my mind, the faith-annihilating *Shoah* and the faith-renewing restoration of Israel are twinned forever. They ceaselessly wrestle for dominance; just when the message of one appears to be triumphant, it is challenged and even overthrown by the phenomenon of the other in an endless, recurring cycle.

As the year came to an end, all these undigested thoughts and experiences threw me into great turmoil. I wanted to move from my professional focus on American and modern intellectual history to some more Jewish activity, but had no idea how to do this. At that time, an academic career in Jewish studies was rare and Holocaust studies almost nonexistent. I also knew that I wanted to deal with the problems posed by Christian religious teachings.

CHRISTIANITY'S PROBLEM—AND MINE

In the course of reading during 1961–1962, I became aware of the pathological images of Jewry and Judaism that Christianity had injected into the bloodstream of European culture. The evidence convinced me that Christian anti-Semitism provided a foundation for the Nazi isolation of and assault on the Jews. I was furious but also frightened. I sensed that there was a real danger of a recurrence of the Holocaust, and I feared for my future children and grandchildren.

A decade or so later, in 1973, Professor Yosef Yerushalmi offered some mitigating factors in judging Christian guilt. He argued that in light of the Nazi genocide, Jews should come to a better appreciation of Christianity. True,

Christian faith had spread hostility toward Judaism for 2,000 years. Christians had persecuted, isolated, expelled, and even engaged in murderous violence toward Jews. However, Christian derogatory teachings were always counterbalanced by some affirmation. Although Judaism was portrayed as a fossilized, soulless religion, it was also credited with having been God's original and true revelation to humanity. While Jews were to be humiliated, they were to be protected—albeit kept in inferior status—as hostile witnesses to the true faith. Thus they would be preserved until the end of days—when they would see the light and become Christians. By contrast, Nazi racist anti-Semitism incorporated hatred without limit and acted out in an attempted total genocide. At that time, I did not fully appreciate Yerushalmi's point that modern anti-Semitism, unlike its earlier incarnations, was more total in nature and far more dangerous to Jews. Later, I came to understand his implicit teaching that in the *Shoah* one could discern pathologies with unlimited murderous potential that lurked within modernity. Over the next decade, I concluded that Jews should reconsider their classification of Christianity as the enemy and rather should consider allying with the Christian faith to check modernity's excesses.

But back in 1961, Christian liturgy, Scriptures, and teaching were still injecting poisonous anti-Jewish images into humanity's mind. Blu and I decided that upon our return to America we would join the Jewish-Christian dialogue. Ecumenism was becoming more visible and more important as the spirit of the sixties—a remarkable opening up of cultures and blossoming of utopian hopes for peace and world transformation—burst forth. Personally I was more motivated by anger than by hope. Mainly we were driven by prudential concerns—stop the hatred and the killing—rather than by a loving opening to Christian faith. I swept down on the dialogue like an avenging angel, demanding that Christians cease spreading evil and demeaning images of my faith. Blu and I frequently smote Christian dialogue partners with the rod of our Holocaust anger, warning that the alternative to repentance and excision of hateful stereotypes was culpability in past and future genocidal assaults.

Our timing was impeccable. The sixties and the American civil rights movement triggered some of the finest impulses in Christianity. Pope John XXIII and the resolutions of the Second Vatican Council unleashed a generation seeking to humanize and democratize the Catholic Church. The activists whom we met were passionate idealists who wanted to correct and make up for 2000 years of mistreatment. Far from resenting our reproof, they validated it and sought to make the church respond. They were eager to connect to the Jewish roots of Christianity, and they drank in our words about Judaism with a purity and intensity that Jewish students would find hard to match.

Some of the finest people we encountered became lifetime friends. We became very attached to Sister Rose Thering, who did the early research on anti-Jewish images in Catholic religious texts and later became a fierce fighter for justice for Jews in the Soviet Union and Israel. She especially loved the Shabbat experience and came to our home often to be with us on that day, a visitor whom our children grew to love as *our* Sister Rose." Ed Flannery became a dialogue partner and John Pawlikowski became a scholarly foil and long-time coworker. To this day, I carry a special place in my heart for Kathleen and Patrick Jordan, who eventually gave up their initial studies toward priesthood and nun's orders in order to marry. Kathleen initially worked as lay servant to the poor. We did not stay in close touch with them, because our professional paths diverged; but every so often there was a letter, a call, or an encounter that cemented the bond of quiet, loving friendship and human concern between us. After our son J. J. died in a tragic accident, they heard the news somehow and wrote a letter of memory and of compassion that reminded us again of the incredible power of Christian love. In the 1970s, we met people like Eva Fleischner, Franklin Littell, J. Coert Rylersdaam, Paul Van Buren, and Ruth Zerner, who attracted us with their human qualities backed by their scholarship and zeal to end Christian abuse and misrepresentations of Jews; they became friends, soul mates, and influences on my thinking. Soon thereafter, I connected with Harry Cargas, Eugene Fisher, and Clark Williamson, and, still later, with Harvey Cox and Krister Stendahl. The power of Christian ethics in all their lives and the beauty of their Christian religious practices gradually revealed to us the intrinsic strength of Christianity.*

 FIRST STEPS IN DIALOGUE

In this early pristine period of dialogue I wrote two essays, one included in this book. Both somewhat reflected my hesitation to make a full disclosure

---

* In our first participation in an Institute of Christian Studies, which incorporated my wife's and my teaching of Judaism, I sat in on a series of lectures by John Dominic Crossan on the development of the New Testament. Crossan's approach moved me in two ways. Firstly, he openly acknowledged that he was driven in his critical studies of the Gospels by the determination to prevent the Gospels from generating anti-Semitism and contempt for Judaism—in order to prevent a repetition of such horrors as the Holocaust. Secondly, his presentation of the spiritual struggle of Jesus' disciples and the next generation to be faithful to their profound religious experience with him and to make sense of the Crucifixion was persuasive and illuminating. Crossan and I did not stay in touch. But, in retrospect I wish to acknowledge that he influenced my articulation of the disciples' relationship to Jesus and how their interpretation of the Crucifixion (and later interpretation, that is, the Resurrection) shaped Christianity. Crossan made me respect the Gospel formation process as driven by profound religious faith, albeit departing from mine.

while my soul remained in a state of undigested, deep spiritual division. The *Shoah* and Israel were already central to my thinking as revelational events comparable to biblical acts of God in history. These new events, I believed, would necessarily reorient the meanings of the inherited biblical experiences that were central to both faiths. Despite my anger, I was listening—so dialogue was a spiritual two-way street. "The New Encounter of Judaism and Christianity" speaks of how each religion can learn from the other and thus correct one-sided tendencies in its own development.

The heart of my essay "The Cultural Revolution and Religious Unity" (not included in this volume) was the contention that the new media and explosion in communications were leading inexorably to a more universal recognition of the human as the image of God. According to my nascent theology, truly knowing the other translated into experiencing the intrinsic human dignities found in every image of God—infinite value, equality, and uniqueness. Ultimately, one could not go on honoring the other's humanity while dismissing the religion in which the other was embedded and that shaped the other's character and values. The inevitable outcome would be the recognition of the other's religion. I dimly perceived that if religions turned out to be as valid and dignified as their practitioners were, one must come up with a new conceptualization of the nature of absolute truth that would allow for the existence of two or more valid yet contradicting faiths. My response was the image of a shift from a Newtonian universe, in which there is only one absolute center point, to an Einsteinian universe, in which many absolute center points exist, each absolute center defined relative to the system in which it was embedded.

It seemed important to me that the Einsteinian physics did not invalidate the Newtonian system but turned it into a limited case (accounting for one snapshot of reality) that existed side by side with other systems in a multifarious universe marked by plural and alternative realities. Over the years, I never could decide if I had discovered a new fundamental understanding or had merely offered a clever metaphor. However, this model became the heart of my effort to distinguish pluralism—in which faiths retain serious authority claims—from relativism—in which all worldviews are true because none is true, other than in some communally agreed, conventional way.

The Christian dialogue experience did not just affect my attitudes toward Christianity; the influence on my thinking impacted on my internal life in the Jewish community and shaped my career in Jewish intrafaith work. Many of the ecumenical conferences and encounters Blu and I joined were far more developed in their theory and practice of dialogue than comparable Jewish programs. Their culture of dialogic civility stipulated showing respect for the other; the breadth of exposures and the variety of backgrounds of the participants turned these events into exhilarating encounters. Although they were deeply rooted in their particular faith, they sought out and listened to contradictory voices—much more so than I was used to in my experience inside the Jewish community.

In 1973, I co-founded CLAL: The National Jewish Center for Learning and Leadership, which became my professional life's project; it seemed then only natural that CLAL should provide a similar setting for its intrafaith dialogue. To my shock, CLAL's work and procedures evoked far more hostility from the conflicting Jewish groups than the comparable Jewish-Christian dialogue had prepared me for. Furthermore, the term *pluralism* was not yet widely understood in a Jewish context; and as my Orthodox community swung to the right in the 1980s and 1990s, the "p-word" became a dirty word. To my great frustration, the Orthodox failed to distinguish between pluralism and relativism; to my failure, I could not persuade them of the essential difference between these positions—in other words, that one could uphold the authority of tradition while making room for other religious systems. Despite these troubles, I never lost my sense of gratitude to Christians for showing the way toward creating a dialogue that truly respects the image of God—the value, equality, and uniqueness of the other.

Driven by the theological and moral issues raised by the Holocaust, I became deeply involved in the mid-1960s with an interdenominational Jewish conversation among theologians meeting in Canada and primarily enabled by my friend and soul mate, David Hartman. The move to interdenominational dialogue did not reflect alienation from Orthodoxy. Rather, in the light of the *Shoah* and the shared fate of all Jews, I felt that all Jewish religious positions should be respected as intrinsically heroic. Also, lacking in answers, I was ready to listen to anybody wrestling with religious questions. I will never forget the new friendships we formed with Eliezer Berkovits and Shubert Spero, and for the first time in our lives with non-Orthodox thinkers—such as Emil Fackenheim, Jakob Petuchowski, Eugene Borowitz, Steven S. Schwarzchild, and Dudley Weinberg, of the Reform movement; and Seymour Siegel, Samuel Dresner, Jacob Neusner, Herschel Matt, and others, of the Conservative movement. I brought my obsession with the Holocaust to the table. At the group's meeting in 1965, I read a first paper on the implications of the Holocaust for Judaism titled "God's Acts in History." Emil Fackenheim responded with great intensity both intellectually and personally. The encounter awakened Fackenheim from his philosophical slumbers, that is, his belief that philosophy and theology incorporate timeless truths, untouched and unaffected by historical events. He went on to write some masterworks of Jewish philosophy through the prism of the *Shoah*. We constantly wrestled with these questions and tried to sustain each other intellectually. Years later, he expressed some regrets to me for not making clearer the nature of my influence; he explained that he had expected that I would publish "God's Acts" immediately so the relationship of our thinking on the *Shoah* would be clear. But I could not bring myself to publish my paper at that time. How could I pour ideas into the fixed mold of print when they were still so molten and bubbling?

A number of the thinkers in this group, including Fackenheim, Petuchowski, and Borowitz, were making important contributions to the dialogue, and they urged us on. Their support was especially helpful because when it came to Jewish-Christian dialogue, I was increasingly on my own in the Orthodox community. Even Eliezer Berkovits, whose liberal modern Orthodoxy was very close to mine and who became a treasured friend and teacher, rejected the Jewish-Christian dialogue. Out of those Canadian meetings, Berkovits took up the challenge of the Holocaust on two fundamental issues, but we took diametrically opposite positions. I concluded that the lesson of the Holocaust was that powerlessness was morally insufferable and that Judaism must reenter history, give priority to the habits and policies of power, and develop a restraining ethic of power. Berkovits responded that the survival of the Jewish people through the *Shoah* proved the power of spiritual force to transcend history. Although Zionism was religiously and morally right, the arena of power politics was the realm of human evil and corruption. The second contradictory conclusion was expressed in his attitude toward Jewish-Christian dialogue. I became convinced that dialogue was an absolute necessity—first to check Christian teaching of contempt and then to revise Jewish negative stereotypes toward Christianity. By contrast, Berkovits saw the event of the Holocaust as constituting a profound condemnation of Christianity's record. Christianity's past behavior and destructive influence on Jewish history made it unfit for dialogue or relationship with Judaism. He was prepared to read Christian theology but rejected personal spiritual interchange and transformation.

In 1967, I was invited to participate in a major Jewish-Christian dialogue conference, organized by the Synagogue Council of America, to take place in Boston. The conference was the apex of the hopes and innocent aspirations of the dialogue during the 1960s. The program was underwritten by the Ford Foundation, then at the peak of its prestige as the new megafoundation, with a program to perfect the world. All of the Jewish and Christian establishment organizations were harnessed to the task of making a "poster child" encounter possible.

By then, Rabbi Joseph B. Soloveitchik, the great intellectual and spiritual leader of modern Orthodoxy, had written an essay on dialogue titled "Confrontation." At first glance, the statement negated serious Jewish theological conversation with Christians. Soloveitchik said that on matters of social action and societal justice, there was room for dialogue and joint action between Jews and Christians. However, in matters doctrinal and theological, all religions spoke their own private language. It would be a violation of the spiritual-theological intimacy between the religious community and God to share the content of the internal conversation with members of another faith. Translating the categories of faith into terminology comprehensible to believers of another tradition would be a betrayal. The resultant portrayal of Jewish Torah would be a distortion in which the views of the minority—that is, Jews—would be placed on a Procrustean bed and would be stretched and cut to the measure of the majority faith. Soloveitchik suspected that a strong conversionist impulse lurked behind Christian dialogue efforts and feared that a tidal wave of interfaith interest might sweep many Jews into the bosom of the church.

Soloveitchik's strictures were troubling because I considered myself to be one of his disciples, having enormous respect for his views and judgments. Yet, by now, I was so caught up in the dialogue and getting so much out of it that I was reluctant to give it up. I could vouch firsthand that the people I was dealing with had not a scintilla of conversionist intentions. I went to see Rabbi Soloveitchik to clear away his objections for myself. First, I said: Rebbe, you taught me that in the halakhic worldview, life is spiritually seamless. But then there is no real distinction between the areas of social action and theology/doctrine. After a moment's pause, he said: Greenberg, you are right.

(To me, the implication was that if dialogue was permitted in matters of social concern, then it was permitted in all areas. I judged "Confrontation" to be a piece of "Marrano writing" [that is to say, the surface words conveyed one message while the substantive depth expressed a very different meaning]. The presumed policy ruling was predicated on a distinction that contradicted one of Soloveitchik's fundamental teachings: that halakhah regulates all of life because all areas of life are intrinsically religious. In my reading, "Confrontation" gave the appearance of prohibiting dialogue; this released the pressure on Soloveitchik from the ultra-Orthodox/yeshivah world that was totally opposed to any joint conversation. But in its actual policy implications, Soloveitchik's statement opened the door to significant areas of joint learning and exchange.)

Then I said: Maybe you meant to say that Jewry is not prepared for such a theological enterprise and that one should restrict it until we are ready.

Again, after a moment's pause, he said: You are right. I responded: You know, many believe that the Orthodox would be in the best position to speak to the spiritual concerns of the church while protecting the distinctive views of Judaism. I myself plan to pursue the dialogue with Christianity because too much is at stake for us not to. He did not object.

(Personally, I had an overwhelming urge to say to him: But if only you had said openly what was really on your mind, then Jews could prepare properly for the dialogue. Now the Orthodox will interpret your view as stating that dialogue is not permitted, and the Jewish community will be even less capable of maintaining a high-quality conversation. However, I did not have the heart or courage to challenge him any more than I had.)

Since the Orthodox had a veto on all substantive commitments of the Synagogue Council of America, the sponsors made an all-out effort to re-shape the agenda of the Boston dialogue to meet Soloveitchik's guidelines (social action, yes; doctrinal conversation, no). Much of the theological substance was removed from the conference program. Shortly before the conference opened, the *New York Times* ran a front-page story (including a conversation with Soloveitchik) announcing that the dialogue heralded a revolutionary opening-up between Christianity and Judaism. The leadership of the ultra-Orthodox/yeshivah world was infuriated. Soloveitchik withdrew his approval. He conceded that the program honored his restrictions, but claimed that the *Times* gave the misleading impression that the dialogue was open-ended and unlimited—and such a conversation was unacceptable. The Orthodox representatives pulled out; the liberal denominations felt morally bound to go forward and honor their commitments to participate, especially since the program had been drawn and quartered to meet Jewish guidelines.

By the time of this episode, Blu and I were already deeply involved in doctrinal and social theological dialogue. In his fair-mindedness, Soloveitchik said that Jews had no right to intervene in—or try to improve—Christian doctrine any more than Christians did to reshape Judaism. But we felt that the only way Christianity would change its traditional "teaching of contempt" for Judaism and Jewry would be if the dialogue dealt with theology—so we had no intention of backing away. You might say that our position was that Christianity was too important to be left to Christians. We felt fully justified to speak our minds theologically because every Christian wrong-teaching about Jews had a direct negative impact on the safety and security of our children and grandchildren. We also felt empowered by the commandment in Leviticus 19:17—a text held sacred by Jews and Christians alike, albeit at different levels of authority—that one should "reprove your fellow".[1] From this verse, I learned that you have a duty to issue reproof to improve the other—in particular, to a person whom you feel connected to as a *fellow* (Jewish Publication Society translation = *kinsman*). While corrections from an outsider were intrinsically less persuasive than from a fellow member of a faith, historically, the discounting reflected the fact that relations between faiths were hostile and polemic. We trusted that Christians would recognize that our critique was motivated by connection, affection, and respect.

Within a decade, I came to see that there was another difference between us. Rabbi Soloveitchik taught that the language of each religion was so private that it should not be shared between believers of different faiths. Yet I was convinced that the Holocaust was a revelational event in at least two religions (Judaism and Christianity). Therefore, it was important to spell out its messages and teach them to practitioners in both faiths.

Can one event be a revelation in two religions? For Christians this was not an unprecedented idea. They upheld Sinai and the other biblical events as revelations in Judaism and in Christianity, albeit they insisted that later events, which were sacred in Christianity, reshaped the meanings of the original revelations. Could Jews accept and teach the idea that an event like the Holocaust constitutes revelation in two faiths? To me the answer was self-evidently: yes. This was a matter not of theological discussion, but of recognizing the facts of what had happened. In the 1960s, I intuitively felt that I was not introducing a foreign theological concept when I taught the implications of the *Shoah* to Christians.

Since I was invited to the Boston conference as an individual, I felt no obligation to pull out. When the official Orthodox representatives discovered this, Rabbi Israel Miller, a major figure in the Rabbinical Council of America (RCA) and, subsequently, a vice president at Yeshiva University where I taught, took me aside and explained that in light of Rabbi Soloveitchik's ruling, it was wrong for any Orthodox Jew to go to the conference.

By then, I was drawing strong spiritual sustenance from my Christian dialogue partners. Therefore, I was not inclined to disappoint Christian friends in order to uphold a mistaken, unjustifiable Orthodox about-face. I explained my theological position to Miller, reported my conversation with Soloveitchik, and argued that it was unfair to drop out of the conference in response to a news story, after the sponsors had gone the extra mile to meet Soloveitchik's requirements. Rabbi Miller replied that all true followers of Rabbi Soloveitchik had to follow his judgment whether or not they agreed with his opinion—to which I responded that the RCA leadership was hiding behind Rabbi Soloveitchik. They wanted him to take a stand and suffer the slings and arrows coming from the right. It was clear to me that were the RCA leadership to take responsibility for the decision to stick with the program, then Rabbi Soloveitchik would likely back them. Instead, they were refusing to take a principled position on their own, and he was crumbling—a scenario that boded ill for modern Orthodoxy's future on many fronts. Rabbi Miller suggested that my attending the conference would not stand me in good stead with the Orthodox leadership. I replied that since I was asking Christians to stand up for Judaism at some personal cost in their communities, I should ask no less of myself than I asked of others. I had learned from my Christian dialogue partners that for the sake of a good cause, one should be willing to suffer some opprobrium even in one's own community, as long as the thinking felt right and one's conscience was clear.

Sadly, this conversation foreshadowed the evolution of my religious thought and of Orthodox life for the next three decades. My years of teaching at Yeshiva University had been spiritually exhilarating for the opportunity to explore and teach a synthesis of Orthodoxy and modernity. However, I was substantially pulled out of the university to serve as Rabbi of Riverdale Jewish Center Synagogue, just when Yeshiva began to slide to the right. The years at the synagogue were soul-stirring and emotionally fulfilling—not least because of the intense contact with religious survivors of the *Shoah*. The experience was so powerful that whatever the later conflict, I remained personally in love with the Orthodox community and its way of life, its thick texture of observance, its strong family and communal bonds, its learning and its passion for Israel. All these qualities nurtured my soul and my family's. However, I was increasingly unhappy with Orthodoxy's spiritual and intellectual complacency. I felt that its leadership was not facing up to the implications of the *Shoah*, and I was troubled by the growing ascendancy of the right wing. In the end, my home Orthodox community in Riverdale and my family sustained my daily religious life. However, my theological journey was quite isolated as modern Orthodoxy retreated on many fronts. Few Orthodox Jewish thinkers were interested in the Holocaust or in the transformation of Christianity. The group of theologians meeting in Canada (most were not Orthodox) gave me some nurture. The departure of David Hartman for Israel, in the early 1970s, was a huge blow. With his aliyah move, I lost my most stimulating reader, inspirer, and critic (although he was personally opposed to Holocaust theology). Soon the Canadian meetings stopped; preoccupied each with our own work, David and I drifted from each other. Except for my father and my wife, and ongoing but occasional meetings with my teacher from rabbinical seminary, Rabbi Yehuda Leib Nekritz, and with Rabbi Soloveitchik, the people who most stimulated my thinking over the next three decades were either dead—Rabbi Israel Salanter (1810–1883) and Rabbi Abraham Isaac Kook (1865–1935)—or Christian.*

In June 1973, a group of Jewish and Christian theologians joined to plan an international symposium on the Holocaust and its implications for Jews and Christians. A year earlier, I had given up my congregation, having concluded that no matter how one tried to refashion it, an Orthodox synagogue was designed to be a community, not a vehicle for theological exploration of the implications of the *Shoah*. As the symposium program developed, I came to understand that the time had come to step forward and publish my views on the Holocaust and its implications for Jews, Christians, and modern culture itself. I also made plans—with the help of a National Endowment for the Humanities fellowship—to take a delayed sabbatical to write a theological approach to the Holocaust. From the summer of 1974 to August 1975, my wife and I—now with five children—spent another year in Jerusalem.

CONFRONTING THE HOLOCAUST—AGAIN

My sabbatical turned into a year of theological déjà vu all over again. I plunged into another full-time experience of study and raw encounter with the *Shoah*. Again I experienced the bitter truth that the Holocaust was a bottomless pit of human torment and suffering. Again sleepless nights were followed by frozen days. The uneasy religious equilibrium I had worked so hard to attain was devastated by the sheer power of evil and death encountered again. Rage at God, anger at man, heartbreak at the suffering, compassion and longing to heal the wounds of the living and the dead—all these emotions struggled within me and gave no peace. Again, my wife and our children, enjoying an idyllic and inspiring year in Jerusalem, pulled me back from the precipice of death, despair, and oblivion to the side of life, time after time.

Three events during the year stand out in my memory. One was the death of my father, Rabbi Eliyahu Chayim Greenberg, in 1975. Although he was a

---

* I was, however, the beneficiary of two Orthodox role models who taught me much over these decades. Michael Wyshogrod exemplified to me the trained, highly qualified theologian, able to integrate insights from Christian thought to enrich the understanding of Judaism, and a person who presented Judaism at a higher level to Jews and Christians alike. (By contrast, I was an amateur autodidact.) Wyshogrod strongly critiqued my argument that the revelation in the Holocaust challenged or reshaped classic religious positions. Nevertheless, I was impressed by his writings on Judaism and Christianity and was influenced by them. From the 1980s on, I also benefited from Professor Steven Katz's first-rate critical writings on philosophy and Jewish thought, including his penetrating albeit sympathetic critique of my ideas. Here, too, whatever the differences, I reflected much on his arguments, and they impacted on the development of my thinking.

teacher of Talmud and not a theologian, my father stimulated and shaped my thought more than anyone else. He was my sounding board, my guide and conscience in matters of *halakhah* and practice. In February, I had a commitment to give a paper on Jewish-Christian relations in Rome. Over the Shabbat, my father suddenly weakened and passed away so swiftly that I never had a chance to make my farewells with him. Nor did I give the paper. The conference was scheduled for Sunday, which turned out to be the day of his funeral. Hastily, I flew back to the United States, but the plane was delayed and I missed the burial. Thenceforth that bitter loss haunted me. My father had opposed our going to Israel for the year, pleading that he would not get to see me again. In truth, he had issued the same warning prior to previous trips; still, there was an admixture of guilt in my grief reaction.

Until that moment in 1975, I had lived a charmed and deeply blessed life. The passing of my father was the first experience I had with the loss of a loved, unique, precious, irreplaceable person. The pain made me grasp for the first time the ultimacy of death and why Judaism and Christianity insist that death must be overcome. My father's death plunged me into a state of sadness and depression; the gloom deepened the aura of total immersion in death and loss that suffused my encounter with the Holocaust. For years afterward, I felt that I was sinking in death, swimming frantically but barely managing to stay afloat while my clothes, my body, my very being were being saturated with evil and death.

My second recollection is of a conference in Hamburg in 1975 that is inextricably connected with Alice and Roy Eckardt. Of all the people Blu and I met in the course of our dialogue, none affected me as profoundly as Alice and Roy. Roy was a disciple of Reinhold Niebuhr and was gifted with the same blend of moral passion and realistic, worldly judgment as his teacher. Roy's personality united a righteousness free of self-righteousness with a piety free of pomposity. His ever-present moral seriousness was always leavened with an unfailing sense of humor and a capacity for laughter (including laughing at himself). As a couple, the Eckardts were extraordinarily appealing to Blu and me. Their white-hot passion for justice for Jews (and others) moved us; their moral realism and acute religious insight inspired us; their unsparing, prophetic self-criticism of Christianity challenged us. I was struggling to move my own Orthodox brethren on many issues involving self-criticism and correction. Time and again, I was tempted to fall silent or to settle in order not to further alienate my community. Then the image of the Eckardts and their unyielding scholarly martyrdom in the service of truth and justice for Jews would appear before my eyes. I would realize that I was not living up to their model and would then try harder. They became my goad and conscience for actions on the internal Jewish front.

Alice and Roy put themselves through the seven fires of Gehenna and risked their own religious sanity in order to make possible true Christian repentance. Eventually their willingness to challenge even such fundamental doctrines as the resurrection of Christ—in order to purge every last source of Christian triumphalism and supersessionism—frightened and upset many of their own Christian colleagues. In their critique of Christianity, they were able to hear their tradition and react to it as if they were Jews. Earlier in the century, Paul Tillich and Reinhold Niebuhr, speaking philosophically out of the Christian tradition, had given Judaism an unprecedented level of dignity as a religion. But their analysis did not approach the level of self-criticism and revision of classic Christian thought that the Eckardts articulated in the light of Judaism's experience at the hand of Christianity. Perhaps for the first time in the history of Christian theology, the Eckardts' analysis put the two religions on a truly equal plane. This enabled them to root out every lingering residue of anti-Semitism, religious triumphalism, stereotype, and caricature in Christian thinking and to purge them mercilessly. I could hardly match their spiritual intensity. At some point, however, the cumulative impact of their witness lifted my Jewish religious life to a new level. Their model broke through my neat categories and leveled the vantage point from which I looked down on Christianity. Thanks to them, I began to vicariously grasp the Christian worldview and experience it without the covert assumptions of superiority and moral judgment that were endemic in Jewish tradition. Soon I felt an obligation to re-present Christianity, within the Jewish world, as a faith with independent value and dignity.

Although fellow Christians were frequently angered by the Eckardts' criticism to the point of accusing them of disloyalty to Christianity, they really were "Christian prophets"—that is, critics from within, so passionately upholding the highest standard of the faith that they often infuriated their contemporaries. Throughout history, the Hebrew prophets had been misread and misused for tendentious purposes against Judaism and Jewry. In the course of the Christian-Jewish polemic, starting with the New Testament, Christians had seized upon prophetic criticism to condemn Jews as a people so evil that their own prophets excoriated them as spiritually unworthy and ethically unfit. In truth, the harshness of the prophets' language did not prove the base behavior of the Hebrews as a people. Rather, the prophets were holding their own people to a higher standard than any other. Behavior that might pass for standard operating procedure among other nations received blistering criticism from the prophets. Christians polemically misread the prophets as signaling the decadence of the Israelites; in fact, the prophets in themselves were signs of the greatness of the Hebrew people and of the traditions that gave rise to them and their searing critique.

Consider how a society with a free press is portrayed compared to one with totalitarian-controlled media. In the American press, a portrait emerges of a bumbling, frequently corrupt, overreaching government in a society full of inequality and dissatisfaction. Read the totalitarian press and a portrait emerges of a well-run, socially egalitarian society whose citizens constitute a well-cared-for and satisfied population. But the actual facts are the reverse. The difference reflects the standards of the commentators, not the facts or the societal situation. The prophets represented the convergence of an extraordinary ethical standard and the moral grandeur of God and of those who serve God. If the people failed to live up to their expectations, the prophets escalated their denunciations. However, as a prophet is the outgrowth of a people (and as the people sustain rather than crush the seer), on balance the prophetic scathing criticism only proves the spiritual greatness of the Israelite people. Only a great religion and people could set such high standards, condemn itself without equivocation for not performing at that level, and eventually raise up a people to live up to the ideal. As a Jew who had discovered the Christian misreading of the prophets to malign Judaism, I came to see that the Eckardts' critique should not be misused to condemn Christianity. Rather, Christians should listen and purify Christianity, and Jews should listen and appreciate the greatness of Christian faith in raising up such "prophets."

In 1975, Professor Uri Tal, a brilliant analyst of the religious background of Nazism and German culture, called and asked me to read a paper in his stead at a forthcoming conference on the Holocaust to be held near Hamburg. Tal was ill, and he appealed to our friendship, as he could not get anyone to step in for him on such short notice. He explained that this was the first such comprehensive conference in Germany on the religious aspects of the *Shoah*. The German participants included Gertrude Luckner, a legendary anti-Nazi Christian who survived being sent to the concentration camps.

Ever since the shock of the Holocaust had sunk in, I had followed in my parents' footsteps in not being able to bring myself to buy German products or to visit the land of Germany. Even though postwar Germany had become a democracy and a major supporter of Israel and had paid significant reparations for its crimes against Jewry, still the crime of the Holocaust was so ultimate that I could not bring myself to do business with Germans. Yet as time had passed and new generations of Germans grew up, I began to feel that this application of the principle of collective guilt was less and less acceptable. But how could one know whether a particular purchase (or visit) might not be a source of profit to a specific person who had murdered or tormented a member of one's own family? After wrestling with my demons for a week, I determined to go to Germany and participate in the conference, after which

20

I would turn neither to the left nor the right but would return directly to Israel without sightseeing, visiting, or buying anything.

At the Hamburg conference, I read a paper from an outline titled "Lessons to Be Learned from the Holocaust." The paper contained an eyewitness account of the most devastating scene in Holocaust sources that I ever encountered. I had just come across this testimony of a prisoner who was in Auschwitz in the summer of 1944, at the peak of the exterminations:

> ". . . When the Hungarian Jews arrived, we used a music camouflage. At the time, the children were burned on big piles of wood. The crematoriums could not work at the time, and therefore, the people were just burned in open fields with those grills, and also children were burned among them. Children were crying helplessly and that is why the camp administration ordered that an orchestra be made by 100 inmates and should play. They played very loud all the time. They played the "Blue Danube" or "Rosamunde," so that even the people in the city of Auschwitz could not hear the screams. Without the orchestra they would have heard the screams of horror . . . The people two kilometers from there could even hear those screams, namely that came from the transports of children. The children were separated from their parents, and then they were put to section III camp. Maybe the number of children was several thousand.
>
> And then, on one special day they started burning them to death. The gas chambers at the time were out of order, at least one of them was out of order, namely, the one near the crematorium; it was destroyed by mutiny in a *sonderkommando* [a detachment of Jewish inmates who handled the victims from the gas chambers to the crematoria – IG] in August 1944. The other three gas chambers were full of the adults and therefore the children were not gassed, but just burned alive.
>
> When one of the SS people sort of had pity on the children, he took the child and beat the head against a stone first before putting it on the pile of fire and wood, so that the child lost consciousness. However, the regular way they did it was by just throwing the children onto the pile.
>
> They used to put a sheet of wood, then the whole thing was sprinkled with gasoline, then wood again, and gasoline and wood, and gasoline—and then people were placed on them. Thereafter, the whole pile was lit"[2]

The absolute need to prevent a recurrence of just such behaviors led the Eckardts to write a sulphurous assault on every Christian teaching that led historically to the demeaning of Judaism and demonization of Jews. In their masterwork, *A Long Night's Journey into Day,* they challenged the absolute meaningfulness of the Crucifixion and sought to demythologize the Resurrection of Jesus—and thus undermine the supersessionism intrinsic to the claim. They quoted the above account of the murder of Jewish children and stated: "Before this kind of event, the death of Jesus upon the cross is lost in relative moral nonsignificance . . . The Godforsakenness of Jesus has proven to be nonabsolute if it ever was absolute, for there is now a

Godforsakenness that is worse by an infinity of infinities—that Godforsakenness of Jewish children which is a final horror" (*A Long Night's Journey into Day*, p. 104). In attacking classic Christian claims of Jesus' absolute status, the Eckardts were truly following Jesus. In order to stop such pure evil as the mass murder of Jewish children from recurring, they were willing to take up the cross and be destroyed themselves. After all, they surely knew they would be spiritually crucified by Christians who were outraged by their relativizing of the core teachings of Christianity. They showed the same courage in the political arena, steadfastly standing up for Israel against a growing demonization and liberal Protestant attacks on the morality and legitimacy of the Jewish state.

The Eckardts' reaction to my Hamburg paper reflected the effect we were having on each other. They would return the favor at a conference in 1977, when Roy's paper challenging God's right to impose the risks of covenant and covenantal living on Jewry created a crisis of my trust in the Eckardts. The resolution of the crisis led me to the transformative insight that the covenant of Israel was being reaccepted in our time; taking this position aroused strong controversy and criticism in my community. Thus the Eckardts, lovingly and unintentionally, reciprocally goaded me into risking communal "martyrdom" out of a desire to follow the directions suggested by the *Shoah*. The Eckardts continuously strained the capacity of their Christian peers to keep up with them theologically. During one of the sessions in the 1975 Hamburg conference, the discomfort that even repentant Christians felt at the Eckardts' relentless criticism of classic Christian concepts and ongoing behaviors boiled over into unmitigated anger. A number of their colleagues present attacked their bona fides as Christians and criticized their speaking so "denigratingly" about Christianity in the presence of Jews.

At this point, I felt obligated to intervene to witness to the group as to the true effect the Eckardts' words were having on me as a Jew. How compelling was the moral grandeur of Christianity in light of its ability to raise up critics of truly prophetic stature such as Roy and Alice in the midst of such a generation! I explained the paradox of the Hebrew prophets' words and witness as to the spiritual power of Judaism, and how the Eckardts were setting a benchmark of religious purification that Jews would have to make a Herculean effort to match. In effect, the Eckardts were calling on the church to have the faith and courage to "die"—to crucify its own worst tendencies even at the risk that classic concepts might also expire—in order to be resurrected as the victor over indigenous forces of evil and death. The group visibly softened and, thereafter, shifted toward a new dynamic of interaction with the Eckardts. The entire conference—which included a journey to Bergen-Belsen, my first encounter with an actual Nazi concentration camp—

confirmed my emotional inclination not to deal with the *Shoah* in an exclusively Jewish framework. Christians would have to be both targets and partners in my wrestling with the demons of the Holocaust.

During this period, I finally brought myself to publish two extended essays on the Holocaust. The first, "Cloud of Smoke, Pillar of Fire: Judaism, Christianity and Modernity After the Holocaust,"[3] captures the condition of raw brokenness in the aftermath of my encounter with the *Shoah*, a state of being torn between "moment faiths" and moments—or days—of doubt, cut off from God and redemption. The piece articulates anger at Christianity and rebellion toward/disillusionment with modernity; it includes biting criticism of any Rabbinic tradition that sought to go on unchanged and expresses wonder at the heroism of Jewish continuity and the marvel of Israel resurrected. I affirmed the Holocaust as a major orienting event that would fundamentally transform Judaism's inner self-understanding. This new self-understanding could not be developed in an exclusively Jewish framework, but rather needed the context of Christianity and modern culture as well. In many ways, the essay looked back; it condensed and codified the conclusions I had derived from 14 years of wrestling with the *Shoah* but only touched upon the new stage of thinking that had begun toward the end of the sabbatical year 1974–1975. In this further reorientation, my focus would shift from anger, self-pity, and blaming God toward a sense of Divine/human shared suffering. I would come to read the Holocaust as signaling the need for greater human responsibility for God's world and plan.

In the second essay, "New Revelations and New Patterns" (published in this volume), I argued that new revelation (in the form of the *Shoah* and the rebirth of Israel) had appeared in both Judaism and Christianity. This renewed revelation paved the way for new self-understanding by both faiths and enabled a reorientation of the inherited, established authoritative traditions. The essay focused on Christianity's sins and sought to articulate the needed Christian paradigm shifts vis-à-vis Judaism. I insisted that the teaching of contempt goes straight back to the original Gospel accounts. The Holocaust had revealed that, at the very heart of Christianity, a shelter for evil existed that must be razed, since hatred was in fundamental contradiction to the gospel of love that is the New Testament's true role and goal. As for Jewish rethinking, I could not go any further at that time than to argue that the restoration of the land of Israel, the covenantal sign, had now released Judaism to ponder anew the significance of Christianity. My fundamental reorientation toward the other faith could only occur in the wake of a personal, transformative religious experience, set in motion by the third pivotal event/memory of that precious, devastating, death-filled, life-filled second year of immersion in the *Shoah* and in the State of Israel.

One day in early 1975, I was sitting in tallit and tefillin, overwhelmed by the terror and suffering of the *Shoah*, raging at God for allowing this to happen, sensing vicariously the humiliation, fear, and pain of the victims, unable to speak a word of prayer or hope. Then I felt a rush of pity, a desire to bind up the wounds, an urge to soothe and heal the Jews who had suffered this torture. While no longer remembering the specific trigger for that emotion, I do recollect vividly an episode from 1961–1962 that conveyed much of the same feeling. In May 1962, when Moshe was 10 months old, we had an opportunity to join a group traveling to Massada and then to the Negev and back. Blu was newly pregnant with our second child, to be named David, and Moshe was still a handful. We concluded that as Blu had been most confined to the house taking care of our son, she should go on the trip. I would stay with Moshe because my primary work, reading and writing, could be done comfortably at home.

That week I learned what immense organizational skills and balancing acts were needed to combine parenting and career. I did not get any writing done and scarcely any reading. My prayers were rushed. Several nights I fell asleep exhausted, fully clothed. One night, in particular, I woke up in the middle of the night and barely managed to recite the evening prayer that I had slept through.

As I am a reading addict, withdrawal symptoms built up steadily. On the fifth day, blessedly, Moshe took the extended afternoon nap that he had skipped for three days. Rushing into the study, I took up a book and began reading ravenously. Unhappily, after a half hour, Moshe stirred in the other room. Like a crazed junkie, I ignored the sounds of my child and continued to read. After another half hour, I sniffed the air and realized that he needed to be changed. Clinging desperately to my book, I tried to go on reading, but in a few minutes he was whimpering. I felt a jolt of annoyance at this interruption. Reluctantly, I got up, feeling somewhat irritated, and marched into his room to change him. He responded with a cry. Then, as I peeled off his soiled diaper, I saw that in the half hour that I had delayed, his skin had reddened and become irritated. Suddenly a memory clicked—a scene I had read countless times but had failed to grasp: families packed in cattle cars, without water or food, unable to move—let alone change a diaper—put on railway journeys for days and days that delivered them to death camps. Had I before now grasped that extra dimension of discomfort, the pain and then the agony of babies whose skin had become raw from not being changed? Had I properly weighed their cries? Or the feelings of their mothers and fathers unable to respond? Even as I reached for the Desitin ointment, the anger switch flicked off. I felt a sudden flood of pity for the child on the table. In this generation, in memory of all the others, he deserved instant loving care, gentle cleansing, and tender dressing. Feeling ashamed of my obsession with reading, I lifted Moshe up to hold him close.

A comparable emotion overwhelmed me that day in 1975. In a flash, it became clear that I had been asking the wrong question: Where was God during the Holocaust? I suddenly understood that God was with God's people—("I will be with him in distress" [Psalm 91:15])—being tortured, degraded, humiliated, murdered. Where else would God be when God's loved ones were being hounded and destroyed? The realization hit how much God had been suffering in the *Shoah,* but the pain had been infinite as only an Infinite Consciousness could experience it. Then I burst into tears; a surge of pity for God flowed through me. A sense of compassion, a desire to heal the Divine, breached the wall of polarized anger and complaint that had arisen between us.

As I reflected more and more on this experience, I came to see that there was an ancient, traditional understanding that offered an alternative to the classic, inherited covenantal claim—expressed in our own day by the Lubavitcher and Satmar rebbes and many leading ultra-Orthodox scholars—that the Holocaust was inflicted by God as punishment for Jewish sins. Despite its prophetic lineage, this assertion, when made in the context of the *Shoah,* filled me with deep moral revulsion. What sin could justify such a horrifying imposition? What kind of God would decree the burning alive of innocent children as a purgative for misbehavior? I also realized that connecting to God's suffering offered a serious alternative to the conclusion that God was dead, or indifferent to human suffering, or (as David Blumenthal was to argue decades later) abusive and tyrannical.

Once my thought moved in this direction, I found many traditional sources that explored God's suffering, alongside the covenantal people, in the midst of historical catastrophe. In time, the true central question came to the fore: Why would God take on such powerlessness in history? I came to interpret this divine self-limitation as a strategy to call humans to greater partnership and responsibility. This insight pointed the way to understanding Israel's torment as that of a suffering servant—the victim of humankind's pathologies and misbehavior—a far more acceptable portrayal of the etiology of Jewish victimization.

Why had I overlooked—or more truthfully, held back—from thinking deeply about God's suffering as a key to grasping the nature of the *Shoah?* The answer was obvious. Such an idea initially sounded very Christian. I—as many other Jewish thinkers—felt compelled to push away the concept of a suffering God as though it were a foreign idea seeking to invade the Jewish inner sanctum. But, in fact, Christians had derived these images from the Hebrew Bible. Increasingly I realized the heavy price Jews had paid in defining Christianity as the totally other. In impoverishing their own religious thought to stay clear of Christian concepts, Jews were rejecting an important part of their own psyche and tradition. In defining Judaism by negating Christianity, Jews paradoxically were being controlled by the very religion to which they were so antagonistic. Aside from bringing me to a new appreciation of Christianity in its own right, these insights stiffened my determination to remain deeply involved in Jewish-Christian dialogue. The interaction was integral to coming to an enlarged and enriched Jewish worldview. Nothing less would allow Jews to begin coping with the religious *mysterium tremendum* posed by the Holocaust.

VOLUNTARY COVENANT, FREEDOM, AND PLURALISM

In 1976, Zachor, the Holocaust Resource Center branch of CLAL, ran a conference for Jewish and Christian scholars titled "The Work of Elie Wiesel and the Holocaust Universe." A good friend and kindred spirit, Professor Alvin Rosenfeld of Indiana University, organized and co-edited a book of the conference papers. For countless people, including myself, Wiesel's life and oeuvre movingly incarnated the devastating impact of the Holocaust and the inescapable transformation that must follow. From his unforgettable classic *Night*, which gave over the phenomenology of the Holocaust in stunning fashion, to *The Gates of the Forest*, whose narrative theology stirred me deeply and thereafter, Wiesel had continuously triggered theological wrestlings in me. At the conference, Michael Berenbaum's paper articulated a powerful theme in Wiesel's writing that, heretofore, I had not marked sufficiently: his assertion of the development of an additional covenant, after the *Shoah*, based on solidarity, witness, and the sanctification of life. But one paper jolted me to the core: Roy Eckardt's "The Recantation of the Covenant?" Said Eckardt: In calling Jews to be God's witnesses and avant-garde for the redemption of the world, God had exposed them to a murderous fury from which there was no escape—as evidenced by the Holocaust. Yet the Lord could not or would not save them. Therefore, God must repent for having endangered the Jews without providing for their protection. Writing with white, scorching fire, Eckardt concluded that the only acceptable *teshuvah* for God would be to recant the divine covenant and thus remove the Jews from the extreme danger they were in. In light of this analysis, any further projection—by God or humans—of a covenant of demand that included the expectation that Jews must live by a higher standard (or else . . .) was outrageous and immoral. That night, I tossed and turned in my bed, blistered by the searing force of Eckardt's statement, recognizing that it rang true yet tormented by a disturbing anomaly in the thesis.

Then I went into crisis. What was the ultimate conclusion of Eckardt's paper? That the divine covenant that had elected the Jews, that had set them on their course as a light unto the nations, for which faithful Jewry had undergone suffering and martyrdom, that to this day was being lived by Jews with heroism and steadfastness—this covenant was to be retracted by God. True, Eckardt made this proclamation in the context of the *Shoah;* reversing classic Christian anti-Judaism, he justified the Jews and "condemned" God for this purported recantation. But in the end, did not his conclusion mean that the best of Christians was nevertheless espousing (behind a much more respectable and enticing front) the old Christian supersessionist doctrine that God withdraw the covenant from the Children of Israel? Had all this dialogic, agonized God-wrestling been nothing more than an empty exercise, leading in the end to the old unacceptable message, deeply planted in the subconscious of even this righteous gentile? Yet why did I resonate in my deepest soul with Eckardt's thesis, even as the cognitive dissonance of his "betrayal" cut off my response?

For years, I struggled with this contradiction. The Eckardts' integrity rang true even under the hammer blow of suspicion. The purity and power of their life journey could not be denied without totally impugning my judgment, my experience, and my instinct—not to mention all my hopes for a better future between Judaism and Christianity. Then at last I came to a realization that reconciled the inner conflicts that were tearing me apart. Roy Eckardt was absolutely right. He was Abraham-like, Jeremiah-like, Job-like in challenging God's justice and demanding *teshuvah*—and in the process, defending and vindicating the people of Israel. But his prophetic insight was "off" in one way. The Abrahamic-Sinaitic covenant was not finished—but the *commanded stage of the covenant* had come to its end. The covenant of demand (for higher standards of behavior from Jews) had been morally passed through the fires of the Holocaust—and had been found wanting. In a world where evil forces had access to extraordinary power while God did not intervene to guarantee the safety of the covenantal people, in such a world, any absolute insistence that the people Israel live by a higher standard—or else—was inherently abusive. Such a demand was illegitimate, and therefore null and void, because it only exposed the Jews to greater danger.

From where then came my inner conviction that all Jews, including myself, were still living the covenant? I believe that the Jewish people, though released from its imposed obligations by every logical and moral consideration of justice, chose to continue its covenantal mission. Some children of Israel were so in love with God; some, with the vision of *tikun olam*

27

(perfecting the world); and some, with all the Jewish people who had ever lived, that they have voluntarily rededicated themselves to the covenant. Amazingly and heroically, knowing full well the risk, they have carried on the covenantal calling. Morally speaking, God could no longer command; but God could lovingly ask for Israel's partnership. And Jewry has responded with love and taken up that partnership again. The renewal of the covenant has led to the highest possible level of commitment, freely given.

Many devout Jews and Christians were alarmed by this concept of a voluntary covenant. They feared that the concept surrendered the classic religious dimension of obligation. For want of making demand, authority would be lost; for want of authority, obedience and observance would be lost. Personally, I was convinced that just as free individuals and societies outperformed authoritarian structures in political, economic, and military matters, so too would voluntary covenantal service prove to be more total and dedicated than any imposed commitments.

After further study and thought, it became clear to me that this concept of renewing the covenant had been a pillar of Judaism in both biblical and talmudic times. At least once previously in Jewish history, the partners' roles had been transformed in the process of renewal. After the destruction of the Second Temple in the first century c.e., according to Rabbinic tradition, God had called Israel to a higher level of power and responsibility in the covenant. This understanding of Jewish history eventually opened a new theological door for me: the idea that covenant was by its very nature intended to unfold in stages.

The fundamental basis of covenant is that out of divine love for humanity, God privileges human dignity and freedom over human obedience. Since the divine goal is to achieve the fullness of human life and capacity, then partnership is essential—because freedom and dignity cannot be bestowed; they must be earned. Therefore, God has self-limited and has invited humans to become partners in the process of perfecting the world. In choosing to redeem reality through the covenantal method, God turns away from three alternative responses to the gap between the ideal and the real world. The Divine renounces coercion of humanity to serve God; nor does the Lord program human beings to do only the right thing; nor does God give up the vision of a perfected world that sustains the full value of human life. The divinely intended outcome of the cosmic process is the creation of a human being with a fulfilled image of God—a creature truly of infinite value, equal, and unique, living in a world that fully sustains these dignities. Whatever the role of command or use of reward and punishment in the interim stages of covenant, the ultimate logic of covenant is a voluntary state. To allow maximum human dignity, God needs to give up all divine demand, force, or coercion and inspire humanity exclusively through education and role modeling to choose life and to do good. It follows that as human capacity grows, as humankind goes from childhood to maturity, the covenantal terms should be jointly adjusted to allow for the increased role and dignity of humanity.*

It took several years for me to be able to articulate the inner dynamics of this concept of covenant; the process culminated in the conclusion that a renewed, voluntary obligation was the immanent outcome of the partnership model. The emergent logic reversed the direction of my own theological drive. From the sixties on, people had generally classified my thought as Holocaust theology. In truth, I was never pleased with that designation, for the category seemed to turn the *Shoah* into the "God" of the system, the source of command and obligation. As an Orthodox Jew, I felt totally commanded by *ha-Shem* and embraced the entire tradition. In 1980, after serving as director of the President's Commission on the Holocaust, I turned down the chance to stay on as director of the proposed United States Holocaust Memorial Museum. I felt that there was a greater crisis to face—the inability to pass on the values and the vision of the covenant in the face of competing ideas and identity in the emerging open, accepting, and totally free society. In light of such a danger, I did not want to concentrate my professional life on Holocaust education solely. Still, there was no gainsaying that my vicarious encounter with the experience of the *Shoah* had been the driving force of my philosophical explorations and professional activities for two decades. The right to demand release from God and the will to renew obligation out of love, freely given, grew out of the *Shoah* experience. Yet as the logic of stages in the covenant grew, I reluctantly concluded, to my surprise, that my encounter with the *Shoah* was the occasion—the adventitious, personal stimulus—but not the essential cause of the needed shift in the religious thinking.

In retrospect, the covenant model always pointed toward the idea that humanity would one day mature into full responsibility. Ideally, the

---

* Although I did not meet Harvey Cox personally until the 1980s, I came across the writings of Dietrich Bonhoeffer and Cox's *The Secular City* in the early 1960s. Although Cox was a bit too celebratory of the secular city, I was powerfully persuaded by his affirmation of the holiness in secularity. Similarly, I was deeply moved by Bonhoeffer's vision of the human being coming of age in relationship to God as well as by his call for a religionless faith, which also was a call to "holy secularism." At the time, I did not consciously incorporate these views in my Jewish theological thinking. However, looking back now, I wonder whether the models they seeded and which I absorbed did not in some way come to fruition in my later religious thinking. In particular, I connect them to my articulation of a second stage (= Rabbinic) and now a third stage (= Lay) in Judaism, marked by a higher level of human responsibility and authority and with a great emphasis on holy secularity. In any event, I acknowledge with gratitude the spiritual and intellectual stimulus that I received from Bonhoeffer and Cox.

development of modern culture with its concomitant explosion of human capacity should have been the occasion for humanity to take up a higher level of leadership in the covenant. However, religious communities missed the signal because they were frightened by the expanding human freedom; they imagined that autonomy was coming at the expense of God's authority. For their part, the secularists too missed the signal, for they were so drunk on the expansion of human power that they welcomed the overthrowing of all restrictions that claimed to be divinely mandated. Ultimately, such human power, out of control, focused on the Jews. This concentrated force (reinforced by centuries of Christian scapegoating of Jews and other sources of hatred) made it feasible to carry out the Holocaust. Therefore, the shock of the *Shoah* must motivate all groups to come to a new understanding about how to take power as human beings and how to limit that same power. God, too, needed to limit further the exercise of divine power. The key to the new equilibrium requires entering into the higher stage of the covenant, with humans taking an expanded leadership role.

As my thinking evolved, I identified three eras of Jewish history, representing three stages of Divine-human covenant. In the biblical era, the self-limited God of covenant, nevertheless, dominated as initiator, instructor (through commandments and prophecy), and senior partner. In the Rabbinic era, God imposed more "stringent" self-limits on God's self, thereby inviting humans to assume a more participatory role. In this spirit, the Divine renounced the mode of prophecy (calling Rabbis to fill the prophets' place) and mediated commands through the human mind and judgment. Finally, in the current post-Holocaust era, God's further *tzimtzum* (self-limitation) summons humans to full responsibility for the outcome of the divine plan. In this emerging stage, humans come of age. No longer intimidated by instant punishment or controlled by overt rewards, human beings are free to act out of love and internalized vision, fulfilling an old promise of Jeremiah (see 31:30–33). The higher technological, medical, scientific power of humanity is part and parcel of this transformation. These new competencies enable human beings to carry out the expansion of life and the upgrading of the dignity of all life in the world, which are the central components of *tikun olam*. These new capacities should be applied to the expansion and moral purification of the religious traditions as well.

Upon further consideration, another conclusion followed: the greater delegation of responsibility to humanity brings with it another corollary, pluralism. In earlier biblical times, prophets could not legitimately contradict one another because God spoke authoritatively; therefore, in cases of prophetic conflict, one of the contenders had to be a false prophet (see Jeremiah 28). In talmudic times, the increased level of human participation in articulating Torah meant that the Rabbis were authorized to use their personal judgment to ascertain God's will. Consequently, Rabbis could disagree on the law, and conflicting positions could both be right. Now, in a post-*Shoah* world where humans have been invited to even greater and more responsible participation in the covenant, the range of pluralism must be extended even more widely. Such a thoroughgoing pluralism constitutes a divine statement of respect for human freedom as well as a conferral of legitimacy on the broadest expression of human variety and uniqueness.

THE STRUGGLE BETWEEN RETHINKING THEOLOGY AND LINKING TO COMMUNITY

These reflections on the evolutionary stages of covenant as well as the broadening of the pluralistic dimension of covenant fed into my ongoing interest in Christianity and my growing admiration for our Christian dialogue partners. This thinking led to the next essay in this series, "The Relationship of Judaism and Christianity: Toward a New Organic Model." The piece was written in response to an invitation from Roy Eckardt, who was editing a special issue on Jewish-Christian relations of the United Church of Christ *Quarterly Review*. Cumulatively, the constellation of my thinking had shifted decisively. Tolerance alone was not dynamic enough to overcome the residues of negative judgment and hostility found in both traditions vis-à-vis the other. In light of the Holocaust, both sides should strive to affirm the fullness of the faith claims of the other, not just offer tolerance. As a thought experiment, I sought to be open to Christian self-understanding—including their claims for theological concepts that are so unconvincing to Jews, such as Jesus' Resurrection and divine Incarnation. I asked myself and other believing Jews: Was there any way to allow for the possible legitimacy of Christians making such claims without yielding our firm conviction that Judaism is a covenant faith, true and permanently valid in history?

"Toward a New Organic Model" presented Christianity not just as a successful religion with which Jews must reckon, but as an organic outgrowth of Hebrew faith. Biblical Judaism looks forward to a future revelation/redemption that is more universal than the Exodus. Therefore, a vital Judaism must stimulate messianic expectations and give rise to movements that seek to realize universal redemption. The question is whether any such messianic movement was meant to happen only once in Jewish history. Or could such a development constructively occur more than once? Could it have been God's purpose to start another religion alongside Judaism to bring the message of redemption to the world in accelerated fashion without breaking up the ongoing election and mission of the original covenanted children of Israel? If this was the case, then Christianity's birth was neither a sign of Judaism's senescence and termination (the classic traditional Christian claim) nor of deviant applications of fundamental Jewish values and concepts (the classic traditional Jewish claim). Rather, the founders of Christianity were being faithful to their remarkable religious experience with Jesus' life and were using Jewish visions, interpretive methods, and thought processes every step of the way, even as their conclusions led them out of Judaism. I argued, however, that they were mistaken in concluding that in order for their experience to be valid, Judaism must be finished.

The most interesting innovation of the whole paper, which, to my regret, has gone almost nowhere with Jews and Christians alike, concerns the status of Jesus. I suggested that Jesus should be recognized not as "a false messiah . . . [that is,] one who has the wrong values . . ." but as "a failed messiah," that is, ". . . one who has the right values, upholds the covenant, but [ultimately] did not attain the final goal."[4]

I truly intended the term "failed messiah" to be honorific—for in the history of humankind, very few individuals have achieved so much good as to be seriously considered a universal redeemer. Even to come close to redeeming the world is beyond the scope of all but a precious few in human history. Christians themselves acknowledge that Jesus' work remains unfinished—and that he will have to come again to complete the redemptive task. It seemed only logical to me that the respectful title "failed messiah" would be acceptable to both Jews and Christians. After all, as I argued in the essay, to fail so nobly places an individual in the highest ranks of moral heroes, comparable to such Jewish heroes as Abraham, Moses, and Jeremiah. They "failed," but how much they achieved in the course of accomplishing their magnificent "failures"! Still, devout Christians recoiled from this term, fearful that calling Jesus a "failed messiah" denied his divinity or undercut his Christian royal title. To me, it seemed that Christians should welcome this classification to encourage them to turn Jesus' "failed" messiahship into a "successful" one by completing the perfection of the world through their own efforts, as soon as possible.

The Jewish world was not ready to redefine Jesus and/or affirm Christianity, either.[5] Most rabbinic and communal interlocutors were not interested in Christian theology, let alone a Jewish rethinking of attitudes toward Christianity. For the most part, I had made no effort to bring the Jewish community, especially my subcommunity Orthodox Judaism, into the search for a new view of the relationship between the faiths. I had my hands full with my other agenda at this time—persuading the Jewish community to reshape its thinking about the Holocaust and to affirm an internal pluralism that would uphold all denominations as legitimate partners in the covenant of fate of the Jewish people. My main activities at CLAL were focused on convincing the Jewish community to become more Jewish in its internal life and to recreate its institutions to meet the challenges of freedom and choice. When the "Organic Model" essay first appeared in a very obscure Christian publication, only a handful of cognoscenti (almost all Christian) paid it any attention. The essay basically sank from sight in the Jewish community without drawing any serious response.

About five years later, an ultra-Orthodox man wandered into a dialogue seminar in which I was teaching "Organic Model" to a group of Jewish and Christian scholars. Angered that his interventions were not taken seriously at the session, he picked up copies of the essay and brought it to the attention of leading *haredi* (ultra-Orthodox) authorities as a case of dangerous deviance. To these rabbinic scholars, who lacked any background in interfaith dialogue, the term "failed messiah" suggested that I was endorsing Jesus as the Messiah, even though I clearly was qualifying his messianic status as "failed." My relationship with the Orthodox community was already strained, since for some years I had been pushing the limits of the community's tolerance by arguing the case for religious pluralism in the light of the Holocaust. With this latest cause célèbre, our frayed relations nearly snapped—for to grant any pluralist legitimacy to Christianity was beyond the pale for most Orthodox colleagues, even in modern Orthodoxy. This latest development added incendiary fuel to the Orthodox community's smoldering anger at my public validations of the Conservative and Reform movements, at a time of growing polarization and antinomian behaviors. Taken together, my intrafaith actions and this new denunciation led to my being brought up on charges of heresy and violation of Orthodox disciplines before my rabbinic organization, the Rabbinical Council of America.

A leading ultra-Orthodox publication denounced me, and then attacked Dr. Norman Lamm, president of Yeshiva University and head of modern Orthodoxy, accusing him of temporizing with heresy and deviation. To thrust the dagger home, the editors charged that he was trafficking and fraternizing with me, the wayward rabbi who had endorsed the religious validity of Jesus and Christianity. Although Rabbi Lamm had been uncomfortable with my views, he had always felt that ideological issues should be avoided, not pursued or persecuted. When Dr. Lamm read my article (cited by the editors of the ultra-Orthodox publication) he was genuinely shocked, especially by my use of Abraham, Moses, etc., as biblical figures who illuminated (and paralleled) Jesus' life. Even some people who had previously defended my pluralist views as an eccentricity and as an unfortunate overreaction to the

Shoah now backed away from what they considered a blatant equating of Judaism and Christianity.

At this point, the main publication of the mainstream Union of Orthodox Jewish Congregations published an article arguing that my affirmations of Christianity had gone far beyond any historically precedented, traditional views of this faith (which was true) and that they constituted acceptance of Jesus as the Messiah as well as endorsement of various other Christian claims (which was false). The author put a spin on every affirmation in my piece that made each one sound as Christological as possible. Under pressure from some lay leaders who supported my other work, the Union gave me the opportunity to reply to these accusations, although I was given a word limit that considerably restricted my ability to refute, point by point, my accuser's skillful distortions. Furthermore, I knew that my readers had no familiarity with the subtleties of thought in this subject and would likely be shocked by whatever I said. Consequently, I had no choice but to explain away any possibility that my thinking was in any way Christological. In the end, I was forced to play down many of the innovative appreciations and nuanced theological insights that I had attributed to Christianity. I minimized the original and daring elements in the essay, stressing instead the most palatable interpretations that would cause the least dissonance in the Orthodox community.

As I wrestled with the writing, I kept thinking: What would Roy Eckardt do? If he had been placed in a parallel situation, Roy would probably have repeated his provocative statements even more boldly, grimly accepting the martyrdom (isolation, loss of legitimacy) that would have been the price of such defiance. My rationalization for not living up to his model was that Roy had the rectitude and unbending courage of the Protestant conscience, ready to live and die by the principle: Here I stand, I can do no other. Yet despite what had just happened, I still dreamt of reshaping the Orthodox community, hoping to regain its understanding and help move it back toward the rest of the Jewish community and toward Christians and society at large. It would have been an exercise in futility and self-defeat for me to argue to the community in a language that it did not speak—especially when people of ill will were standing by to put a sinister twist on my every word. All in all, this episode, one I am not proud of, was a painful lesson on the dangers of being too far ahead of one's community.

For a while it looked as though my affirmative views on Christianity had unleashed an irresistible force and that I would be impeached. To this day, I do not know all that transpired behind the scenes. The RCA looked to Rabbi Lamm for guidance, although he held no formal title in the organization. At some point, Dr. Lamm was persuaded that he must intervene to stop the process because the publicity would be very unflattering to Orthodoxy and appalling to the donors of Yeshiva University. Still, momentum was strong for condemning me. Here the ultimate irony of Orthodox nonparticipation in the Jewish-Christian dialogue made its impact felt. Many moderates feared that a conviction for heresy would generate a negative picture of an intolerant Orthodoxy that would cause public relations damage to the community. Other of my opponents viewed Christians through the old premodern perspective—as dangerous authorities, liable to erupt at any moment in anger against Jews, even to the point of violence. Some others in the community feared that persecuting and condemning ecumenical, "innocent" Yitz Greenberg for the crime of being soft on Christianity could lead to a serious backlash against Jews. The old medieval principle that Jews should do (and should not do) certain things to avoid arousing the hatred of gentiles also came into play. So, the "Christian factor" first put me on trial, and then in the final agreement with the RCA, freed me from prosecution—lest the trial become public.

As one can see, the ironies that arose in this situation abound. Despite refusing to back down on the principle of pluralism, I agreed to take steps to make it clearer that the value of pluralism did not abolish distinctions between religious positions; nor did it lead to dismissal of halakhic contradictions between Orthodoxy and the liberal movements. While reserving the right to go on teaching Torah in Conservative, Reform, and Reconstructionist congregations—in fact, anywhere people would invite me in—I agreed not to take public ritual honors in the liturgies of these communities, lest it be interpreted that I denied there were halakhic objections to specific aspects of liberal services. In point of fact, I did—and do—recognize that various aspects of liberal practice do break with halakhic tradition. However, my position remains that these denominations are valid partners in the covenant of the Jewish people, and that their prayers are heard and accepted by God. They constitute legitimate Jewish communities whose members fulfill their obligations of prayer and Torah study as they participate in such activities. But my positions and activities vis-à-vis the Christian issues were left off the table altogether for fear that if any of this leaked, the outcome could be explosive. In essence, I went on in the Jewish-Christian dialogue as if nothing had happened. However, the entire affair left a permanent residue of mistrust toward me in the Orthodox community and did damage to my standing.

CONFLICTS OVER A POSITIVE THEOLOGY OF CHRISTIANITY

What heresy hunters could not accomplish, the internal and external enemies of Jewry could. A full 10 years passed between publication of

"Organic Model" and its corollary essay, "Judaism and Christianity: Their Respective Roles in the Strategy of Redemption." The main reason for the delay was my personal preoccupation with the growing assault on Israel's legitimacy in the aftermath of the Israeli war in Lebanon from 1982 to 1985. That war and its outcome made clear—to my deep angst—that Sadat's initiative in 1979 and the subsequent breakthrough peace accord between Israel and Egypt were not going to translate into a universal peace between Israel and its Arab neighbors. Over the next two decades, the image of Israel in the eyes of the world shifted steadily from a David resisting an Arab Goliath that sought its destruction, to Israel as the giant trampling on its neighbors; in particular, the Palestinians in the territories. I earnestly believed that the Jewish state, in protecting itself, was exercising a genuine ethic of power—one subject to flaws and errors, overreactions and mixed motives, yet restrained, defensive, designed to minimize the suffering of others, at real cost to its own in terms of lives and capital. Given the Arabs' refusal to affirm the legitimacy of Israel, I felt (and feel) that morally equating the two sides (not to mention depicting the Israelis as colonialist aggressors, if not Nazis) constituted collaboration to undermine Israel's right to exist, leaving it vulnerable to future genocide. Therefore, I turned from my other ideological agendas in order to write on the ethics of Jewish power and the defense of Israel. I have never lost the belief that in taking and properly using power, Israel is carrying out a central covenantal task. I continue to hold that Israel is a moral and theological response to the intolerable powerlessness of the victims of the Holocaust and serves as a modest, but needed, light unto the nations as to how to exercise power under conditions of extended attack and unrelenting tension.

At the same time, Jewish denominational polarization was reaching unprecedented intensity. A genuine, perhaps irremediable, split loomed, a breach that would cripple the community's capacity to deal with the challenge of freedom and to reach out to the unaffiliated. CLAL multiplied its efforts to find ways to promote unity and to offer pluralism as the alternative to polarization. Perforce, I had to reduce my time in Jewish-Christian dialogue. I missed the experience and remember often complaining to Christian friends that if only the churches would give more help to Israel, I could spend more time working to bring Jews and Christians closer to each other.

My hopes were in vain. Indeed, as Christian sympathy eroded, I was experiencing doubt that Christian-Jewish dialogue was in fact engendering meaningful changes and generating new understanding between Jews and Christians. In 1967, the deafening silence of most Christian churches during the tense period leading up to the Six-Day War, when Israel faced genocidal threats and a military assault by the united Arab nations, had shaken many

Jewish participants in the dialogue. The apathy within the Christian community made us wonder whether Christian faith had built into it a permanent coldness toward Jewish fate that could never be overcome. Most Christian groups countered that, until then, they had no idea that the State of Israel was so central to Jewish life and faith, especially since the Jewish state mostly had been left out of the ongoing dialogue. This point was, alas, only too true. Both sides concluded that the only solution was to pay more attention to the significance of Israel, rather than to withdraw from the dialogue. The topic of Israel was feverishly added to a thousand dialogue programs.

In 1973, during the Yom Kippur War, Christians did somewhat better in understanding and supporting Jewish concerns. Over the next three decades, the Catholic Church and other official Christian bodies continuously moved forward, improving teachings or correcting historical mistreatments of Jewish religion. More and more affirmations of the ongoing validity of Judaism were articulated by mainstream churches and pioneering theologians, each in its own way. The most notable example came in Pope John Paul's declaration in the course of a visit to a synagogue in Rome that Judaism was an ongoing, valid covenant. Still, crises continued to flare periodically, especially when past sins were denied or when various Christian bodies tilted toward the Arab side. One example: John Paul II—theologically the most advanced pope in history in recognizing Judaism's current validity—nevertheless sought to beatify Pius XII. Many Jews were driven to despair by this aggressive defense of a pope who had miserably failed to defend Jews in the Holocaust. Whenever such moments of conflict occur, some Jewish leaders question the fundamental value of new encounter between Christians and Jews. (And given the role of the Gospels as a primary source of anti-Semitic images and action, can any permanent corrective be accomplished through dialogue?)

Unfortunately, such periodic crises of trust stir up a great deal of anger and inherited suspicion on both sides. Nevertheless, many Jewish dialogue participants, myself among them, resist the urge to pull out of the dialogue, refusing to make the enterprise of repentance and mutual re-visioning over the past half century an exercise in futility. Admittedly, I am not a disinterested observer. Still, in my best judgment, the hope quickened by this dialogue should far outweigh the despair periodically engendered by incidents of Christian regression. True, the process is not complete and past negative sources and attitudes are not yet permanently vanquished. Still, the rearticulation of Christian attitudes toward Judaism and the determination to end the teaching of contempt toward the Jewish religion already constitute one of the great moral cleansing revolutions of all time—in any religion. (This statement assumes that these breakthroughs are never reversed; however, it is still too soon to know whether these changes are in fact final and irreversible.)

I believe that re-visioning the Christian-Jewish relationship through bilateral self-revision is the mission of this generation and that persistence will bring the needed permanent breakthrough. Trying for complete healing, even if the project fails, constitutes nobler, more responsible behavior than perpetuating the cruel and contentious history that has thus far cursed both groups. Moreover, I still believe that, with God's help, success will crown these efforts and both traditions will be uplifted. Therefore, whatever my internal oscillations, I have never abandoned the work, especially since it was our Christian friends and soul mates who were among the leaders upholding Christian responsibilities toward Israel and the Jewish people.

The "Respective Roles" essay was the next step on my continuing journey. "Respective Roles" argued that Judaism and Christianity shared one central message: the triumph of life. Both faiths share the belief that the process of redeeming the world operates through the covenant, that is, a Divine-human partnership. However, the covenant process generates many paradoxical and dialectical effects that can only be balanced properly by having different communities explore and realize the polar and tension-filled possibilities. Therefore, the two faiths *need each other* to maximize the good and to offset the negative tendencies inherent in both as they follow their own distinctive paths. The two faiths must learn to see themselves as two aspects of a general divine strategy of redemption. The essay included concrete examples of the self-revisions implicit in this new partnership and how this could lead to mutual growth and to greater service for humanity. Summing up the previous two decades of thinking, I argued that "the mission of this generation [is] to renew revelation, to continue the covenantal way, and to discover each other . . . Let these two religions model the truth that the love of God leads to the total discovery of the image of God in the other, not to its distortion or elimination."

Looking back, I am struck by the one obvious omission in the essay. I never openly said that God actively willed the opening of Sinai's revelation and covenant to the gentiles through the formation of a new religion, Christianity, emerging out of Judaism and the Jewish people. Understandably, one hesitates to make such a statement since it goes beyond the millennia-old consensus of the Jewish people vis-à-vis Christianity. I also feared then, as I fear now, that some Jews might unjustly use my teaching to justify their religious syncretism. Nevertheless, in reflecting back, I wonder now if this omission did not, in the end, result from my unwillingness, certainly unconscious, to go through another inquisition at the hands of my community.

CENTERING ON LIFE: COVENANTAL PLURALISM

But my silence did not last long. By now, I was deeply involved in working out a theology of Judaism as the religion that teaches, models, and works for the triumph of life. This centering on life was in part a delayed reaction to decades of immersion in the Holocaust and death; the more affirmative tone also reflected coming to terms to some extent with my father's death and the lifting of my deep depression. In the light of the new theological focus, I saw both religions as truly committed to the same ideal of *tikun olam*. Moreover, I became convinced that in a secularized and media-wired world, the moral and cultural credibility of both Judaism and Christianity would depend increasingly on overcoming the legacy of their interacting hatefulness. They would hardly get a hearing for their individual messages unless each faith tradition was able to set a standard of mutual respect that at least equaled the pluralist norms of modern culture. Any religion professing the goal of perfecting the world to enable the victory of life over death should enthusiastically welcome any and all other faiths willing to partner with it in such a daunting task. Furthermore, after the *Shoah*, every religion should be so hungry to rebalance the world back toward life that it should be prepared to overcome barriers, stereotypes, and shameful histories in order to forge such partnerships. I concluded that we needed to develop a comprehensive and positive Jewish theology of Christianity.

Of course, from the early days of entry into the Jewish-Christian dialogue, I was aware that Franz Rosenzveig had developed a powerful theology affirming Christianity as a second covenant, as God's channel to reach out to the gentiles. I always admired Rosenzveig's comprehensive theology of Judaism, its sophistication, its ability to articulate Jewish perspectives unintimidated by modernist norms and conventional wisdom. But I was distanced from Rosenzveig's thinking about the relationship between Judaism and Christianity—and the Holocaust was a huge barrier between us on this matter. He positioned Judaism as "outside" of history, dwelling directly with God—while Christians, as the people of a pilgrim faith, entered into the trials and vicissitudes of history in the course of trying to bring humanity to God. Since the Holocaust was driving my thinking, it seemed all too obvious that Judaism was not outside the maelstrom of history. To my mind, Judaism was always charged with the task of journeying through history, showing the way for humanity toward *tikun olam*. Furthermore, the Jewish calling after the *Shoah* was to enter into history with both feet and strive to move the entire world toward redemption. To me, Judaism was as much a pilgrim religion as Christianity; it could work alongside Christianity but it could not turn its mission over to that faith. In my judgment, Rosenzveig, writing before the rebirth of the State of Israel, was glorifying Jewish powerlessness and giving over much too much of the task of witnessing to the nations. Moreover, I wanted to focus on the triumph of life through covenantal action as the central teaching of Judaism—and of Christianity. When I tried to articulate the three fundamental stories of the Jewish narrative, they came out to be Creation, Covenant, and Redemption, whereas Rosenzveig's second story was Revelation.

The next essay in this series, "Covenantal Pluralism," expressed these new directions. The article was reworked from a presentation at a conference organized by Rabbi David Rosen in Jerusalem in 1994 and published in 1997. What a sense of excitement and hope that conference engendered, especially because Cardinal Ratzinger participated on behalf of the Vatican. Ratzinger's own speech was fairly cautious, constituting a modest statement of the positive Catholic theology of Judaism developed since Vatican II. However, his mere presence as Catholicism's chief supervisor of doctrinal purity spoke volumes. As well, a few of his words seemed to bestow his blessing on the emerging pluralism that affirmed Judaism and Christianity as ongoing, valid covenantal religions (in the spirit of John Paul II's talk in 1986 at the Rome synagogue). Thus, it was quite a comedown six years later to read the Ratzinger-inspired declaration "Dominus Iesus," which focused on protecting the supremacy of Christ and the Catholic Church as the sole channel of salvation. This declaration very much pulled back from the earlier generosity of spirit expressed in the cardinal's words in 1994.

"Covenantal Pluralism" presented a different theological universe than my earlier, more cautious articulations that Christianity was a valid, necessary outgrowth from Judaism, albeit not for Jews. The new essay started by affirming a joint role in history for the two faiths and upheld a distinctive unity between Jews and Christians. The essay began with the assertion that "the people of Israel" have been chosen to witness to their loving God and to the divine plan for humanity and the cosmos. I hinted that "the people of Israel" were not Israelis or Jews only, but Christians and Muslims as well. The members of the other faiths could be recognized as Abraham's cherished children, but only when they purged themselves of hatred of Jews and of supersessionist claims.

Reading the essay now, I realize that, at the time, I was under the spell of the hopes raised by the Oslo peace accords between Israel and the Palestinians. Although I did not expect that all conflicts would be resolved speedily, I mistakenly assumed that Israel's pariah status in the world would soon come to an end. If this happened, then future conflict, even war, would not pose the threat of genocide, in the event that Israel lost. Unconsciously I blinded myself to the spread of radical Islam with its message of hatred for the West and destruction for the Jews. I wishfully looked away from the unrepentant, almost unchecked supersessionism that has come to dominate current Islamic thinking and theology, the kind of thinking that once ruled Christianity and Judaism prior to the modernizing process. Were this essay being written today, I would not have equated Christians and Muslims. Rather, I would have acknowledged regretfully that the Muslim mainstream is, by and large, far from purging itself of supersessionism and hatred.

"Covenantal Pluralism" focused theologically on the stories of Creation ("the divine vision of an intended perfect world"), Covenant ("that process operating through a Divine-human partnership whereby our imperfect world will be brought to that state of perfection") and Redemption ("the culmination and realization of the process"). All three together added up to a master narrative of the triumph of life. In effect, I argued that with respect to the first and third stories (Creation and Redemption), the two religions are of one mind; in the second story (Covenant), they are parallel. Both religious communities strive to work toward perfection of the world. Both have served as teachers, role models, and coworkers to move the world toward perfection.

In retrospect, the entire essay is suffused with unrestrained utopian hope (probably implicit in the very concept of the triumph of life). Some of the unbridled optimism stemmed from the collapse of the Communist empire in 1989, which led me to the conviction that the triumph of democracy and the growth of pluralism were rooted in human nature and therefore unstoppable. I was further buoyed by the economic boom in America in the 1990s that so clearly benefited the people I was teaching or working with professionally; by our foundation's success in creating affluent partnerships to revive American Judaism; and by my own personal good fortune in being able to work daily with my son with a closeness and easy mutuality of ideas that few fathers can even dream about. All of these positive signs seemed to reinforce the heady visions of covenantal pluralism. I do not apologize for my exaggerated optimism in that essay; at least there was nothing foolish or cruel in it. But much has happened since then to temper my hopes, diminish my expectations, and lengthen the timetables for achieving goals.

"Covenantal Pluralism" argued that both Judaism and Christianity have paid a heavy price for their original readings of the split between them. Although officially, they taught their followers to choose life and love, in their relationship to each other they communicated a message of hatred and death. As an alternative reading of their original separation, I proposed that it was God's plan to bring the vision of redemption and covenant in a new iteration to a wider group of humanity, i.e., the Christians. Founders of this

41

new faith needed to emerge out of the family and covenantal community of Israel. Therefore, Judaism should affirm Christianity as born in the fullness of Judaism's time. However—reversing Paul's classic image in the New Testament—God's intention in making way for Christianity should be understood as the grafting of a shoot of the stalk of Abraham onto the tree of the gentiles. Christianity thus represented neither replacement nor repudiation of Judaism but instead the creation of an offshoot, a reaching out to new masses. Christians misread their origins within Judaism as a sign that the new faith was intended to replace the original faith. Jews were threatened by the Christian claim of election and read the claim of supersessionism as proof of Christianity's falsity. The triumphalism, rejectionism, cruelty, and mutual defamation grew out of human need for reassurances that "indeed, I am the favorite son." This sense of rivalry for God's favor led both communities astray. Both faiths needed to abandon their historical allegiance to their own chosenness at the expense of the other's election. Rather, they needed to understand that divine election was a case of multiple choice. God as a divine parent was capable of loving each child infinitely without loving any less. I argued in the essay that "There is enough love in God to choose again and again."

The good news was that Christian and Jewish interest in a Jewish theology of Christianity was growing. Within a year after publishing this essay, I again overrode my reluctance to go to Germany in order to participate in a conference with people with unblemished records of authentic dialogue and concern for Jews and Israel, the International Council of Christians and Jews. The purpose was to present a follow-up paper titled "Pluralism and Partnership." The paper's argument was built on the assumption that this was a time of great breakthroughs in recognizing the image of God in the other, which is the basis of principled pluralism. This reasoning also leads us to acknowledge that another's religion is valid because it has trained and nurtured human beings in the image of God. In turn, this insight (into the other faith's achievements) leads us to admit the limits of our own faith and truth, however absolute. Our own religion must make room for the independent dignity of the other and the faith of the other. That is, our own religion must necessarily impose self-limits in order to allow the other's faith to exist in its own right. This model, if applied to the relationship of Judaism and Christianity, would allow us to leave behind our freighted history and negatively charged past categorizations. This model can equally be applied to revisioned relationships with other world religions as well.

Finally, the essay argued that it was urgent for Jews and for Christians to go beyond pluralism into partnership with each other and with every faith willing to help to perfect the world. In pluralism, one faith accepts the existence of the other, even seeks to recast its own self-understanding to affirm the ongoing validity and dignity of the other, and eventually is able to integrate insights from the other. Partnership, however, involves going one step further. Each partner affirms that its truth/faith/system alone cannot fulfill God's dreams. The world needs the contribution that the other religion can make for the sake of achieving wholeness and perfection for all. A partner affirms (today, I would say: celebrates) that God assigns different roles and different contributions to different groups.

COVENANTS IN PARTNERSHIP

By the late 1990s, the circle of Jews interested in reaching out theologically to positively affirm Christianity had grown. Happily, the Institute of Christian and Jewish Studies in Baltimore, the cutting-edge institution in developing a two-way theological discourse, undertook to create a major Jewish statement publicly affirming Christianity as a religion. The statement, issued in 2000 under the title *Dabru Emet (Speak Truth): A Jewish Statement on Christians and Christianity*, was supported and given depth by a book of invited essays dealing with Jewish perspectives on Christianity, each of these paired with a response by a Christian scholar from a Christian perspective. I hoped to write two essays, but I could not clear adequate time and composed only the essay published herein, entitled "Judaism and Christianity: Covenants of Redemption."

"Covenants of Redemption" used the grammar of biblical covenant to demonstrate the logic of Judaism and Christianity's coexistence as partner religions. The fundamental and universal biblical statement is that God wants Creation (the world as it is now) to be redeemed. Out of love for humanity, God imposes self-limits and calls humans to be partners in the process of *tikun olam*. God commits to uphold the laws of nature that allow humans to live constructive, dignified lives within the framework of a stable, dependable natural order. Humans pledge to live in harmony with the rhythms of the universe—that is, God's plan—to increase life and improve nature and society to fully sustain the value of life, especially human life with its fundamental dignities. This is the universal covenant with all humanity, biblically called the covenant of Noah. This covenant is never superseded. Every religion that accepts these values and goals derives its legitimacy, its direct access to God, and its partnership with the Deity from this covenant open to all people, all the time.

The Abrahamic/Sinaitic covenant of Israel is an additional, particular covenant initiated by divine wisdom and love, to remove the danger of completely centralized spiritual and political power. Particular covenants have their advantages, including freedom to experiment and diversify on a human scale; more local, intimate connections; and distinctive human textures, languages, and memories. While the particular covenants are intended to serve as models and as sources of blessing for all humans, such covenants raise other risks—of parochialism, tribalism, or amoral familism (that is, a Mafia-like morality), and loss of solidarity and of responsibility for all humanity. Therefore, particular covenants need to be corrected and refreshed by encounters with other particular covenants and by ongoing contact with humanity at large as well as with the universal covenant.

In my view, Christianity itself is another one of the particular covenants that God has called into being in order to engage more and more humans in the process of *tikun olam*. The issues of precedence between Judaism and Christianity and the nature of the split are really secondary. Christianity was intended as part of God's plan to bring the vision of redemption and the covenantal way more widely to the attention of humanity. In "Covenants of Redemption," I speculated that the timing of Christianity's birth reflected the fact that the Jewish people had sufficiently internalized the process of being in covenant to be able to take on new levels of responsibility. This maturation equipped Jewry to sustain the shock of the destruction of the Temple and to give birth to Christianity as a rival (and soon after, a dominant rival) without crumbling. The proof of God's sound judgment is that Jewry was able to give rise to Rabbinic Judaism and enter another stage of the covenant without losing its faith or its way. Christianity's arrival was timed perfectly to take advantage of the spiritual search taking place within the Hellenistic world.

The tragedy in their separation was that each faith could only conceive that its own genuine religious experiences as well as its inner coherence and vitality required that the religious truth of the other group be finished or false. (A caveat: The two groups followed different courses in attempting to invalidate the truth of each other's faiths. Christianity developed its replacement theology in a more proactive, aggressive way; Judaism was more reactive and defensive.) Each religion paid a price in dismissing the other. Christianity skewed toward dualism, minimizing the religious significance of carnal matters, the law, and the body. Judaism slid into denigrating political and military power, and narrowed its concern vis-à-vis non-Jews. Both faiths stepped away from history as a meaningful theater of operations for God and humanity, at great cost to their inner spiritual strength, to their constituencies, and to the world around them. Additionally, Christianity was led to terrible excesses vis-à-vis the Jewish faith and people.

My conclusion was that in order to correct itself by removing degrading traditions toward other faiths as well as filtering out the residue of negative attitudes toward outsiders inherited from the past, each religion should now affirm and seek to validate (rather than refute) the legitimate claims and hopes of the other. Comfortable in the conviction that Christianity's large role in the world is not diminished by Judaism's ongoing vitality, Christians should celebrate the Jewish renewal of the covenant and the Jews' return to the land as a signal of God's faithfulness and the eternity of God's promises. Comfortable in the interpretation that the founding events of Christianity were meant to be accepted by Christians only and were not intended to undermine the ongoing validity of the Jewish way, Jews should understand that Resurrection and Incarnation were not putative facts to be argued over; they were signals intended for and recognized by the Christian community to bring them closer to God. The conclusion of "Covenants of Redemption" was that the achievements of both religions trump their vexed histories with each other; both have contributed much to the world. Both faiths have transmitted God's message and worked toward the final redemption. But both have fallen short of their ultimate goals. Therefore, both must come to recognize that they need each other's efforts and those of others to realize their deepest hopes.

Let me conclude this argument by pointing out that one should beware of focusing new thinking just on the internal Jewish or Christian historical experience, however remarkable. The new developments are taking place within the framework of a broader civilizational transformation for humanity. Both faiths are reacting to modernity—the Promethean human effort to take charge of humanity's destiny—that led to the flowering of science, technology, liberalism, and democracy. But that surge set off a moral/political/cultural disequilibrium, incarnated in a tidal wave of totalitarianism and in the Holocaust, which simultaneously climaxed and undermined modernity. The ineluctable outcome was the emerging era of postmodernity marked by even greater human assumption of power, by the arousal of powerful counterforces such as conservatism and fundamentalism, as well as the pluralization of religion, culture, and values. Within this constellation, the re-creation of Israel is the particular Jewish paradigm of humanity come-of-age in its relationship to science, politics, economics, religion, and God.

Judaism and Christianity ignore these trends only at the cost of their own relevance; in fact, neither has turned away from the time of their new visitation, i.e., their new revelations. Since the classic role of each community has been to be "a covenant people, a light unto nations," one can guess that a transformation in each one's self-understanding will carry with it a message for other religions. A successful, positive change in the relationship to each other can point the way to better future understandings between all nations and religions of the earth.

WHERE DO WE STAND NOW?

Where do we stand now? I stand, often bruised and disappointed—when Christians regress into supersessionist thinking; when they deny, belittle, or evade their past sins. In the year 2004, Mel Gibson produced a film, *The Passion of the Christ*, which featured a powerful fundamentalist retelling of the Gospel story. The movie highlighted (literally) the Jewish authorities as the dominant persecutors (whitewashing Pontius Pilate and inventing his kindly wife, Claudia, wishing to save Jesus). By contrast, the Jewish authorities and mob are hook-nosed, cruel, bloodthirsty, unmoved by Jesus' innocence and agony, insistent on his death, and in league with the devil (literally portrayed in feminine form). This was in flagrant violation of Vatican II's "Nostra Aetate" declaration, and of other official Protestant strictures warning against such representations that historically spread hatred of Jews. The film won approval from many evangelicals (and even conservative Catholics, including some who affirm Judaism's validity) for its powerful narrative of Christ's life. This support was given notwithstanding that the movie repeated the sin of slander and hate-mongering vis-à-vis Jews for which many official Church bodies had confessed guilt and expressed repentance. The American Bishops never spoke out against the violation of their guidelines. Will the Gospel of Love never stop generating hate for Jews?

Similarly, I stand angered when Christians turn on Israel or buy the approbation of others at the expense of their erstwhile victims. Since the outbreak of the second *intifada* in 2000, hateful images of Israel's behavior (and concomitant demonization of the Jews) have been spread relentlessly by Arab media and rhetoric—aided and abetted by many Western (indeed, most European) media. These practices have injected a constant flow of poisonous, genocidal impulses into the bloodstream of Islam. Tragically, I do not see, at this time, enough healthy antibodies in the mainstream of Islam to fight and eliminate this infection. I have not given up on Jewish-Muslim dialogue, as I hope and pray that Islam as a universal religion will find the inner resources to restore its moral and cultural health. But in the interim, I feel that Christians must step in to protect Jews and Judaism—especially in light of their faith community's responsibility for creating the penumbra of hateful stereotyping around Jews and for lending credibility to the demonization of Jews. I worry that out of alliances with Christian communities living within the Middle East and out of residual historical coldness to Jews, Christians may betray Israel or stand by in the face of Islamic anti-Semitism.

Still, I remain full of hope that Christian faithfulness will overcome the past. I remain no less full of admiration for Christianity as a continuing source for human ethics, for sacrificial service to humanity, and spiritual fidelity to God. I continue to explore with wonder and thanksgiving the possibility that this generation is the one worthy enough to bring a new birth of freedom and variety to the Divine-human relationship. We should be humbled and grateful that we can bring a fresh pulse of love and compassion for all humans into our religious ways of life: If this generation wills it, it can restore to the fabric of Jewish and Christian religions the beauty and the breadth of God's vision and love for all. If such a healing is accomplished, then Judaism and Christianity in partnership could lead the world toward messianic accomplishments in upgrading human life, dignity, and peace.

Will I live to see a decisive transformation of the relationship so that both faiths can never again be a source of hatred toward each other or any other religious community? Will my grandchildren, and Roy Eckardt's, comfortably embrace the fullness of other believers' spiritual lives while fulfilling and witnessing their own? Will the renaissance of Jewish life triumph over the destruction inflicted in this age? Will religious renewal overcome the assimilation and ignorance that afflict Jewry at this time? Only God knows the answer, and God asks our help to make the right outcome happen. I consider myself blessed to be alive at such a time, to be a participant in the greatest story ever told, and to be given a chance to help shape a happy ending.

1960s
- "The Cultural Revolution and Religious Unity," *Religious Education,* vol. 62, no. 2 (March 1967), pp. 98–104.
- "The New Encounter of Judaism and Christianity," *Barat Review,* vol. 3, no. 2 (June 1967), pp. 113–125.

1970s
- "Cloud of Smoke, Pillar of Fire: Judaism, Christianity and Modernity After the Holocaust," in *Auschwitz: Beginning of a New Era?* ed. Eva Fleischner (New York: KTAV, 1977), pp. 7–55, 441–446.
- "New Revelations and New Patterns in the Relationship of Judaism and Christianity," *Journal of Ecumenical Studies,* vol. 16, no. 2 (Spring 1979), pp. 249–267.

1980s
- "The Relationship of Judaism and Christianity: Toward a New Organic Model," in *Twenty Years of Jewish/Catholic Relations,* eds. Eugene Fisher, James Rudin, and Marc Tanenbaum (NY: Paulist Press, 1986), pp. 191–211.

1990s

- "Judaism and Christianity: Their Respective Roles in the Divine Strategy of Redemption," in *Visions of the Other: Jewish and Christian Theologians Assess the Dialogue,* ed. Eugene J. Fisher (Mahwah, NY: Paulist Press, 1994), pp. 7–27.
- "Covenantal Pluralism," *Journal of Ecumenical Studies,* vol. 34, no. 3 (Summer 1997), pp. 425–436.
- "Pluralism and Partnership," in *Unity Without Uniformity: The Challenge of Pluralism,* Martin Buber House Publication Number 26 (International Council of Christians and Jews, Spring 1999), pp. 68–81.

2000s

- "Judaism and Christianity: Covenants of Redemption," in *Christianity in Jewish Terms,* eds. Tikva Frymer-Kensy, David Novak, Peter Ochs, David Fox Sandmel, Michael A. Signer (Boulder, CO: Westview Press, 2000), pp. 141–158.

Notes

1. Anchor Bible translation.
2. My translation, as cited in Roy and Alice E. Eckardt, *A Long Night's Journey into Day* (Detroit: Wayne State University Press, 1982), p. 104.
3. To be reprinted by The Jewish Publication Society in a second volume of collected essays (forthcoming).
4. A decade after this essay appeared, the death of the Lubavitcher Rebbe—one of the most influential Jews of the twentieth century—proved the essential validity and necessity of such a distinction. Rabbi Schneerson's followers, electrified by the scope of their achievements under his inspired leadership, were swept up in a messianic fever, declaring him to be the long-awaited redeemer. But with his death, in 1994, the Rebbe fell short of bringing universal redemption, although he clearly had been teaching right values and positive Jewish behaviors. The unwillingness of his followers to admit this failure hardly turned him into a false messiah—as his detractors and critics of Chabad now styled him.
5. Now, however, see Bernice Bruteau, ed., *Jesus through Jewish Eyes* (Maryknoll, NY: Orbis Books, 2001). Byron Sherwin, in the article "'Who Do You Say That I Am' (Mark 8:29): A New Jewish View of Jesus," (*Journal of Ecumenical Studies,* vol. 31, nos. 3–4 [summer–fall 1994]), reprinted in *Jesus through Jewish Eyes* (pp. 31–44), took up the proposal that Jesus be affirmed as a failed messiah. However, Sherwin then focused on identifying Jesus with messiah son of Joseph, i.e., a traditional Jewish model of a first would-be messiah who gets killed and fails his mission, and is followed by the second, ultimately successful messiah son of David. I was trying to suggest a model of a messiah who comes within a non-Jewish framework and act as a redeemer for the gentiles but who did not accomplish the full mission in his first attempt.

Covenantal Partners in a Postmodern World

This essay strives to reimagine the relationship between Judaism and Christianity by reexamining the encounter between these two faiths. It is an historical narrative constructed with a theological goal: to make the argument that both Judaism and Christianity were jointly and severally intended to play a part in an Infinite Creator's plan to perfect the world. This proposed narrative, rooted in an awareness of the image of God found in Jews and Christians alike, affirms the independent dignity of each tradition, their intertwined destiny, and their potential partnership to perfect the world.

This account attempts to break out of the ethnocentric parameters and conflict-ridden historical context within which the two faiths have primarily related over the past two millennia. I am tempted to say that the perspective of the narrative is theocentric. That is to say, it seeks to look at the patterns of interaction from the vantage point of an imagined divine intention to bring into being two covenantal communities working side by side for *tikun olam*. Of course, one cannot write from a truly theocentric perspective; in the end, we are human and not God. We are locked in our mortal bodies, embedded in our socio-economic-cultural contexts, which filter our received evidence and shape our interpretive schema. Nevertheless, much of sacred Scripture seeks to lift our gaze up to the mountains and beyond to the vastness of Creation. The divine word strives to inspire us to see life not from the narrow confines of fleeting, 80-year-life-expectant, mortal flesh-and-blood creatures. Rather, we are to find our place in a world that we now understand was created eons before we came into being by a Creator who existed eternities before this universe was shaped; a world whose idealized

49

perfection may well be realized ages after we are gone from the scene. If humans can see the world even a little bit from these perspectives, they will recognize their modest place; their judgments will be less distorted by the skewing that power, wealth, social standing, cultural cocoon, and religious membership generate. They will be more able to find their proper role in the process of perfecting the world. They will act closer to the norms of love, justice, and dignity, which are the proper responses to the value of their fellow creatures.

Humans—including theologians—should walk in God's ways (Deut. 10:12) and try to inspire people by offering broader vistas. Then, if this essay helps Jews and Christians envision playing a more positive role in a drama that has a wider frame than either religion alone can provide, if it can stretch the imagination of religious leadership just a bit so as to make more room for the dignity of other faiths in the process of perfecting the world, then it will have made its contribution. I should add that while this historical-theological narrative will appeal primarily to postmodern Jews and Christians, it is intended for all people of good faith who work to define and live a good life that includes respect for all faiths and dignity for all humans. Also, while the narrative begins with the biblical stories, it seeks to speak to people with a wide range of approaches to these accounts—from the traditional Jewish and Christian to that of other faith adherents, and to those with secularizing humanist stances. It is written in the belief that the correlation of these narratives to the wisdom of life experiences will make this model credible to just such a wide variety of people, many of whom do not necessarily share my beliefs or the full assumptions that undergird the biblical accounts.

CREATION, REDEMPTION, AND THE GOOD LIFE

Judaism starts with the fundamental affirmation that life is precious and history is meaningful. Christianity, which grew out of Judaism's biblical phase, is also built on this core value. We live in a universe that is neither accidental nor chaotic. The world, despite its infinite variety and size, which seem to outstrip all explanation and elude all human categories, is best described as a creation—that is, an infrastructure designed for life. The stability of matter and the finely calibrated interaction of the life-sustaining laws of nature are signals. They point to a pattern of meaning and purpose in the cosmos.

In turn, the paradigm of Creation signifies the existence of a creator, a force that drives existence, the ground that sustains being. Judaism proclaims the unity of existence and the interconnection of all life bound up with this universal sustaining presence. Since the Creator is not visible, one must learn to see through the surface of reality to plumb the depth at which authentic reality is found; this is where the presence of the Divine is grasped. In truth, the Divine is everywhere, but we must be trained and focused to uncover that presence. As long as the world is full of evil and suffering, the hidden God can only be detected rather than really known; until the world is perfected, we see God dimly, as through a glass, darkly. Once one discovers the presence of God in this imperfect world, however, life is never the same again. You are never alone. Though I walk through a valley in the shadow of death, I fear no evil, for God is with me (Ps. 23:4—my translation).

Whole schools of thought arose in Judaism and Christianity seeking to grasp the full implications of God's presence. To some it meant that the one who walks with God cannot be harmed: "A thousand may fall at your left side, ten thousand at your right, but it [the scourge] shall not reach you" (Ps. 91:7). To others it meant that every event in one's life (as every rain and every drought in national life) is a providential treatment by God in response to one's behavior (see Deut. 11). Still others understood that God upholds the individual in need; God even suffers with the person—but offers no magic protection. To live all of life sustained by the eternal loving arms of God is in itself the reward of trust. In all human sorrows, the Divine is in sorrow; in all human joy, the Lord is gladdened. Once the presence of God is internalized, the healing balm and the enabling power of conscience, which the *Shekhinah* (literally, "Presence") bestows, can never be taken away. This is not to deny that many believers have experienced the agony of abandonment and/or the hiddenness of God. People of faith are particularly vulnerable to this devastating affliction when they labor through periods of innocent suffering or historic oppression. Yet most believers have cried out but persisted, or they have summoned up the memory of past redemptions to sustain them through such dark nights of the soul.

Biblical faith teaches that God's caring, which we experience in our personal lives, is expressed in the vast Creation itself. The Creation Force—whom people call God, Yahweh, *Elohim*, and many other names—is like an infinite Person, omniscient, omnipotent, omnipresent, omnivorously relating to everything. Out of love, the Creator has brought existence into being and continues to dote on it. Out of love, God self-limits to make room for the being of others. Out of love, God has structured a universe with natural laws stable enough that living organisms can grow within it. Out of love, the Divine sustains a reality dependable enough that every human being can potentially develop into a dignified self, living a responsible life.

The cumulative effect of this biblical proclamation of God's caring was a cultural and psychological revolution. Living in a world in which life was nasty, brutish, and short, humans saw the universe as a theater of conflicting supernatural powers that toyed with them. Surrounded by arbitrary, unpredictable, demanding, tyrannical gods, humans sought to appease these authorities by any means possible—by the first fruit, first flock, first blood—any sacrifice that would buy peace, even the ritual surrender of one's own child. People sought out every formula, incantation, and ritual script that could manipulate the divine forces and guarantee a good outcome. The presentation of a law-abiding, humanity-respecting God paved the way for self-affirming human beings—bonding, loving, following, judging, and partnering with God. With the desacralization of natural bodies, nature becomes the dwelling place of God. The conclusion follows that nature should be approached with reverence, but it is not a supernal, independent, or hostile power. Human beings are free to study nature, to master it, or improve it.

The Bible links this narrative of the Creator "hidden" and present in Creation with a future story: the perfection of the world, or Redemption. Biblical religion witnesses that the present, fractured, evil-flecked, death-filled status quo will be overcome. God's intended outcome of Creation is a world filled with life, especially life in its highest, most developed form—humanity—with conditions that completely sustain the fullest dignities of all life. No one should settle for the world as it is, for there is a promise from an Infinite Being that the world will be perfected. Then God will be fully known. When that day comes, "they shall do no evil nor cause any harm throughout My Holy Mountain [= Earth]; for the Earth shall be full of the knowledge of the Lord, as the waters cover the sea" (Isa. 11:9; my translation). The Bible calls this end result Redemption. This condition will initiate a final paradise on earth, for nothing less could do justice to the infinite value, equality, and uniqueness of human beings created in the image of God.

But if there is a loving Creator and an intended ideal outcome, why is the current world a vale of sorrow and tears? Why is Creation not perfect now? To explain this flawed, tormented existence—which is even more heartrending if one believes in a loving Creator—various schools of thought have arisen in Judaism and Christianity. Out of fidelity to the God of Creation, these schools interpret the record of nature and history, of revelation and reason with unceasing commentary, in the hope of reconciling the contradiction.

Many say that the only answer is mystery—an incomprehensibility that should not blind us to the ever-present Redeemer behind reality. Others explain that God made the world perfect, but humanity sinned and spoiled it. (This minority Jewish position became the prevailing view in Christianity until modern times.) Some theologians argued that Creation takes place in cosmic time, in which eons are like a watch in the night; the final perfection will come, but the world must go through the process. Mystics averred that

Creation's flaws reflect a cosmic catastrophe. The inherent contradiction of bringing into being a vast but finite universe intended to be the Place of an Infinite Being led to a rupture in the fabric of creation. This disaster left behind a fragmented universe filled with forces of evil and conflicting power vectors that await Redemption. Still other mystics, both Jewish and Christian, have argued that this world is an illusion, that evil is only a surface phenomenon. True existence is in God, and this existence is perfect, devoid of evil.

Many Jewish and Christian sages concluded that perfected existence could only be reached in a spiritual world to come where the body is discarded. This teaching implies that the world of flesh and blood is a brief interlude, an entrance hall, where humans can earn (or forfeit) their worthiness to enter the eternal perfect world of heaven. (This otherworldly view was dominant in both religions in medieval times.) Other spiritual masters taught that spiritual perfection can be achieved in this world but that this process demands renunciation of worldliness and liberation from ego and self. In modern times, a longtime minority view has become prominent in both faiths: Out of respect for human freedom—or out of a necessity dictated by the dignity of human free will—the world is left flawed and unfinished by God, so that human beings can complete it.

All of these schools have grown in the soil of the living community of faith. Their interpretations are shaped by the interaction of inherited tradition and historical experience, and illuminated by frames of meaning derived from extant cultures and values. By a continuous process of interpretation, all these schools link the past to the present and supply continuity in the face of the frequent, often drastic, discontinuities that arise out of historical change or transformed living conditions. Parallel schools have emerged in both Judaism and Christianity—sometimes in different times—before and after the two faiths separated. All of these schools agree that, in giving religion, God's goal was to help people work through the contradiction between the divine dream and reality. Torah and, later, Talmud and Gospel teach people how to live their lives so as to reconcile the ideal and the real and thus enable the world to achieve Redemption.

Creation teaches us that the universe is infused with values and shaped in accordance with a divine plan to maximize life in the world. One should live—and judge—life by standards that advance this plan. A neutral or wasted life is one that does nothing to advance the cause of Creation; an evil life is one spent in diminishing life or in opposition to the perfecting of the world.

How do we know how to live the good life? The short and simple answer of Israelite religion is that the Creator infused certain rhythms into Creation to move it toward the desired outcome. To live the good life is to live in harmony with these movements to advance, not hinder, the divine plan. Out of love, God gave direction to humans to enable them to go with the flow of Creation. In the words of the Jewish prayer book: "You loved the House of Israel, your people, with an endless Love; [so] you taught us Torah and the commandments." And again: "Our Father, our King, for the sake of our forebears who trusted in you, so *you taught them the laws of life,* be gracious to us and teach us also."[1]

The first chapter of Genesis describes the three primary movements of Creation. The cosmos moves *from chaos (tohu va'vohu) to order (Shabbat);* it moves *from nonlife to life;* finally, *life itself develops* qualitatively as it gains more consciousness, power, capacity for relationship (especially love), freedom, and longevity. In biblical imagery, life develops *from being less to becoming more and more like God.* The climax of this development is the creation of a human being—a creature so conscious, so powerful, so capable of loving, so free as to be an image of God. The possession of these godlike capabilities enables humans to understand the nature of reality, to grasp the presence of the Divine, to recognize the rhythms of Creation—and to choose to live in harmony with them.

The emergence of human beings was a turning point in the history of Creation. Up to this epoch, the development of Creation was governed by the laws of nature and the chemical/genetic programming of all forms of life to maximize reproductive success and populate the world. Of the living creatures, humans alone have the consciousness to understand these laws of life and to choose freely to act in accordance with them. Of course, this same freedom can be used to counter the rhythms of Creation, and thus fight, even set back, the divine plan.

Out of love, and respect for human dignity (which is expressed in humans' exercise of freedom), God elects to honor rigorously the laws of nature. Thanks to this discipline, God does not divert nature to sustain only moral human life, or to punish evil demonstratively. The price of this restraint is that rain falls on the lands of the guilty and the innocent alike; gravity does not release the blameless from its pull in order to spare them from a crash. As Maimonides says, nature runs its course. To humans, therefore, the cosmos often appears to operate as a morally blind machine—although if they delve deeply into existence they will discover that humans enjoy the benefits of the anthropic principle, the built-in bias for nature to sustain higher forms of life. The one way in which God "openly" intervenes on the side of the moral and the needy is through communicating Torah (or equivalent revelation) to humans. This holy wisdom guides people to live by the laws of life, in harmony with Creation.

COVENANT: THE PROCESS OF TIKUN OLAM

Bound by divine self-limitation through the laws of nature and intertwined in the matrix of a reliable reality, God further renounced power. God entered into covenant (partnership) with people in order to engage humanity in its own liberation. The Lord promised not to complete the redemption by coercion or divine force majeure. This was a remarkable act of love and respect, for in giving humans an indispensable role in perfecting the world, God accepted the inescapable outcome: a considerably longer duration for the process of *tikun olam* (repairing the world). Humans operate at a human pace and are motivated by material, conflicting interests; some interests go against the flow of Creation. Given human freedom, all divine plans are subject to setback by willful human misbehavior. In the interim, until Redemption, God suffers—as only an infinite consciousness can suffer—every pain inflicted or agony endured by God's creatures. In effect, God took on boundless suffering to enable human beings to grow into dignified and responsible partners in perfecting the world.

The Noahide Covenant

In this next step of divine pedagogy, God reached out to humanity in its flawed historical context. To encourage human beings to be active and valuable partners, God summoned humanity to join in the process of *tikun olam.* Humans were called to be fruitful and multiply (Gen. 1:28; 8:17; 9:1), to increase the overall presence of life in the world by working and guarding Creation (Gen. 2:15), and to revere, value, and uphold the dignity of every form of life (Gen. 9:4–6). The children of Noah—all of humanity—were offered this covenant of life to live by.

Although the desired outcome is a paradise on earth, the covenant operates out of the unredeemed reality in which people are embedded. To live covenantally, humans should shape every act, in some small or large way, to move the world closer to the ideal state. Therefore, the revelation of the Noahide covenant incorporates models of covenantal behavior that show how to reconcile the ideal and the real. In an ideal world (the Garden of Eden), humans would eat no meat so that their life would not be sustained by the death of other (animal) life (Gen. 1:27–30). In an imperfect world, humans are permitted to eat meat (Gen. 9:3). But the principle of reverence for life is upheld by prohibiting the consumption of blood (Gen. 9:4; cp. 9, 5–6), "for the life of the flesh is in the blood" (Lev. 17:11). Thus, even as the act of eating sustains life, so the restriction upon eating upholds the ideal of a world that maximizes life. In some small way, this behavioral modification moves the world closer to the day when life will triumph. The deeper lesson is that every act of living can advance or set back the movement toward perfection. Every act that is in accordance with the covenant echoes the three fundamental rhythms of the universe: It will favor order over chaos, it will be for life against death, and it will support becoming more like God instead of degrading the qualities of life.

As the laws of nature are given to all forms of life, so is the covenant of Noah offered to all of humanity. This covenant is not repealed or superseded by later covenants (see Isa. 54, especially verses 4–10), for God's promise is eternal and God's covenantal commitment is totally reliable. Human behavior cannot invalidate the covenant any more than it can exhaust the infinite divine mother-love. The covenant of Noah is of greater moment than later Rabbinic tradition indicates. It is more than a covenant of seven commandments that opens the way, but is inferior, to the Abrahamic/Mosaic covenant of 613 commandments. It is more than the Maimonidean framework by which gentiles connect to the way of life that earns them personal salvation in the world to come. The Noahide covenant is no less than the master paradigm of the structured love relationship that links the Divine to the human and humans to the Creator's cosmic plan.

The Noahide covenant reveals that God bonds with humanity and shares in its finite existence. In Joseph B. Soloveitchik's words about the covenantal community, "Finitude and infinity, temporality and eternity, creature and creator become involved in the same community. They bind themselves together and participate in a unitive existence."[2] In the Noahide covenant, the universal Creator agreed to sustain the cosmos and to care for the welfare of all its denizens, from the least to the greatest. The pact extends a universal commandment to humanity: to revere life and to increase it. The sign and reminder of the covenant, the rainbow, is open to and shared by all people. The heart of covenant is the freedom, reciprocity, and equality experienced in the link between God and humanity. Still, people entering covenant initially recognize God as an absolute, not-to-be-reasoned-with-sovereign; they project as God's will their unequal and inferior status before authority. (This is the historical daily fate of most humans.) Thus, unlike Abraham, Noah never argued with God, whatever the divine decree. However, as the covenantal relationship unfolds, the fullness of its implied partnership comes out. Over the millennia, the covenant educates for full human equality and dignity in relationship with God and with humans.

This is not to say that the Noahide covenant is the alpha and omega of covenantal living. The particularist covenants that were established after the

Noahide pact are more comprehensive and more distinctive; they offer a way of life that is rooted in the culture, language, and heritage of the covenanted group. Above all, the more detailed covenants offer a channel to God and structures of relationship, spirituality, and service that provide a distinctive path for the souls of their participants.

The universality of the Noahide covenant does mean, however, that henceforth every religion that works to repair the world—and thus advance the triumph of life—is a valid expression of this divine pact with humanity. Every religion that nurtures the quantity and quality of life (especially if it upholds the dignity and value of life in the image of God) derives its authority and its eternal validity from this divine commitment. Abraham's covenant—a pioneering, world-transforming revelation that teaches God's presence, concern, and obligation—is but one in a series of divine initiatives to redeem suffering humanity. Thus the Hebrew Bible refers to other divine revelations and other nations' access to God (see, for example, Gen. 14:18–20; Num. 22–24; Amos 9:7; see also Mic. 4:5).

Of course, this recognition is in tension with the tendency of monotheistic faith to polarize the world spiritually between its worship of God and idolatry. The universal, pluralizing spirit within Israelite religion also wrestles with the in-group versus out-group ethical system that unfolds in biblical history. Still, the power of the covenantal model is that God's gracious election of one people (the people Israel) leaves room for more than one integral divine relationship with humans. God can single out and redeem even peoples of clashing interests and beliefs. By contrast, had the Hebrew Scripture proclaimed not a metaphor of loving relationship, but rather one of ultimate truth as the message of divine revelation, this would have left scarcely any room for legitimating divergent or contradictory messages possessed by other peoples and faiths.

The Covenant of Abraham and Sarah

Once God extended a covenant to all of humanity, the next step in the divine plan of redemption was to call into being a distinctive, particular covenant people. God wants humanity to keep the way of the Lord by doing what is just and right (Gen.18:19). The best way to instruct people to raise their standards of ethics and relationship to the Divine without using coercive tactics is to inspire them with a human model that freely and lovingly sets an example. This divine purpose is achieved by establishing a particular covenant, historically and culturally located, such as the Abrahamic covenant. God singled out Abraham and Sarah with love. To be known

(Gen. 18:19) lovingly is the most profound confirmation of the value and uniqueness of the individual. The beloved experiences being loved as having been set aside out of the mass of humankind—and feels strengthened and challenged to live more intensely. The knowledge of being chosen leads to a feeling of gratitude. It engenders an inner search to discover which distinctive capacities and what intrinsic values have evoked such love. This feeling also generates a wish to discover the distinctive task for which these capacities are suited and the calling that one's soul must answer.

In the covenant of Abraham (and others), being chosen translates into a mission to bring God and the divine blessing to a world that needs them. The covenantal behaviors of the chosen are intended to instruct all people and stimulate them to higher responsibility for *tikun olam*. This, then, is the stuff of which the Abrahamic covenant's behaviors are made: human mundane activities, oriented toward the Divine by being directed toward repairing the world.

On the surface, the election of a particular group to carry on the covenant appears to privilege this group. But in fact, the election of a distinct group affirms the uniqueness of individual humans while validating all groups' potential for parallel roles as an avant-garde. That is why God, in making Abraham and Sarah God's beloved, promised that their blessing would be a blessing to all of humanity (Gen. 12:2–3). Once God singled out one group lovingly, then God, acting out of love, could follow that precedent with another group, without dismissing or demeaning the first. Henceforth, every person elected could experience being equal in value and dignity to every other while being sent on the path of life that is uniquely suited for his or her soul. Creating multiple particular covenants allows for a variety of experiments to find right ways of covenantal living; this division of labor also protects the human scale of efforts to perfect the world. Equally important, pluralization undercuts the danger of one centralized group controlling the process of redemption. Exclusive power inevitably tempts human groups into dominating others or corrupts them into an abuse of power, such as confusing their own establishment with the divinely intended redeemed state.

Why were a sheikh in Bronze Age Mesopotamia, Abraham, and his wife, Sarah, given a central, pioneering role in actualizing the next stage of covenantal development? Why was this couple—and their descendants—worthy of so singular a mission? The answer the Bible gives is as arbitrary and as unexpected as love. ". . . God desired your ancestors, to love them; then God chose their children after them . . ." (Deut. 10:1—my translation). Christian commentary has tended to focus more on God's grace in choosing, that is, on the unmerited gift of infinite love. Jewish tradition has focused more on finding the virtues of Abraham and Sarah that evoked the Divine mother-love. However, both religions—in the spectrum of their views—incorporate both elements of explanation, as does Islam, which places even greater stress on the divine action that determines election.

To join the covenant, Abraham and Sarah gave up their groundedness in their "homeland, birthplace, and father's house" (Gen. 12:1—my translation)—not to become rootless cosmopolitans but to strike roots in another God-designated home country . From this experience, they learned that the cherished value of being at home was not to be translated into lording it over the strangers in their midst or into worshiping local god(s). They exchanged the safety of anonymity and cultural assimilation for the risk of representing the Divine and the opportunity to teach the way of righteousness and justice. Taking this step demanded great faith in God because visibility often evokes jealousy and resentment. As a reward, they were promised eternal fame as the initial carriers of God's covenant. But Abraham and Sarah took on the covenant not for personal gain, but to show their fellow humans the way to tap into the blessing. (In the Bible, blessing represents the power of proliferation and expansion that God had built into all living phenomena.) The founding couple exemplified how to live in harmony with the divine plan so that humanity could benefit from the blessing that God infused into the Creation. Thus Abraham and Sarah became a source of blessing for all the families of the earth (Gen. 12:3).

Living their lives, Abraham and Sarah learned the paradoxes of the covenantal way, in particular the worth and limit of every human value. The covenant of the triumph of life works through the family because the family is uniquely capable of creating life, nurturing its full capabilities, and passing on the values and the goal of a perfect world to the next generation. Yet maintaining the family creates needs and counterforces that often conflict with the ideals of the covenant—so limits must be placed on the family's claims. Still, covenant members are trained to treasure the family and not to trample human connections for the sake of the higher values—so limits are placed on the covenant's claims as well.

Abraham learned one of the most daring implications of the reciprocity of covenant: God, too, should be held to the standard of justice and righteousness. Abraham initiated a signature Jewish expression of love for God by protesting to his Creator against injustice in the world. God is to be held accountable to covenantal norms. That is what the patriarch argued when he pleaded with God not to destroy Sodom and Gomorrah so that the righteous should not be harmed along with the wicked. But even the divine covenantal values have limits, as Abraham learned when told to sacrifice his son, Isaac. This instruction seemed to breach both the teachings of righteousness and justice to which he had dedicated his life, and the dependability of God's compassion and promises, in which he had trusted without limit. Yet, in the end, he was told not to hurt the child. All of his hopes, teachings about God, and ways of living were given back to him, but with the knowledge that they were infinitely more precious—and more limited in scope and validity—than he had initially realized. The religious message is that the presence of God relativizes all things human without taking away the preciousness and intrinsic significance of all things human.

The Covenantal Process in History

"The events of the fathers' lives are a sign [pointing the way] for the children's lives," says the Talmud. Abraham and Sarah and their descendants wrestled with their mission and learned to live out the covenant, through the state of being outsiders in exile, through slavery and persecution, through the experience of liberation. At Sinai, the family covenant was renewed and extended to cover a whole nation, including outsiders who joined in the Exodus. This expansion made clear that despite its embodiment in family, the covenant was not a genetic endowment or a tribal constitution. It takes a community to create institutions; it takes a people to generate a society to model how the whole human enterprise should be lived covenantally.

The people continued forward through history as a paradigm for others, as "a covenant people, a light of nations" (Isa. 42:6). Bestowal of covenant did not lift them out of this world, so they had to wrestle with the military challenges of homecoming and conquest; later, with trial and error, they fumbled their way through state formation and developing the art of government—especially in the effort to reconcile realpolitik and covenantal values. Possessing the covenant did not release them from the grip of surrounding cultures. They often borrowed and adapted other civilizations' thinking as well as religious and legal institutions. Yet, had they swallowed those frameworks whole, they would have betrayed their mission or lost themselves forever. In its small size, the State of the Israelites appears to be insignificant, dwarfed by mighty imperial powers. Yet its Lord and its cosmic mission sustained the people; their nation outlasted conquerors and world empires.

One might argue that the annals of a third-rate Middle Eastern ministate should be of no interest to the Cosmic Lord of all eternity. But the deeper teaching of the biblical tradition is that nothing human is trivial in God's eyes. In history, in everyday reality, the divine plan is being tested and lived out. In the embodied, evanescent, material world, inhabited by flesh-and-blood human beings, God is present, waiting to be discovered, yearning to be liberated from the suffering and pain that racks the image of God. Here, in the realm of the five senses, God prays to be healed from the sicknesses that afflict the world and all who dwell within it.

How to go about the process of redemption? The teaching of the Sinai covenant is to start with one land and strive to build a society of law and justice for the mighty and the weak alike. In this space, set up a community in which righteousness spells mutual responsibility and the will that none should go hungry. Then extend this realm to the rest of the world.

As there is not enough available wealth and human energy to treat every member of humankind as infinitely valuable, equal, and unique, then start with one people. In this circle, let the experience of love and of knowing the other create a framework to structure socially responsible, emotionally responsive behavior. In this society, let each man learn to love his neighbor as himself. In this collectivity, let each woman imitate God and extend her mother love to all of God's creatures. From there, the circle will expand to more and more distant cousins until, someday, it will embrace the entire human family—and beyond.

As it is impossible in any society to liberate all of the slaves at once, or to free totally all laborers from the grind of labor, then start with one day. On the Sabbath day, let the world be experienced as whole and perfect, so that all people—free and slave alike—are released from commerce and work to focus on relationships and love. On this day, let the weeklong slave rest like a free person; let the animal be unyoked. On this day, let the hungry be provided with abundant food so that a prayer of thanksgiving and pure ecstasy of relationship can go up from mortals to the Immortal Source. Then let the Sabbath day be extended steadily into the six days that follow, until the entire work week is transformed into a time of perpetual peace and wholeness, or, at least, into a time when labor is exclusively chosen, creative and dignified, and not undertaken out of the coercion of economic necessity.

Early on in this covenantal national society, a tabernacle was built, followed by a sanctuary, in Shechem and then Shiloh, and then a central temple in Jerusalem, to represent the realm of pure life, the incarnate presence of the Lord in the midst of the people. In this house no human death could enter, nor could a human whose contact with death had not been overcome by ritual rebirth. For God is totally on the side of life. The people who served before God in this house had to be physically perfect—representing the future when all humanity would be healed and made whole. This house—this microcosm—foreshadowed the day when God's reign would cover the earth, when evil and death would be utterly vanquished and "the world would be full of the knowledge of God as the waters cover the sea" (Isa. 11:9—my translation). Because this house incarnated the redeemed future of the cosmos, it was at once the heart of the nation and the navel of the world, the place toward which all eyes turned.

In its external form, this building was not so different from the house of God as envisioned by neighboring cultures. Inside, the vivid, overpowering tangibility of the Divine Presence in this place evoked terror of the *mysterium tremendum* and fear that one misstep, one inappropriate handling, could lead to instant death. Therefore, priests were set aside to carry out its rituals. They and the sacrifices they offered on behalf of the people served as intermediaries, as channels of blessing that brought humans closer to God and God closer to humans. But the priests were not superhuman. Some of them routinized the dynamic interaction with the ineffable, while others turned the house and its liturgy into a bastion of patronage and self-seeking privilege. Some turned the worship into machinery for manipulating the Divine by cutting the ritual loose from the ethical regimen of the covenant. Other priests made common cause with the kings whose support they craved and to whose power they hitched their stars. In neighboring lands, the king tended to be the intermediary between the kingdom of the transcendental and the realm of the mundane. Here, High Priest and Temple played that role, but the kings sought to win over and control the priestly leadership. Even the servants of the Cosmic Lord are not above self-interested attempts to manipulate the Divine.

The Bible teaches that even though the Lord condemns wrong behavior, God accepts this cost of relating to humans. God is prepared to undergo the trials and tribulations of human history out of desire to realize the Eternal in the mundane. Thus biblical religion affirms the significance of history. The God of Eternity enters into, and is deeply concerned with, humanity's historical journey. The Torah, as covenant, upholds the dignity of human life in this world despite mortals' inherent flaws and distortions of the divine will.

When social inequality spread and the weak were victimized, when the Temple was patronized by oppressors who thought to buy off God with their ill-gotten gains, a group of people arose to protest. They were the prophets of Israel. Some stood up as individuals, some as members of schools; some came from the outside and some from court-retained inside groups. They proclaimed that God the Mighty One who dwells on High resides with the oppressed and humble in spirit—and would not tolerate this exploitation. They spoke truth to power and challenged the sinning king: You are the Man [who sinned grievously] (2 Sam. 12:7—my translation); have you murdered and now wish to inherit [the victim]? (1 Kings 21:19—my translation). They warned that God hated sacrifices brought by heartless exploiters (Jer. 6:13–15, 20), that the Lord was surfeited with rivers of fat and streams of blood (Isa. 1:11; Mic. 6:7) and rather asked for people to do justice, to love goodness, and to walk humbly with God (Mic. 6:7; Isa. 1:16–17). This is not to say that the prophets were twentieth-century democratic reformers. They, too, often served as intermediaries between the people and the vast Ruler of the universe.

The prophets taught, again and again, that God would not be owned or manipulated. They insisted that the Divine Presence was always infinite and beyond human control. All human absolutes constitute idolatry; systems that worship them represent humans worshiping their own handiwork. Therefore, the divine ethic must be honored ahead of human power and human conventions. Royal orders and priestly dictates were to be obeyed only if they were ethical, for these were subordinate to the word of God. The people who listened to the prophets were often torn between their love of the king and the reward he offered (or fear of royal punishment) and their awe at the word of God, which debunks the absoluteness of all human systems and symbols. In the end, as Elijah insisted, humans must choose between God and idolatry. In the end, as Jeremiah insisted, ritual and sacrifice were no magic bullets; God would reject God's home and let the people go into exile rather than allow Jerusalem and the Temple to continue as a den of thieves and oppressors (Jer. 7).

In time, the Temple was destroyed and the Israelite nation went into exile. There they learned again that God was not only in the sacred building or the holy city, but everywhere. God was not a tribal chieftain whose favor could be bought with gifts. God was not merely present Spirit, manifest in a Temple, but the invisible, universal Creator of the cosmos, one who went into exile with the Chosen People. In Babylon, a remnant of the nation learned to approach God through a greater understanding of God's Torah and through walking in God's way of righteousness and justice. Later, in Jerusalem, a restored fragment of the people renewed their covenant, prayed to the Creator who singled out the children of Israel, worshiped more modestly in a more modest temple, and sought to understand God's will.

Hundreds of years passed. The Greek Empire succeeded the Persian Empire, which followed the Babylonian Empire. The Israelites further internalized the values of Torah. As human capacity and scientific understanding grew in the realm of Hellenism, a far wider swath of humanity began to lose faith in the gods of nature and culture and the demons of necessity and hidden powers. Within the Hellenistic civilization—the world where European and Oriental culture met and matched and elevated human comprehension of existence—Judaism survived a military suppression and a cultural assault to renew and maintain its vitality.

JUDAISM AND CHRISTIANITY IN CONFRONTATION

The Birth and Separation of a New Covenant

One may say that in the spread of Hellenistic civilization, the human ground was prepared for a new birth of religion. The reign of the gods of nature and paganism's hold over people were weakened. Millions of people were open as never before to good news about God's love for humanity and the unfolding of human dignity that must follow. This became clear in the remarkable widespread response to Jewish and Christian proselytization and in the differential positive response of downtrodden groups (including women) to missionary Judaism and Christianity. For its part, the Jewish community's capacity to take on a new stage of covenantal responsibility was in place as well. This was the fullness of time for a new unfolding of the divine plan to engage humanity more broadly in the covenantal process. Both Judaism and a new religion, born out of its body, organized to witness to the nations about a loving God; each brought instruction as to how to lead the good life.

Both Judaism and its nascent offspring—sometimes united and sometimes clashing as bitter rivals—brought a powerful message to the gentiles. The universe was a Creation filled with meaning by its Creator. God's eye was on the lowliest bird or blade, and every human being was an image of God. Although humans lived all-too-brief lives in a world of suffering and personal sin, God loved them and promised to bring them redemption, in this world and the next. While the emperor and other ruling authorities should be given their due, all humans were equal in the sight of God. While there were many ritual practices and holy days to express membership in the religious community, the universal commandments were to love God and love one's neighbor as one's self. Justice and responsibility were the obligations between one person and another. Whatever goodness one did to the weak, the poor, and the needy was done to God, who would reciprocate. Both creeds spoke of prayer and repentance. As time went on, Jews spoke about the merit of the ancestors and the efficacy of prayer in place of the once and future sacrifices. Christians spoke of the efficacy of Jesus as the final sacrifice, brought for human sin in his life and forever more. As time went on, Christians treated the holidays of the Bible as the foreshadowing events now made secondary by the reenactment of the ways of Jesus' life. Thus, Christians focused more on the individual's salvation while Jews stressed the significance of the collective history of God's revelation and liberation. Both groups agreed that the end time was near, that God was bringing great saving events to lead humanity to a golden age.

Was Jesus the fulfillment of the biblical hope for a messiah? To the over-whelming majority of Jews, then and now, who understood ultimate re-demption to include the political, economic, and social liberation of humanity—as well as the achievement of love and harmony between all hu-mans and between God and humanity—the answer to this question was clearly no. They experienced no restoration of political dignity and, spiritu-ally, no transformation in God's availability. Given the facts on the ground, this person was no messiah. As open and anxious as they were for a new age, they heard no new signal of revelation. They were not deaf, but they heard a different call—to a greater level of participation in a renewed covenant of Israel. To many gentiles who heard the narrative of Jesus' life and experienced spiritual regeneration, Jesus became the Christ, a messianic figure who had come to them. To those who encountered God reaching out in a new way to forgive their sins, spiritually creating a new heaven and earth, Jesus was the fulfillment of the biblical promises taught to them, and so they joined the faith in his name.

One should not miss the nuances of the situation. Many gentile pagans went on with life as usual. Many Jews never heard of Jesus and his ministry in the first century. A minority of Jews embraced Jesus' life as a redemptive religious event for themselves and others. Some of these Jews were inspired to become missionaries to the gentiles; enough Jews followed this new ar-ticulation of their faith to keep it alive until it struck roots in Hellenistic cul-ture, where it spread rapidly, eventually becoming the dominant religion and separating from Judaism.

Had the believers of both faiths been more modest in their self-under-standing or, alternatively, had they more fully grasped a wider divine pur-pose, they might have recognized that here was a hoped-for broadening of the realm of liberation. They might have remembered God's promise to Abraham that he would become a father of a multitude of nations (Gen. 17:1–5). Christianity would bring an expansion of the time, the places, and the peoples in covenantal relationship with God, even as Judaism would transform itself and reach out as well. Unfortunately, Christians failed to rec-oncile their soul-stirring fervor in generating a new covenantal movement with the dignity and continuing vitality of the traditional people of Israel. And Jews were so enthused by the Rabbinic renewal of their covenant that they could not imagine that a spin-off vanguard could be a second channel of God's blessing for the world. The two faith groups separated, broadening the availability of the covenant. Yet as they increasingly became rivals and bitter enemies, they also narrowed the availability and credibility of the covenant.

What happened to turn a teacher who came to reclaim the lost sheep of the House of Israel into the focal point of a new faith whose disciples traveled over land and sea to spread the Gospel? What signal triggered the arrival of the Kingdom of God for a group of people, a sign so moving that it overrode the contradictory evidence that the world was as unredeemed as ever? Undoubtedly it was the aftermath of the crucifixion of a good man who died broken, feeling abandoned, crushing the hopes of his followers. Yet they clung to his message of a loving, redeeming God, his father; and before long, stunningly, they experienced his presence in their midst again. Thus Christianity's birth is a triumph of human fidelity in the face of tragedy that was rewarded with such powerful religious experiences as to enable the steadfast to know God's presence in the midst of the faith community.

Non-Christians and some Christians will welcome the conclusions of modern critical scholarship that this process of unwinding God's absence took a generation or more. In fact, the Gospels are the distilled understanding of later Hellenistic gentile converts as much as—actually, more than—that of Jesus' Hebrew contemporaries. For contemporary critical scholarship, the ongoing life of Jewry and the renewal of its covenant pose no ideological problem; the pluralism of covenants reflects the diversity and power of human responses to God. In this postmodern view, the twenty-first century—with its open media and universal communication channels—is an ideal time to accept the variety of human narratives that speak to humanity.

But what of those believers—the substantial majority of Christians—for whom the Gospels speak a more unmediated word of God? The key to pluralism is not the denial of the ultimacy of religious authority, but the acceptance of limits. The believer may accept the Gospels as the absolute word of God, yet believe that their authority was not intended to obliterate the norms of the Hebrew faith that preceded it (or of other religions that precede or parallel it).

There are plural possibilities in understanding the Resurrection. Classically, Christian witness insisted that the Incarnation and the Resurrection were so radiant that only the willfully blind refused to see them and be captured by their message. The Incarnation, then, constituted a divine entering into history on an unprecedented scale, and the Resurrection was the decisive divine witness to the supremacy of Christianity.

However, there are two more modest ways to articulate the founding experiences of Christianity. One is that in the circle of faith, experiences occurred that could not be replicated in the world at large. God was manifest and the redemption was visible inside—but only inside—the community of disciples and followers. This appearance was not delusional; it was the expression of the truth that God is close to those who call God's name, whose yearning born out of love and fidelity calls out truthfully and sincerely to the Lord (Ps. 145:18). This humbler understanding allows God to be present with a different name and a different manifestation in another faithful community—say the original covenantal Israel, or, later, the Abrahamic faith of Islam or yet another religion. Such a Presence may occur even in a religion that does not experience a monotheistic God bringing redemption. Such a modest understanding of Christianity can be honored by Jews and other non-Christians without yielding the ultimacy and consistency of their own ongoing covenantal way. Non-Christians could recognize that God acts in and through Christian faith to reach billions of humans even as God acts in and through other religions that—at the very same time—continue to serve and witness.

Secondly, Christians who affirm that Incarnation and Resurrection were objectively visible events can, nevertheless, in good faith, accept a covenantal, religiously appropriate limit on their religion. They must only recognize that God reveals divine wisdom and participates in other faith communities' lives as well. (This is what Paul was teaching when he said: ". . . God's choice [of the Jews] stands . . . for the gracious gifts of God and his calling are irrevocable . . ." [Rom. 11:28–29].) As extraordinary as their tradition is and as blessed with Divine Presence as they feel they are, Christians can acknowledge modestly that their gifts do not exhaust the infinite presence and blessing of the Lord. Christians need not cease sharing their exaltation with others; they need only give up the implied arrogance that no other faith communities can equally experience God in their midst. They need only walk humbly with God and drop the claim that no one else can contribute to the perfection of the world beyond or in a different way than they can. One wing of this approach may choose to focus more on Jesus bringing people to God rather than on Jesus as the self-contained, exclusive manifestation of the Divine.

There is another dimension to this approach. The claim that God became incarnated in a particular human body at a unique moment in history has always been denied by faithful Jews as contradictory to God's essence and unjustified in light of the human capacity to turn to God directly. Similarly, Jews insisted that, to be valid, the messianic resurrection must include all of humanity. But one can uphold the presence of ultimates and, at the same time, honor limits. Why is it necessary for Jews (or other religionists) to insist that the truth of their historical experience with God extends into Christian communities and negates Christianity's claims? It is sufficient for Jews to affirm that they have no interest in restricting God's choice of tactics and methods of revelation. Exactly what happened in the first century is of limited import to Jews. They need not rule that the Trinity constitutes idolatry or degradation of pure monotheism. They need only insist that as open as they were, God did not give them the Christian signal—because God had another mission and purpose for them.

Of course, idolatry is as idolatry does. If Christianity comes dealing death or spreading contempt that encourages others to degrade and kill Jews, then it is idolatrous, that is, the faith of death. But if Christianity repents and comes bearing love and affirmation of the spiritual and physical life of Israel, then blessed be all who come in the name of the Lord.* Then Judaism can retrospectively and joyfully affirm that it partly fulfilled its mission to be a blessing for the world when it gave birth to Christianity as an independent faith. This religion took Jewish core teachings, interpreted its own authority and witness to be foreshadowed in the previous divine revelations to Israel, set forth on its own journey to bring a surplus of love, ethical instruction, and meaning to billions of human beings—and is not yet done. As long as Christianity represses its past hostility and negative portrayals of Jews, as long as Christian faith makes room for the validity and dignity of Judaism (and of other religions), as long as Christianity does unto Jews what it would have others do unto it, then Jews can strive to see beyond past denials to an affirmation that God works in wondrous ways through many channels. Then Jews can retrospectively say that the new expression of the Abrahamic covenant was designed to reach out to gentiles.

The Christian approach opened up the partnership and offered membership in a people fundamentally defined by faith rather than birth. While Christianity would see itself as a family, its creation separated the phenomenon of covenant from the historic language and blood relationships of the people Israel. Yet this was not intended to be a repudiation of the covenant of Israel—including its emphasis on the centrality of family in the process of creating and nurturing life and of cultural transmission. The two arms of outreach were complementary; the gentiles were joining another subpartnership, another iteration of the Noahide covenant. Entering this new faith removed the risk that, in joining the covenant of Israel, they would be deemed second-class citizens in the Israelite partnership because they were not genetic descendants of the original stock.

---

* The most important traditional authority who makes the unequivocal statement that Christianity is not idolatry is Menachem HaMeiri of Provence. HaMeiri also identifies the fundamental distinction as based on the fact that idolatry is characterized by lawlessness and death-dealing, and that is how idolaters behave, so they forfeit all moral obligations to them. By contrast, Christianity (and other such religions) teach morality, teach that God expects and recompenses moral behavior and creates morally responsible people. See on all this Moshe Halbertal, "Ones Possessed of Religion: Religious Tolerance in the Teachings of the Me'iri," in The Edah Journal, 1:1 (2000), on-line, 24 pages.

Their introduction to a Universal Lord would distance the new believers from this Godhead that was a far more cosmic and transcendently Other than that with which they were familiar. It thus became essential—and appropriate—that a strong mediating presence enable the new relationship with the gentiles. This is precisely what Christianity preached and offered in the new religion.

To Jews, the process was very different. Having internalized the Divine Presence, having already connected to the "manifest" Spirit in their midst, they continued in a renewed phase of the covenant. In this stage, the Divine Presence intensified its hiddenness in order to call forth a more active human role in the partnership.

Rabbinic Judaism and Christianity

In the Rabbinic Era, which coincided with the early centuries of Christianity, the Rabbis taught that the age of miraculous, overt divine intervention was over; henceforth, God would operate more behind the scenes and through human agency. The great redemptive event of the Bible is the Exodus, with the Divine Warrior inflicting the Ten Plagues and smashing the Egyptian army at the Reed Sea. But for the Rabbis, the new age redemptive event would be Purim; in that episode, a hidden God, operating behind the facade of chance and irony, saved the Jewish people from genocide through the efforts of Esther and Mordecai. The ultimate logic of this development was that in the life of the individual also, the age of visible divine messengers and constant miracles was over. Explaining personal tragedies as the outcome of providential punishments for individual misbehavior loses its credibility in an age when the Divine self-limits and summons humans to act on its behalf. But it would take two millennia before these conclusions were fully drawn.

In tandem with taking greater responsibility for the intended covenantal outcome, *tikun olam*, humans were also called to a heightened level of authority in the partnership itself. Thus the age of prophecy ended in Jewish tradition, and the era of Rabbinic leadership came into being. Whereas the prophet presents as the channel of divine instruction, the Rabbi presents as a human being studying the past record of God's actions and words in order to uncover what God asks of us here and now. The prophet was empowered by miracles and divine punishment for those who disobeyed. The Rabbi was empowered by the force of his argument and his capacity to persuade the people. When the prophet spoke, the one who contradicted his message was a false prophet. Rabbis freely disagreed, and alternate views were legitimate.

In the Rabbinic system, majority vote decided the position to be followed, and the Heavenly Court accepted the authoritative ruling. This role development advanced the long-term goal of the covenant that human freedom in political, economic, and social areas be matched by human freedom in the relationship to God.

In the century following the destruction of the Temple in 70 C.E., the Jews, led by an emergent band of Rabbis, surmounted the shocking crisis of the destruction with an affirmation that this tragedy heralded the new *tzimtzum* (self-limitation) of God, which paved the way for expanded human activity. In Jewish understanding, the hidden God was actually coming closer to Israel, but in more "secular," less "visible," and less spiritually terrifying ways. To respond adequately, people had to refocus their spiritual capacity to detect this subtler Divine Presence. The education of the laity and its leadership through the central mitzvah of Talmud Torah (Torah study) was the key adjustment. A more developed consciousness, combined with increased knowledge, gave access to this more concealed Divinity. This heightened literacy supported the further growth of a new teaching class, the Rabbis. Thus the ancient people of Israel heard the signal intended for them and responded— even as the gentiles heard their message and responded.

All of these developments paved the way for the expanded role of the Oral Law *(Torah she-be-al peh)* in relation to the written Scripture of biblical faith. Over centuries, the Talmud was articulated by the Rabbis to exposit, interpret, and reinterpret the inherited tradition. Thus, facets of the Sinaitic revelation obscured in the first stage—Judaism's biblical stage—by the splendor of God "visibly" present in the Temple and the awesome nature of its sacramental worship were now uncovered. The hiddenness of God also paved the way for an expansion of the loci of holiness to secular areas, such as homes, workplaces, wedding halls, sickbeds, and funeral places. The role of the Rabbi, while often played out in the inherited priestly mode (as mediator between distant God and present population), shifted steadily toward that of teacher and enabler as people became increasingly equipped to turn directly to the ever-present Lord. Rabbinic Judaism elaborated the law into the shaping force of an expanded way of life, bringing in its wake a new universal "priesthood of the people." The genetic priesthood fell back as its central locus was destroyed; Rabbinic/lay successors took their erstwhile leadership role as prayer became the dominant liturgy of turning to God.

Paradoxically enough, this philosophy of human empowerment soon confronted the reality of an exiled and stateless condition for the Jewish people. This political powerlessness was considerably intensified when the nascent religious offshoot of Judaism won the struggle to dominate the Roman Empire. Christianity became the official state-sponsored religion and used the governing power to suppress or restrict all of its rivals, including Judaism, the original covenant out of which it grew. Given the difference in the condition of the two religions, Christianity (as a majority faith) became the religion offering guidance and legitimacy to the exercise of political power. Judaism became the faith that guided and gave legitimacy to people in the state of political powerlessness. The Rabbis used their empowered theology to develop an ethic of powerlessness that sustained the Jews morally—strong internal life, a sense of chosenness and ethical superiority—and religiously—God in exile with the Jewish people, the irrelevance of politics and economic power, and the centrality of the spiritual reality that God and Israel forged together. They taught that the ultimate messianic redemption would be carried out by the Lord. World redemption would retroactively validate Judaism and Jewry; ultimately, believers in the daughter religions and all other faiths would acknowledge the emptiness of their religious traditions and unite in the worship of the true God under the leadership of the Jewish people.

It should be added that this was the dominant understanding of the Jewish community from the first century down to modern times. From time to time, important figures (such as Maimonides in twelfth-century Spain) discerned dimly that Christianity (and Islam) was advancing the messianic kingdom in important ways. Still others, like Menachem HaMeiri of Provence (1249–1316) taught that Christians (and Muslims) should be judged as participating in a God-worshiping, humanity-civilizing mission. Meeting this standard gave the religions validity and their practitioners a dignity to be respected and honored by Jews. However, through the unfolding history of Rabbinic Judaism, most Jews reciprocated Christian denial and Islamic denigration of Judaism with a dismissal of the other religion's validity.

In the first century C.E., the core founders of the new wave of the Abrahamic covenant grew in the bosom of biblical religion; the essential teaching of the faith they initiated—Creation made new and perfected (Redemption) through covenantal actions of God and humanity—was grounded in that earlier Revelation. The believers had to survive the shock of the Crucifixion and the further degradation in the apparently robbed tomb of their charismatic leader. They took his proclamation of imminent divine breakthroughs to Jews, and then some of them took it to the gentiles as well. (The disciples closest to Jesus naturally took the message primarily to their brethren; some of the newcomers took it to the gentiles.) The Jews responded little, in accordance with the divine plan to bring gentiles into the covenant and mission of Israel—not to redirect the channels of redemption carried by the Children of Israel. The new movement soon surmounted the defeat of the Crucifixion with the experience/conviction that their leader had been resurrected—a profoundly Jewish signal that the final redemption was underway. (This development meant that henceforth both Rabbinic Judaism and Christianity would share a core teaching. For both religions, the central metaphor of the divinely desired total triumph of life in the world would be the promise of a universal resurrection.)

As Christians brought the message of hope to Hellenized gentiles, the new audience heard the proclamation about Jesus, the son of God, bringing them closer to God. According to the Jewish tradition, metaphorically, all people are the children of God. The newcomers understood the message in a more literal way. They accepted with gratitude the news that God sought to close the gap between humanity and the Divine by crossing over and sharing human experience in the flesh. God sharing human experience was an established Jewish idea, but the conclusion that this identification took the form of Divine Incarnation, literally, was ultimately deemed by Jews to be in conflict with the monotheistic idea. The gentile Christians came to understand that the newness that Jesus and his disciples experienced was not a renewal of spirit within tradition but a radically new covenant. Because Jesus' initial followers were so deeply grounded in the original covenant, they were motivated to reinterpret those inherited symbols and messages as having foreshadowed their experience. They found a hermeneutic key in the life, Crucifixion, and Resurrection of Jesus, now understood to be the Christ, and then, literally, the Son, and then, literally, the very substance of God.

However, so powerful was the continuing Jewish influence on the emerging Christianity that even this radical departure—Jesus' sonship and divinity—was ascribed to an aspect of the One God. To honor the principle of monotheism, Jesus was not described as a co-God or as a separate Divine Being. Historically, Judaism rejected what it saw as the divinization of a man. Many Jewish sages rated the Trinitarian teachings as idolatry or, at best, as the dilution of the monotheistic principle. Yet, the Trinity represents Christianity's effort to honor the Jewish normative understanding of God's Oneness at the cost of placing a paradoxical, logic-scandalizing affirmation of a triune God at the center of its faith. (To be fair, one should add that it is also trying to be faithful to its religious experience with the One God it worships.)

In retrospect, it was essential that the nascent offspring religion incorporate definitional "DNA" elements that would evoke "antibodies," which would cause Jews to reject this creed as a foreign body. This transubstantiation was the impact of declaring Jesus to be Son and substance of God. Otherwise, this new formulation could have stayed within the body of Jewry, seeking to take over its mother tradition.* If successful, this new iteration would have monopolized the understanding of the existing covenant. But it was the divine intention not to replace the original, but to reach a new set of nations with a new modulation of the message of creation, redemption, and covenant. For that matter, had the Nazarenes not been cast loose, it is likely that the Jewish ethnic elements of the Gospel would have been strengthened, making the new faith more difficult for gentiles to join. While the inner Jewish mission reached millions of gentiles, many were moved but held back from joining due to the ritual requirements of biblical Judaism. Others were deterred by the gap between its spiritual articulation and their present religious attitudes. In these groups, Christianity found many receptive followers, and it spread more swiftly and widely. For its part, had Judaism not continued, the facets of past revelation uncovered by Rabbinic Judaism would have remained unrevealed, further compressing the richness of the divine communication.

Yet even Paul, who led the charge in turning to the gentiles and who brilliantly interpreted the rootedness of Christianity in Judaism, could not fathom the fullness of the divine pluralism. On the one hand, even as he turned the emerging creed in decisive new directions ("Christ ends the law . . ." [Rom. 10:4]), he expected Jewish Christians (but not gentile Christians) to continue their traditional observances. On the other hand, Paul found it hard to affirm that the divine plan included two independent channels of redemption, operating side by side. He grasped that, notwithstanding his own personal religious experience that Christ reconciled humans to God in a new way, God had not rejected the original covenantal community, "the [Jewish] people which He acknowledged of old as His own" (11:2). He affirmed "God's choice stands . . . for the gracious gifts of God and His calling are irrevocable" (11:28–29). (Otherwise, how could the newcomers trust the promises they were hearing?) Still, in the end, Paul could only imagine that the majority of the Jews were afflicted with "partial blindness"

---

* There was a medieval Jewish folk tradition that committed Rabbinic Jews helped formulate the Gospels (evangelion) in order to facilitate a decisive theological break, hence separation, between Jews and (gentile) Christians. This view considered the original Jewish Christians to be the most threatening element because they sought to rearticulate Judaism itself as culminating in a Jesus religion. See Sid Z. Leiman, "The Scroll of Fasts: The Ninth of Tebeth," *Jewish Quarterly Review*, vol. 74, no. 2 (October 1983), pp. 174–195. While the historicity of such traditions is dubious and the intention was polemic, the deeper truth behind them is that the separation strengthened Judaism's inner coherence. Even as separation enabled the followers of Jesus to create a new, highly successful missionary religion, Judaism was freed to move into a more participatory, humanly creative phase, Rabbinic Judaism. See also Babylonian Talmud, *Berachot* 28b, Tanu Rabbanan, Shimon Ha-Pakuli, etc., and the uncensored Rashi on Babylonian Talmud, *Avodah Zarah* 10a.

(11:25) in order to pave the way for "salvation [to] . . . come to the gentiles" (11:11). This state would last "only until the gentiles have been admitted in full strength" (11:25) whereupon, by the end of days, the Jews would see the light and all would be saved (by the new dispensation) (11:26).

Paul's heroic efforts to respect Jewry and the original covenant were undercut by later Christians precisely because of the hermeneutic that derived Christian teachings from the Bible and because Jesus spoke so strongly as a Jew. Given the authority of the original covenant that Jesus upheld and from which Christianity derived its claims, the persistence of the Israelites with a contradictory interpretation was deeply troubling. The Jewish proclamation that the Messiah had not yet come, for the world was not redeemed—that God had not sacrificed his own Son to atone for humanity's sin because God had no biological son, and *teshuva* (repentance) was the way to forgiveness—undercut Christianity's truth claims. In the eyes of the Christians, only one group could be right. The Christians soon claimed that the original chosenness of the Jews was forfeited due to the Hebrews' own denial of God's further revelation. Furthermore, the New Covenant superseded the Old Covenant; the original no longer had any right to exist as a live option.

Paul warned gentiles not to become arrogant out of the conviction that they were saved or by painting the Jews as rejected for willful defiance of the new redeemer (Rom. 11:13–32). But his successors took his words "blind eyes," "deaf ears," "ignore God's ways of righteousness" and applied them cruelly and belittlingly. They went far beyond those words to characterize Jews as "hypocrites," "children of the devil," and "killers of God"—terms taken from the New Testament itself. The fact that these wounding, degrading terms initially were hurled by Jewish Christians during a fight in the family (for they were still inside the religion of Judaism) was lost on gentile Christians. They heard this terminology as revealed words of God describing a strange, that is to say, uncanny people whom many of them had never met. They were inflamed by the descriptions and were all too willing to lash out at this stiff-necked people whose very existence denied the truth of their faith and the authority of their redeemer. As the centuries went on, the language became more demonic and the persecution more cruel. Thus a Gospel of love for the gentiles became a teaching of hatred toward the Jews.

For their part, the Jews closed ranks that Christianity was an illicit offspring, an invalid faith that truckled to gentiles' understandings and conceded too much to their idolatrous ways. Suppressed by Christianity's use of power, Jews became even more devoted to their understanding of Jewish faith. Challenged and dismissed as a superseded faith, they checked their own vital signs and found them strong. They accepted the Christian insistence that only one understanding of the covenant could be valid—and rejected Christianity as a legitimate religion. Jews, too, could not conceive that this oppressive development for them was in fact God's intended word of liberation for the gentiles. How could Christianity be the will of God when it compromised the purity of monotheism and glorified an antinomian reading of the covenant? And how could the new religion be true revelation when its adherents were blatantly denying the inherited true faith? How could a loving God be present in a community that was abusing the faithful continuers of Abraham's way?

The Cost of Conflict

The Trinitarian view and Paul's influence on theological development, including his mission to the gentiles, had other effects as well. A view of human nature as essentially evil won out in Christianity. The primary explanation of how a good God created a human being in God's own image, yet evil in nature, was articulated by Paul and further crystallized by Augustine in the fifth century. The intrinsically flawed human character was ascribed to the effect of the original sin of Adam and Eve, which injected a permanent fount of evil behavior into human makeup. This view implied a greater gap between mortals and divinity and made the logic of God crossing the divide and sacrificing a son more compelling. The two judgments—about divine and human nature—interactively strengthened each other in Christianity.

In Judaism, there were parallel interpretations of human nature and the polluting effect of Adam and Eve's sin. However, the teaching that human nature is balanced, torn between a good inclination and an evil inclination, became the dominant one. Again, this more benign view of human nature strengthened the affirmation that humans could turn to God and save themselves through their own efforts and God's merciful grace. Not that Jews did not instinctively turn to scholars, saintly types, ancestors, and angels to serve as intermediaries to help them with the Divine; still, the Christian extreme solution that God's own Son provided the essential vicarious atonement for sinful humanity and that without that intervention humans were beyond salvation appeared in Jewish eyes to be excessive to the problem and offensive to the principle of monotheism. This clash in judgment about divine and human nature drove a widening wedge between the two religious communities.

As Christianity pulled away from the Jewish religion, its teachers tended somewhat to reduce the weight of the teachings of the Hebrew Scripture

(= Old Testament). This withdrawal intensified the influence of Hellenistic values, including the dualism that set body against soul. In turn, Pauline Christianity held up a paradigm of an existential struggle between the human spirit seeking to rise up and unite with the Lord and the body whose wrongful desires dragged individuals into sin and alienation from God. The body's impulses fought against the law's directions and turned the law into a source of torment, that is, an unreachable standard. Thus, the law (in which Paul's inmost self took delight) was transformed by the willful body into a frustrating judgmentalism that made the sinner feel guilty and condemned him to death. The only way out was for the bodily desires and the carnal law to die so the spirit could be set free. Then one could live by the Gospel of faith, the law of the spirit.

Judaism also came under the influence of Hellenism. Down through the medieval period, a dualism of body and soul, of this world and the next, gained prominence. Under this emphasis, the law was upheld but interpreted as a curb on bad impulses, a channel to direct bodily desires to higher, more sacred behaviors. Nevertheless, the residual, stronger influence of Hebrew Scripture kept the balance somewhat more affirmative to physical life and the mortal body. Each creed carried on many of the same themes, but what was minor in one was major in the other and vice versa.

A good example of this parallelism and distinctiveness is reflected in the attitude toward sexuality. Given the denigration of the body and the glorification of purity expressed in the concept of the Virgin Birth, it is not surprising that celibacy ended up as a heroic religious category in Christianity. In Catholic Christianity, this value interacted with Hellenistic ascetic models and concern for protecting the church's property, and a tradition of mandatory clerical celibacy emerged. This heroic purity qualified priests to serve as channels of mediation with the Divine—as in their transmuting the wafer and wine into the atoning flesh and blood of Christ through the Mass.

Jews are fond of contrasting this ascetic rigor with the Jewish affirmation of sexuality in marriage, but this comparison is too simplistic. It is true that the Rabbinic leadership was not priestly and sacramental in its function; therefore, it was easier and more natural for the tradition to define rabbis as parents and family men. Nevertheless, there is a strong current in the Talmud that views sexuality as a dangerous force, always ready to erupt and undermine proper religious behavior. The conclusion of this view was that sexuality was best curbed sharply. "There is an organ in a person, which if starved, is satisfied, but if satisfied, becomes ravenously hungry," says the Talmud.[3] This view led, in medieval times, to the rulings of Maimonides (and later Yosef Caro in the authoritative Shulchan Arukh [Code of Jewish Law]): Sexual activity should be undertaken primarily for procreation; secondarily, to satisfy the wife's needs (which bespeaks her weaker, more fleshly character); and lastly (worst case), to relieve the sexual urges that may otherwise lead a man to sin. Caro urged husbands not to seek personal pleasure, but only to fulfill their obligations to satisfy their wives. (Compare Paul's Christian teaching that "it is better to marry than to burn.") Strikingly, however, when Caro had mystical conversations with an angel and sought release from his conjugal obligations so he could ascend higher in spiritual illumination, he was instructed to remain grounded, to meet his sexual responsibilities in a holy manner. One should note that alongside its monastic orders and sacerdotal celibacy, Catholicism does make marriage a sacramental activity. While one cannot deny the more affirmative practice in Judaism, a range of patterns is familiar to both.[4]

The contrast in sexual values highlights one of the more consistent shadings between the two religions. Operating off the model of Jesus as the fruit of a Virgin Birth, as the perfect sacrifice, as the untainted divine undergoing crucifixion, Christianity tended to valorize purified, sacrificial religious activity. Saints were saintly; they lived and died heroically. Priests and nuns devoted their lives to Christ and practiced celibacy, poverty, and service. Jews operated off the biblical models of the patriarchs, Moses, David, and others, who were exemplary but flawed human beings. Rabbinic religion valorized the sanctification of everyday activities instead of extraordinary acts that distinguish the behavior of leaders from that of the rank and file. Yet, again, one cannot draw stark contrasts. An important trend in Rabbinic tradition "painted out" the flaws of biblical characters and glorified scholars who broke away from the compromises of every day to live lives of total dedication. In sum, major themes in one religion are sometimes minor in the other, but similar themes are found in both. The weight and interaction of values often shift, and, frequently, this process works in parallel ways in both traditions. It is all the more the pity that out of antagonism, the chance to interchange and rebalance one's models out of encounter with the other was, for millennia, mostly unavailable.

Sometimes elements rejected in one century were picked up in another. Thus Catholic Christianity, which inherited the Christian repudiation of the law, nevertheless established sacraments that became its defining *halakhah*, the way through life of the universal church. This parallel was further intensified in the development of the canon law. Judaism, which moved to neutralize messianism in reaction to the destruction of the Temple and the rise of Christianity, repeatedly generated new messianic movements, some of which reenacted the antinomian thrusts of Christianity.

Over the years, the two faiths grew ever more alienated from each other. Judaism focused on the peoplehood of Israel and the distinctive (one is tempted to say, genetic) spiritual physiognomy of Jewry as well as the land to which it sought restoration. Torah was unfolded with ever greater stress on the observances and works that made up its distinctive way of life. The urgency of God's universal redemption and the Jewish role as a light unto the nations were de-emphasized even as the origins and common elements between the two faiths were played down. Christianity unfolded and stressed its theological claims, dismissing Judaism as carnal and its observances as works too trivial to merit grace in the eyes of God. The stress on faith in Jesus became so defining as to sometimes make the concept of a secular (or even a merely born) Christian into an oxymoron—whereas for most Jewish authorities, a sinner or a nonbeliever did not lose membership in the holy people.

Christianity triumphed in the world that Jews inhabited; it attained both political power and numerical majority. Christians interpreted this as proof of its theological supremacy. Judaism was portrayed as a superseded and, indeed, dead religion. Far from acknowledging its core figure as Jewish and crediting his mother Torah, the new faith painted Jesus and his disciples (except for Judas) as Christians; his enemies and the foes of God were depicted as "the Jews." Judaism's ongoing life was explained away as a sinister phenomenon; the devil was sustaining this otherwise lifeless faith. The synagogue was a charnel house, full of death. The children of the devil acted devilishly; blood libels and awful behaviors were attributed to the Jews. The absence of this people was a desideratum; whether that outcome was achieved by forced conversion, by locking them away behind ghetto walls, by expulsion, or by killing depended on the anger and degree of Christian hostility. The oppressive behavior varied from place to place and century to century. Thus a privileged sanctuary for hatred was carved out within the universe of the Gospel of love.

Christianity paid two other heavy prices for the preferential option of religious polarization and political dominance. Having established itself with the model of possessing exclusive revealed truth, Christianity did not need to make theological room for the existence of any other legitimate religion. The faith blinded itself to the ever-renewing life and development of Judaism; it failed to see that "dead" Judaism inseminated yet another daughter religion: Islam (a creed that Christianity rejected just as firmly and fought with even greater conflict). Thereafter, Christian triumphalist theology combined with its political power and alliances to lead it into imperialist behavior toward all the religions it met as it spread over land and sea. Even as in Jesus' name the descendants and members of his people, Jewry, were cruelly treated and religiously violated, so the remarkable proclamation of God's saving love throughout the world was tainted by a domineering theology. The conviction of possessing a revelation without limit soon turned into abuse of dissenting views outside—as well as inside—the religion. Thus, out of Christian religious fidelity and trust in God, millions of God's creatures were harmed or religiously coerced. (Let it be acknowledged that simultaneously tens of millions were liberated, helped, and consoled.)

Additionally, to override Jewish objections, and to explain away the contradictory state of the world, the church was motivated to spiritualize redemption. "The Kingdom of God is within you" is a true statement, but it reduces the redeemed realm and abandons present political/economic/cultural space to Mammon. This thrust toward the spiritualization of faith was reinforced by the tendency to label Judaism as a carnal religion. Too often, the wholeness of redemption "shrank" into spiritual completion of the individual's world.

These otherworldly tendencies in Christianity subtly steered the religion away from the political redemption and economic social justice themes of the Hebrew prophets. By emphasizing the unworthiness of the body and the joys of eternal heavenly bliss, Christianity reinforced the status quo in the world. The creed provided a form of escape from the sufferings of the poor that encouraged political and social passivity. (In the modern period, this influence was bitingly dismissed as proof that religion was "the opium of the masses.") From time to time, the poor or the dispossessed classes were driven to rebel; then they read the texts of the Hebrew Scripture in revolutionary fashion ("when Adam delved and Eve span, who was then the gentleman?"). All too often, as an established church, Christianity rallied to the side of the ruling class, compounding this bias toward upholding the status quo. Christian teachings minimized the import of suffering, instead offering compensation in the world to come. Here again, the exact impact of the mutual disregard is hard to measure. Still, the inability to cross-check positively between Christianity and Judaism, the absence of openness to the neglected elements in each one's own crystallization of the Mosaic tradition by learning from the other, played some role in the neutralization of religion's egalitarian and worldly redemptive themes.

Judaism, too, paid a heavy price for the total alienation between the sister religions. A faith, whose founding document begins with the Spirit of God creating the vast universe and all within it, turned inward. One tradition avowed that after the Destruction and Exile, all that God had left in the world were the four cubits of *halakhah*. In a survival mode, universal visions of redemption were pushed to the background; moral instruction for the general society was often put aside as unwanted by the host. The sense of responsibility for the fate of the world shriveled; alternatively, it was spiritualized into halakhic behaviors and kabbalistic exercises.

The biblical idea that God had lovingly liberated the Philistines and Arameans just as God had redeemed the Hebrews receded. The Isaianic vision that God's House would be a house of prayer for all nations—and from those populations, priests and Levites would be recruited—was turned triumphalist. For the most part, Judaism hardened its heart toward the legitimacy of other religions, especially under the blows of oppression. Thus Christianity was primarily categorized as idolatry, which means a faith with no redeeming spiritual value. Its myths (Virgin Birth and Incarnation) were ridiculed; its veneration of saints and use of statues were folded into Trinitarian articulations of God and popularly labeled as idol worship. While Islam was given some greater recognition as a monotheistic faith, the general consensus was that other faiths had little standing in the eyes of God.

As in Christianity's internal development, the logic of the worthlessness of other faiths inexorably led to reduced respect for the decency and humanity of their practitioners. A powerful and widespread moral judgment grew in which gentiles were considered less than fully human or less than images of God; non-Jews were less worthy of ethical responsibility, the objects of fewer obligations to help and to heal. In 1965, Rabbi Jehiel Jacob Weinberg, a towering figure in the world of modern Orthodoxy, wrote a private letter articulating an impassioned protest at the cumulative moral cost of these attitudes. "In my opinion, it is fitting to put an end to the hatred of the religions for each other. More than Christianity hates Judaism, Judaism hates Christianity. There is a dispute if stealing from Gentiles is forbidden from the Torah. . . . The law of a Gentile is the same as that of an animal. . . . We must solemnly and formally declare that in our day this does not apply. . . . Meiri [Rabbi Menachem HaMeiri of Provence, 1249–1316—IG] wrote as such, but the teachers and the Ramim [teachers in advanced Yeshiva studies—IG] whisper in the ears of the students that all this was written because of the censor."[5] Also, to be fair, Jews did not act on these hatreds as Christians did—partly because Jews were powerless and Christians were in power as the dominant culture. That having been said, the total cost in moral attitudes and denial of dignity of others was high. There is a legitimate argument that these categories were the mirror of gentile behavior toward Jews; this explains but cannot undo the value reduction.

Judaism also paid a heavy price in modern times for the resultant internalization of the gentile's otherness. The coherence of Jewish culture and the strength of identity were held together by a sense of moral superiority and quasi-genetic distinctiveness. This feeling eroded rapidly as modern culture opened up and gentiles accepted the Jews. Still other Jews were seized by the exhilarating universal redemptive visions that flowered in modernity (from democracy and liberalism to socialism and communism to cultural liberation movements); such Jews were prone to abandon (or actively suppress) Judaism, justifying their betrayal by labeling Jews as perversely tribal and guilty of denigrating the value of others.

One might also suggest that by defining Christianity as the negative pole of religion, Judaism was encouraged to play down theology and overemphasize religious behavior; this tendency can too often turn *halakhah* into legalism. To define the contrast between the two faiths, some Jews were led to belittle the political realm and overcompensate the kabbalistic spheres. The triumph of the Kabbalah weakened the role of philosophy and reason in the Jewish religious economy. In reaction to the spread of Christianity, some Jews were led to renounce the mission to other nations and exaggerate the significance of birth and possession of a Jewish soul.

Of course, in actual interaction over the centuries, all of these shifts and moral stances were modified by humanizing contacts between Jews and Christians, between Jew and gentile. There were even periods of symbiosis and affirmative attitudes. But the big picture was isolation, alienation, and negation. To round out the picture, one should add that there were constructive mutual influences as well. The medieval pietists of German Jewry were energized by the surrounding piety. The impact of Christian values is highlighted in the triumph of monogamy in Judaism. In the zone of Islam, with the Koranic upholding of polygamy, the residual polygamous tradition in Judaism remained legal until the twentieth century. Jewry and Judaism played a mediating role in bringing Greek philosophy and science and Muslim culture to Christians and the West; Christians made biblical and Jewish values part and parcel of European civilization. Jewish Bible scholarship was useful to Christians; mystics of both traditions influenced across faith lines.

Judaism and Christianity provided universal values that transcended national and ethnic boundaries. They also provided an ethical critique that raised standards and civilized behavior, especially communicating the importance of caring for one's neighbor and communal compassion for the needy. Christianity reached and incorporated many more people; this was achieved in no small measure by bringing God closer to where the people were through preaching Jesus' person and Jesus' sacrifice—not to mention the Virgin Mary and a host of other intermediaries to the intermediary. Christians amplified the message by tirelessly pursuing a mission to bring the Gospel to every corner of the globe. As a result, and to its eternal credit, Christianity brought the two faiths' common message of God's love and human value, of responsibility to fellow human beings and accountability to a Higher Power, of the individual's need for family and community to hundreds of millions of people throughout the world.

Conflict and Exile

From the time that Judaism and Christianity separated, the new faith spread throughout the Roman Empire and then became dominant in medieval Europe. The extraordinary growth went hand in hand with the creation of a broad class of clergy; an important fraction of that group became teachers, scholars, and intellectuals who developed a rich and variegated tradition of philosophy, theology, and canon law. As Christianity's influence grew, its values, themes, and narratives penetrated the realms of art, music, and literature, inspiring many masterworks of high art as well as a broad scale popular culture. Christianity and the Bible may be credited with shaping the view of a nondeified nature and a sense of natural law that sustained the growth of science and scientific thinking. From late medieval times on, as the West expanded through geographic exploration, Christianity rode alongside, bringing—sometimes, imposing—its worldview on the newly colonized territories. In these centuries, and down through the modern period, Western culture was dynamic, productive, and expansive, and it brought much of the world into its purview—and under the banner of Christianity. The population aggregations were staggering, and they made Christianity a world religion. Sometimes, the price for such growth was the absorption of millions whose Christianity remained a surface phenomenon while the underlying culture and world of spirit remained relatively untouched. One must add that Western conquests brought with them warfare, suppression, decimating illnesses, and economic exploitation, as well as civilizing blessings. Christianity sometimes mitigated but often aided and abetted the imperialist misbehaviors.

As it spread, Christianity showed the ability to relate to local cultures and modulate its messages and imagery to be more compatible with local cultural idioms and frameworks. The one thing Christianity did not learn was a sense of its own limits. The faith presented itself as representing the single, all-powerful God of the universe who had uniquely intervened in history through it; as well, it was the carrier and avatar of the most powerful human civilization in the world. It was not clear where one cause stopped and the other claim took over. In any case, Christianity felt and seemed unstoppable. The combination of European superiority and Christian triumphalism, however, meant that frequently, local religions and cultures were pulverized in the encounter.

Judaism spent these centuries restricted politically and embattled religiously and culturally. Despite this, the religion grew in strength as it shaped the life and destiny of Jewry. One of its signal impacts was to catalyze and influence the birth and shaping of Islam. However, that religion was so zealous and powerful in its growth that it too turned against Judaism and reduced the Jews to second-class status. Despite casting a seed of blessing on the world and shaping another monotheistic faith as it emerged out of Arab paganism, Judaism remained derogated and under siege. Nevertheless, the vast encyclopedic ocean of the Talmud was completed. This was followed by the development of halakhic literature, ethical and mystical schools of thought, and, especially in Muslim lands, the growth of philosophy, literature, and Bible commentary as well.

It was no small accomplishment for the Jewish religion to make the successful transition from Iron Age to ancient civilization and from the ancient world to medieval Europe. Judaism developed from a religion of an agricultural peasantry to one of artisans and urban dwellers, from a cult rooted in land and homeland to a liturgy and way of life thriving in an exilic existence—all done through a continuous process of interpretation and institutional innovation that enabled the Torah to stay relevant and effective under trying circumstances. Affirmation of this world—not just the world to come—combined with the economic needs of the Jews who were excluded from land ownership to lead Judaism to develop a positive attitude toward business and commerce. This combination, plus the need of some Jews to live by moneylending, led Judaism to develop a religious ruling called a *heter iska* that allowed receiving interest on one's money—this at a time when Western Christianity and Islam clung to the biblical norm prohibiting interest. The continued prohibition on interest in Christianity and Islam reflected an inability to grasp the dynamics of commerce and its moral potential. Economic transformation moved people beyond the *gemeinschaft* (personal-linked) economy and the primacy of helping the poor into a more impersonal, but expanding, economy that made capital productive and lifted the status of the needy through wealth creation.

Judaism fostered values and convictions— the dignity of labor, the belief in the legitimacy of economic efforts—that made Jews early carriers of commerce and business development and later of the capitalist ethos, albeit one shaped by and subject to religious norms. Thus Judaism continued to affirm the dignity and value of this-worldly economic effort when other religions were tempted to spiritualize their values and validate only pious devotion to otherworldly and nonmundane activities.

During the centuries of landlessness and outsider, minority status, Jews also learned how to live in exile. People normally orient themselves morally and spiritually by the familiar landmarks of home territory and rooted memory; for example, ancestors' values, historic institutions, and familiar practices. Exile is a deeply trying experience because it shatters the familiar and gives the sense of being an interloper. Minority status is intimidating and leads one to question one's own judgment. Is it not correct that in Rome one should do as the Romans do, rather than insist on the internalized set of values brought from the old country?

Exile probes the capacity of a people to recognize that it is dialectically rooted in God as well as in land. Minority status tests the depth of a value system. Is a person or group capable and ready to be foolish in the eyes of the surrounding society and all its human denizens—and, withal, unwilling to deny its Maker or its mission? Exile is, thus, a test of both independence and steadfastness, of faith and of courage, of trust and of sacrifice. On the other hand, exile can be productive. The outsider can detect problematic societal phenomena that the entrenched cannot perceive because familiarity or self-interest has blinded them.

The key to successfully navigating through exile is to be in the world, but at the same time, not totally of the world. In a profound moment of insight, the talmudic and the kabbalistic traditions grasped that going through exile without losing one's self constitutes *imitatio Dei* of the highest order. In an unredeemed world, with a suffering humanity, God is also out of sorts and in pain. Yet the Lord persists in presence, comforts the afflicted, upholds eternal values, and works indefatigably toward liberation and perfection. The partners who follow God undergo exile willingly out of identification with the Divine and are upheld by the Presence as they go through the experience together.

Perhaps the key adjustment is to learn and affirm one's limits. On the one hand, there is an internal boundary—no invasion, no criticism by the outside world should be allowed to undermine the believer's soul and wholeness of being. At the same time, one must recognize that even one's most absolute insights and truths do not cover the whole world; they are not self-evidently dominant or triumphant. They are constantly contradicted, or at least under review, in the eyes of the world. In exile one learns to affirm one's claims powerfully, while recognizing the limits of those claims. Religious people who successfully integrate the lessons of exile become more modest in self-presentation. They become more inner-directed and are not intimidated by the contrary opinion of the majority, yet, simultaneously, they are more capable of accepting the differences of the other without being threatened by them.

For triumphant Christianity, exile did not arrive until the nineteenth and twentieth centuries, when the negative side effects of modernity began to hit home. Then, pressed between the sheer massiveness of the billions of members of other faiths who were not Christian and the growing number of secularizing Westerners who were de-Christianizing, Christians came to know themselves as a minority, as members of a particularist covenant, not as a putative universal church. The outcome of this experience is not yet certain, but the effect was chastening, then humbling. Sometimes, the encounter led to paralyzing guilt and strong, even excessive, identification with the downtrodden. Overall, however, the process opened the door to a more pluralistic Christian faith, more respectful and more willing to listen to others.

Judaism and Christianity Encounter Modernity

First, Judaism and Christianity had to go through the process of modernity and into postmodernity. At the risk of oversimplification, one can describe modern civilization, in all its immensity and variety, as humanity's attempt to come of age and take charge of its own destiny. In the Modern Era, the age-old Jewish and Christian promise of a world made whole for life seemed realizable by human efforts. Major scientific advances led to breakthroughs in technology and industrialization. These developments, in turn, led to dynamic expansions of commerce, massive urbanization, and the rapid spread of communication and media. There followed a rise in standards of living and dramatic improvements in public health and life expectancy, particularly in the West. As the safety and dignity of daily life conditions improved, the availability of life's pleasures expanded. Gradually, but steadily, cultural and personal attitudes shifted toward affirming the worthwhileness of this world. Human beings' sense of competence expanded exponentially.

Other cultural, religious, and ethical transformations followed closely in modernity's wake. With the breakup of the static surface in a host of areas, revolutionary movements repeatedly erupted all over the world. Conservative and restorationist responses were not far behind. The unifying theme in these movements was the breakdown of the given, the end of the assumption that people are fixed for life in the social, economic, political, cultural, and even biological condition into which they are born. The associated theme was that humans must shift from passive acceptance of their fate to activity that can improve their lives and perfect the world. Both themes grew steadily more resonant and more influential as modernity spread and evolved.

The nature and understanding of religion was powerfully reshaped by modern civilization. For one, the ascendancy of scientific thinking broke down the qualitative distinction between the heavens and the earth. The belief in a transcendent God, sitting on a throne, looking down at the world and giving its people their due through constant interventions, receded—especially as the iron rule and cosmic reach of natural laws became ever clearer. Both Judaism and Christianity showed an amazing degree of resilience in incorporating these radical transformations of understanding without losing their central teachings about God and the good life. Admittedly, these adjustments unleashed profound modernizing, secularizing, and revisionist movements within both faiths, which shook them, split them, and reoriented whole groups within them. Still, by reinterpreting classic texts and inherited traditions, both faiths newly articulated their core beliefs and upheld them, albeit in subtler, more naturalistic, and more worldly forms. Instead of dying a death of a thousand qualifications, both religions emerged with serious reserves of power, needing to be as reckoned with as ever.

The modern message of human power and initiative, however, was spelled out in the religious realm in polar opposite ways. For many modernists, abandoning the Divine was the point of the exercise. Marxists believed that atheism would focus people's minds on the injustices in the world and lead to revolt and liberation. Psychoanalysts believed that releasing humankind from the repressive, castrating Father figure would lead to self-fulfillment. Scientists who "had no need for that hypothesis" believed that untrammeled science would achieve more good. All these and a host of other movements supposed that the death of God would make everything possible. (They got more than they bargained for; as Dostoyevsky and Nietzsche predicted, the proclaimed event meant that *everything* was permitted—and possible.) Certainly, for millions of people God talk became notional, and religious loyalty became nominal.

The counterpoint was that the new sense of human capacity could also be understood as enabling a higher level of human covenantal performance and accountability to God. A truly infinite, more cosmic God was revealed as the vastness of the universe was grasped on a new scale. The wonders of Creation, as the hidden signature of the invisible Creator, became clearer even as the consistency and the random orderliness of the cosmic process became more manifest. A host of religious movements seeking to recover the worldly dimension of justice and redemption developed, bringing universal ethical commandments to the forefront of Jewish and Christian concerns. Mysticism and aesthetic appreciation of God's presence surged as a host of demons, devils, and angels melted away under the sun of scientific and philosophical analysis. Awareness of the humanity of all humans spread powerfully, evoking the sacred obligations owed to the image of God and challenging the in-group/out-group dichotomies that had become entrenched in both Judaism and Christianity. This shock of recognition led to new levels of tolerance between faiths, though sometimes it led to indifferentism and relativism.

Both faiths were transplanted into the soil of the emerging democracies, which required yielding religious monopolies, albeit reluctantly. Both religions were challenged by the tension between the freedoms protected by law and their demands for prescribed behavior and thought. Both learned that liberal, democratic values could erode some of their believers' sense of being chosen—while simultaneously energizing others, out of freedom and choice, to move into higher, more consistent levels of faithfulness. In these two faiths, modernization led to remarkable ferment and soul-searching, great creativity, and an efflorescence of scholarship. In both faiths, large blocs of believers were swept into secularizing tendencies, and this led to powerful fundamentalist reactions. Ironically enough, the upsurge of fundamentalism only proved that "you can't go home again" to traditionalism. Rather, the authority, stability, and certainty promised by return to the fundamentals could only be achieved by turning inherited beliefs and behaviors into conscious commitments, reformulated in contradiction to the new cultural situation.

In Christianity's case, the effect of modernity was central because it was the West's dominant religion. Thus the cultural battle was fought within the body of Christianity; it absorbed the greatest blows, suffered the most intense struggles, and generated the widest range of creative religious responses. Interestingly, the secularizing effects of modernity were somewhat offset by the new channels of communication and outreach that brought Christianity to hundreds of millions around the world—masses who were less affected by the modernizing process and who absorbed a more traditional understanding of Christianity. This development strengthened these traditional values within the overall body of Christendom.

Perhaps one can again conceptualize the religious significance of the modern age from a "theocentric" perspective and assume that Judaism and Christianity were jointly and severally intended to serve as role models in the unfolding divine plan to perfect the world. From this vantage point, one may argue that modernity uplifted humanity's godlike capacities. The new culture strengthened and disciplined reason—indeed, expanded consciousness—increased human power, intensified emotional expressiveness while deepening individualism and the range of relationships, widened freedom, and extended life. This paved the way for a more internalized faith, "purer" in that it was less the expression of infantilized dependency. This inner empowerment opened the door for a more competent humanity to turn to God out of dignity and disinterested attraction. In the divine will, modern civilization was intended to liberate human capacity to the fullest, making otiose the God of the gaps, the Omnipotent One worshiped by human beings out of fear, need, intent to bribe, and other unworthy motives. Empowered humans could now come to God out of love, out of a feeling of fundamental rootedness, out of a sense of capacity that expresses itself in gratitude and celebration of life. If people chose properly, humans could use their astonishing aggregations of power to make whole their fellow human beings. Together, God and humanity could heal the world and increase its capacity to sustain life.

If Judaism and Christianity had responded appropriately to the new possibilities in the human condition, by seeking to serve God for God's own sake, they would have played down their own claims of special merit and striven to serve as models of selfless service. They would have welcomed every laborer for *tikun olam* as partner and coworker. They would have striven to eliminate every teaching that generates hostility and disrespect to others, and thereby also hurts the credibility of those who testify to God's presence and love. They would have worked to temper excessive concentrations of power, giving up their own to show the way. They would have upheld and unfolded human greatness, while warning against giving blank checks to (and even worshiping) the human exercise of power.

The Holocaust

Unfortunately, this is not the way modernity was actualized. In some cases, the growth of the good metastasized and important elements of the culture turned pathological. The rise in the standard of living led, in various forms, to a materialism that knew the prices of a better life, but forgot the value of life itself. The growth in human power outstripped the forces of containment. At times, this productivity explosion threatened the environment's capacity to survive the manipulation and pollution that followed in its wake. Some people translated the new levels of change and choice into an erosion of values and moral anarchy. Revolutions turned into visions of radical perfectionism; some rejected all political limits and metamorphosed into movements of utopian totalitarianism. In the absence of checks and out of the growing feeling that neither God nor humans could intervene, untrammeled concentrations of power were unleashed against those deemed to be standing in the way. Thus the century of human dignity turned into the century of mass murder and oppression—in the name of one noble cause or another.

In the twentieth century, human power, worshiped, metamorphosed into a life-consuming absolute. This is the archetype of idolatry—a human, finite power breaks out of its limit, is turned into a pseudo-absolute, and becomes the source of death, instead of life. The ultimate expression of this moral/religious cancer was the Holocaust, and not only because of its all-out infliction of death. The *Shoah* was the fruit of unlimited human freedom and power. Nazism claimed to synthesize economic equality with communal/corporate wholeness and spiritual unity. Out of desire to install a human as

God and thus pave the way for a final perfection, the human authority decided to get rid of the people of God. Achieving this goal, by implication, would wipe out every signal and reference to a higher power that could check and condemn this overweening human self-worship. (Some Nazis were believers in God. But one can say that the God they invoked was not the free, transcendent One who judges humans and condemns murder as an ultimate evil. Rather, as exemplified by the SS mass killers who wore belt buckles marked *Gott mit uns* [God is with us], their God was a human manipulated totem, carried before the army to provide "supernatural" cover for their evil, genocidal actions.)

Contrary to triumphalist Christianity's claims, when Nazism, the force of concentrated evil, turned on God, it recognized that the carnal children of Israel had not lost their charisma as the sign of God-in-our-midst. Therefore, it set out to destroy Jewry. It also turned out that in accordance with Jewish and Christian claims that God is the source of total life, the opposite power, the antimatter of God, constitutes total death. The Nazi goal was to obliterate the people of God and thus the presence of God. The intended outcome was to achieve the final paradise for the full realization of humankind. The actual outcome was the creation of a kingdom of death and the systematic degradation of the human being as the image of God. This event made clear that a human-willed death of God brings death, not life, to the world.

The devastation wrought by modernity-out-of-control unleashed a frenzy of cultural self-criticism and a search for limits on human power, beliefs, political hopes, and authority claims. Chastened traditions turned to soul-searching and purification. A vast range of reductionist analyses and pluralizing movements set as their priority to break up all concentrations of power—political, moral, cultural, religious, epistemological, scientific, gendered, among others. Thus, the aftershock of the Holocaust powerfully strengthened the forces that turned into postmodernity.

TOWARD A NEW UNDERSTANDING: JUDAISM AND CHRISTIANITY IN PARTNERSHIP

The Impact of the Holocaust

I shall not detail the implications of the Holocaust for Judaism and Christianity, as these are dealt with in various other essays in this book. Suffice it to say that, globally speaking, Christians wise enough to learn the lessons of the *Shoah* absorbed two transformative insights: the need for repentance and the drive for regeneration. Although Nazism was antagonistic to Christianity and Nazis persecuted some of its sincerest practitioners, Christian triumphalism played an indispensable role in setting up the Jews as the target of annihilationist hatred. The Christian contempt tradition and its supersessionist theology mutated into secular forms and entered Nazism directly. Back in their Christian home base, these teachings made Nazi enmity for Jews conceivable and credible. These inherited attitudes also weakened the likelihood that bystanders would attempt to check the destruction. In effect, after the Holocaust, Christianity was on notice that it needed to burn out the hatred in its core or the evil within would overweigh its good. After a period of stunned moral confusion, Christianity's life-giving capacity for guilt and repentance asserted itself. The mainstream of Western Christianity, paced by the Catholic Church (and especially American Christians), set out on a decades-long journey to reimagine itself in relation to the original covenantal community, God, and humanity. The outward expression of this inner rethinking was a move toward a pluralistic affirmation of Judaism's covenant.

The second insight driving Christian rethinking was the realization that the religion had not sufficiently regenerated its believers' moral and religious capacities. Sixteen hundred years after the triumph of Christianity, the population had absorbed its teachings in so limited a way as to permit a murderous generation to arise from within Christian civilization and operate genocidally, unchecked by their Christian neighbors. This outcome pointed to the need for a new Christianization process based on a higher level of human spiritual and ethical activity. Somehow, the availability of God through Jesus and the unlimited power of forgiveness had to be tempered to evoke a more elemental moral responsibility. The challenge was to achieve a much higher level of moral regeneration as the threshold of becoming a Christian; this would demand a more total capacity to see through conventional human norms and be willing to meet standards that were credible in God's presence and under God's judgment. Then it would be necessary to train these new model Christians to express their identity in a more rigorous practice of *tikun olam* and responsibility for others. To achieve this outcome, as Dietrich Bonhoeffer argued, Christianity would have to affirm human empowerment and nurture a more competent, more activist, more selfless, and more direct relationship between humans and God. Jesus would become the model of this service; for many, he would become the one who brings people to God rather than the God who came down and lifted the burden of human action from the backs of mortals.

For their part, Jews now have to understand that their triumphant assertion that the Messiah has not come is not a victory for Judaism. There can be no complacency about the fact that the world was not redeemed—as claimed by Jesus' followers—for this flawed reality bred evil forces that threatened

Jewry's very existence. Thus Judaism needs to reach out to every movement that hopes to bring the Messiah, jointly working to temper the absolutist, utopian elements in this commitment, while seeking to attain redemption as soon as possible. To avoid doing unto others what was done unto it, Jewry now has to search out and destroy every teaching of contempt and dehumanization of the other that lurks within its traditions. This goal cannot be realized without self-criticism, repentance, and the internalization of higher standards of moral responsibility for Jews and all human beings. Nor will this goal be reached without establishing a much higher level of connection and feeling of obligation toward Christians and followers of other faiths.

For both Judaism and Christianity, God's self-restraint in not preventing the Holocaust was a divine cry to humans to step up and stop the evil; it was time for the human partner to take greater responsibility in the unfolding of the covenant and the redemption of the world. This is not to say that God withdrew into deistic apathy toward the historical process. The self-limited God is more ever-present, sharing human fate, bonding, loving, calling, accompanying, empathizing, suffering, and judging—but no longer playing the role of deus ex machina. This is God contracting divine power in order to empower humanity. This is the Lord of the covenant seeking to elicit more mature, selfless, and humanly responsible activity in the world, from Jews, Christians, and all who would heed the still, small voice. This divine *tzimtzum* suggests that God is entering a deeper shadow of concealment and that both faiths are called to follow and find the Lord, even in the most secular settings. For both faiths to speak truthfully and credibly in such an age, they must downplay elements of formal sacrality and intermediary figures and teach believers to serve God with greater purity—for God's sake, and not for reward or victory.

It may be argued that, for Christians, Vatican II opened the door to the "democratization" of the religious process, with greater participation and consequent greater personal responsibility for the laity acting collectively as the people of God. This same trend is reflected in—and strengthened by—the spread of certain charismatic forms of Christianity, which also stress a more powerful personal transformation as well as the need for more total experience of God in one's life. Among Jews, the equivalent is the shift from the centrality of the rabbi to the growth of lay-led renewal movements and greater stress on living out religious values in every aspect of mundane life. People search for God and express their relationship with the Divine less under the badge of formal religion and more in the everyday activities that improve and heal the world. In this unfolding scenario, people encounter God primordially in serving and nurturing the (human) image of God. This expanded articulation of higher values and search for God's presence in the secular realms of life has sometimes been called "holy secularism."

The covenant is, essentially, a divine, loving, and pedagogic process. As humans become more competent, God invites them to take up a more active role in the task of *tikun olam*. Christianity, then, may be entering the equivalent of its own "Rabbinic era," an age marked by less direct revelation and less hierarchically controlled channels to God. In this scheme, the lay people of God play a more influential role in discerning God's purposes and carrying out divine mandates.

This tendency is present in theologies, like Bonhoeffer's mentioned above, in which God the Father is understood as a more accessible, loving parent and Jesus is more a messenger for the Divine than a Divine Messenger. This trend has evoked more Jewish theological willingness to affirm that Jews and Christians worship the same God. Any such step to "soften" the emphasis on Trinity and underscore the "One" side of the triune paradox reduces a major ideological obstacle to Jewish appreciation of Christianity as a dignified monotheism.

In any event, because the Holocaust signals that God is more self-limiting, both religions must encourage humans to seek power to protect themselves and others. Both religions came to understand that rampant evil threatens to obliterate the presence of God in the world. Therefore, they must rejoin the historical process fully and throw their weight on the side of justice and dignity for the downtrodden—and the comfortable. In response, post-Holocaust Judaism must seek to guide the exercise of power by Jews while serving as a light unto the nations in this area.[6] Post-*Shoah* Christianity must seek to renounce its past excesses and guide policy at a higher, purer level without repeating the errors of its past—avoiding excessive identification with power. At the same time, both religions need to develop an ethic that will check the inherent tendency of power—in all forms and when exercised by any authority—to corrupt and to lead to abuse of others. Both traditions have to learn to enhance human capacity and creativity to advance the process of *tikun olam* operating in the world while holding these forces accountable before God and humanity.

Both faiths grasped dimly that the experience of the *Shoah* provided a hermeneutic principle by which to understand their inherited traditions. Using the light that the *Shoah* cast, it was time to illuminate all the facets of cumulative revelation that they possessed in their heritage, to purge the dross and to enhance the life-giving elements. At their deepest level, both Judaism and Christianity have long recognized that revelation was not limited to their formative, axial age. In the past, both have affirmed—albeit on different occasions and in response to different experiences—that later historical events reshape the understanding of earlier teachings. Both have recognized that inasmuch as all the generations are in partnership to realize the goals of the covenant, later generations are authorized to interpret anew the classic sources and to generate guidance and commandments for their age. Both believe this reinterpretation can and must be done respectfully, giving full faith and credit to the unique Divine Presence and guidance recorded in their canonical texts. Thus, Judaism and Christianity must summon the courage to absorb and critique the revelations found in the greatest age of transformation—the modern—as well as the revelations embodied in its unique historical catastrophe—the Holocaust—and in the Exodus of our time—the rebirth of the State of Israel. To his eternal credit, Pope John XXIII responded to all three catalysts when he opened up the Catholic Church to the world by convening the Second Vatican Council. Jewry has yet to generate a comparable religious figure with an equivalent response. Of course, we are all at the beginning of the way. The risk is high, but the potential for renaissance is exhilarating. The responsibility is staggering, and, undoubtedly, this generation will not finish the task, but no one is exempt from undertaking it.

Pluralism and Peoplehood

For both Judaism and Christianity, this is a time to reinterpret their relationships to one another.* This new analysis must include an understanding of God's pluralism—that no religion has a monopoly on God's love. The Noahide covenant lives; both faiths articulate and extend its mandate, but, in so doing, they do not have an exclusive divine mission that renders other religions irrelevant. On the contrary, they need the help of other religions to accomplish *tikun olam,* and they can instruct and enrich the others along the way. Judaism and Christianity are the two ancient faiths that have most experienced the freedom and power, and most internalized the reconceptualization of human

* Even as I write, I acknowledge that the sweeping nature of the proposals for transforming the relationship between Jews and Christians will be difficult for traditional Jews to consider. In my own Orthodox community, in particular, the question will be raised: By what authority are these suggestions made? The primary validation, I believe, is derived from the overriding moral and theological necessity to respond to the Holocaust and the recognition that the *Shoah* is a revelational event. This response is driven by and directly connected to the recognition of the image of God in Christians (and others). I have followed the logic of these responses and I take the responsibility upon myself. Nevertheless, for those for whom some great tree is needed to hang such ideas on, I call attention to Menachem HaMeiri's broad-scale views declaring that Christians (and Muslims) are a "people bound [or: restricted--IG] by religion which removes their religion from the category of idolatry and places them fully within the universe of moral obligation of Jews." See on this Moshe Halbertal's treatment of Meiri in his volume *Bein Hokhmah Le-Torah* (Jerusalem: Hebrew University, Magnes Press, 2000). Major portions of chapter 3 of that book have been translated in *The Edah Journal,* vol. 1, no. 1 (2000), on-line. Meiri's willingness to apply the halakhic guidelines to behavior by bringing Christians inside the mutual obligation universe is based on his philosophic analysis of the various religions' status; this aspect of his approach is particularly important as a precedent.

understanding that is the outcome of modernity. These are also the two religions that have seen close up the failures and experienced directly the pathologies of modernity. Both have much to digest and much to teach other faiths and cultures by analysis and role-modeling. The modeling must start with the two erstwhile antagonists, who built their religious claims on the invalidity of the other, affirming each other's independent dignity as ongoing, legitimate covenantal faiths. Yet, at the same time, this mutual affirmation does not negate the ongoing areas of disagreement, theological and otherwise.

But mere achievement of pluralism will not do justice to the uniqueness of the Jewish-Christian connection. Even if the two faiths enrich pluralism—by developing language and teaching models of deepened self-commitment combined with mutual affirmation—they will still only scratch the surface. The two self-described peoples of Israel must come to grips with the fact that they are both the children of Abraham—albeit they attain this status in different ways. The patriarch and Sarah were both promised that they would become the ancestors of many nations and that this development would be a blessing to the world (see Gen. 17:4–7 and 17:15–16). Theologians of several traditions have argued that the promise to Abraham is fulfilled in Ishmael and in the Muslim *umma*, which identifies Hagar's son as its eponymous hero. However, taking Sarah's blessing seriously implies that yet another nation will grow out of—or join as a branch of—her descendants, Isaac and/or Jacob/Israel.

Jewish tradition has long recognized that one need not be a genetic descendant of Abraham to become one of his children. Since the family is on a mission to teach, exemplify, and realize the covenant of redemption, one who accepts this calling can be born into the people of Israel through conversion. Once this joining takes place, all future descendants who carry on this line of the covenant are part of the people Israel. Given this fact, Judaism should factor in some understanding of the billions of gentiles who joined in the covenantal mission *en masse* even if they joined through a different narrative and lived as another (separate) part of the family. True, that part of the family once denied the legitimacy of this part; but when they acknowledge their error and stop the false denial, their conscious membership in Abraham's family should be integrated in some way.

Many Jews will respond to this proposal: Absolutely not! The gentiles who joined the Abrahamic covenant (as they understood it) did not meet any of Judaism's conversion standards; they did not embrace the life and practices of the Jewish people. Therefore, their intentions carry no religious weight in Judaism, and their commitments represent no ethical claim for recognition. Some would reject this proposal even more sharply. "Would you murder and take possession?" (1 Kings 21:19). After 2,000 years of Christianity demeaning Judaism as well as persecuting and killing Jews while trying to seize the name Israel by force, will Jews now voluntarily surrender the crown of a good name to Christianity's believers? Just because some Christians are sorry for what they did and some others want reconciliation?

To this argument, the counterresponse is: Do Christians not also merit recognition under Isaiah's thrice repeated rubric "so you [the people of Israel] are My witnesses, declares the Lord—and I am God" (Isa. 43:12; see also 43:10, 44:8)? Are there not hundreds of millions of human beings who had never heard of the God of Creation until Christians sought them out and testified to them about the God of Israel, who is the God of Creation, who loves them and wants them to be redeemed? Even if Christians spoke to gentiles about Jesus as Lord, did they not, in the end, bring these people to the God of Israel whom Jesus worshiped as Lord? These untold millions would never have known of the God of Israel but for Christians' repeated witness to them, until the people were convinced; and when they heard that the Lord had taken note of them and that God had seen their plight, then they bowed low in homage. And what about Isaiah's vision that some day "My house will be a house of prayer for all the nations" (Isa. 56:7)? Will this prophecy be fulfilled only by complete world conversion to Judaism? Is there no credit to Christianity for bringing billions to pray to the God of Israel? Is there no recognition that those Christians overwhelmingly acknowledge Jerusalem as a holy city and the Land of Israel as a special place of Divine Presence? Is it so that our Father in heaven has only one blessing for one child and none for all the other children of God—even those who, in good faith, consciously intended to join Abraham's family covenant? Is there not a precedent for reconciliation and sharing the blessing that after many years of distance and alienation, Isaac and Ishmael came together to honor their common father, Abraham (see Gen. 25:9; see also verses 10–18)? The children of the two sons remained distinct families, pursuing their own histories; yet at the same time, in honoring their common father, did the brothers not recognize themselves as branches of one family? Can this account in Genesis not serve as model and precedent for linking Jews and Christians today in a bond of family?

True, according to an established (albeit hostile) Jewish tradition, Esau is the progenitor of the Christians, so it can be argued that precedents drawn from Ishmael's life can have no application to Christians. Well, Esau too gets a blessing and a chronicle in the Torah—albeit a secondary, subordinate one. Now that Christians come and acknowledge Jewry's birthright and seek to join rather than usurp Abraham and Sarah's ancestry, is there not room for an expanded and more dignified blessing for these relatives?

The proposal to recognize Christians as a branch of the people Israel is made with real diffidence. One of the defining differences between Judaism and

Christianity is the Jewish insistence that birth and membership in a people is religiously significant. Judaism combines membership in a faith and membership in a people in one holistic union. This unity is partly due to Judaism's interpreting birth and genetic selection as an a priori (but not definitive) signal of chosenness; a person is elected to be a Jew when he or she is born. The signal is not absolutely determinative because Judaism and the Jewish people can be joined by conversion, a consciously willed adoption of the fate and mission of the people/religion. Note that the traditional Jewish conversion consists of two elements: physical rebirth (male circumcision and male/female total immersion in a *mikveh,* a ritual bath), as well as a freely chosen, moral commitment to the religion. By contrast, Christianity, essentially, repudiated lineality; rather, one becomes Christian only by being born again to faith in Christ.

The centrality of peoplehood in Judaism is also due to its ongoing focus on the self as a body-soul unity. The body embodies many of the religious messages even as the self (the body-soul unity) carries them out through ritual and ethical deeds. Similarly, the good life is to be actualized in real world society and within human history. By contrast, Christianity broke with genetic transmission and the paradigm of a political peoplehood in order to present the church as a fellowship of believers, defined by faith in Jesus. Christianity spiritualized peoplehood and territoriality as it shifted the balance toward the world of the spirit. Christian faith privileged the spiritual, timeless realm over the political and historical one.

The proposal that Christianity constitutes a branch of the Abrahamic family should not be interpreted as a diminution of Jewry's concrete peoplehood or its contemporary expression through Zionism. In effect, I am proposing that Christians are "honorary" members of the House of Israel, spiritual descendants of Abraham and Sarah. According to Jewish tradition, all human beings are members of one family; in biblical language, all humans are the children of Adam and Eve. From this biological heritage comes the universal dignity of equality and the principle that all human beings are created in the image of God. However, Christians are even more closely related to Jews— much as first cousins are closer than distant relatives. The articulation of this relationship is an attempt to capture the special connection to the mission of Israel and the intention to join the people Israel, which Christians express by dint of being Christian.

Jews who resist giving any greater weight to Christianity as a religion or to Christians as a possible branch of the people Israel should ask themselves the following question. What religious weight should be given to the fact that one of the central dignities of their own existence as a Chosen People is to be a blessing to the families of the earth and a light unto the nations? Some important part of the fulfillment of these promises and hallmarks has

96

come about through—and only through—the existence of Christianity. Christians not only brought to billions of people the good news of the loving God of Israel who seeks the redemption of humans and the ethic/commandment to love your neighbor as yourself. Christian faith also brought the Bible and Jewish values and thinking to bear in the formation of Western civilization, thus magnifying Jewish importance manyfold. Judaism's claim to be a world religion, and Jewry's self-understanding as a singled-out people central to history, as well as planetary witnesses to God, would be far more marginal were it not for Christianity's teaching. Do Jews owe Christians something in return? If so, what happened to the Jewish religious virtue of gratitude and returning good to others? Again, the reply may well be: Christians misrepresented the condition of Jewish specialness and twisted it into a state of uncanniness and demonic possession. They stole Judaism's best clothes and dressed themselves as the only child of the blessing. But if this history totally disqualifies all the good Christianity did for the world and for Jewry, then Jews must ask themselves: Why did God allow Christianity to spread so far and achieve so much? Shall all the gains be discounted as the outcome of purely human activity with no enabling or approval from God?

Let it be repeated that the affirmation of Christians as a branch of the people Israel is dependent on their ceasing and desisting from the degradation and usurpation of Judaism. They must put away their pride of power and act like loving brothers and sisters. One of the great moments of Jewish history and Torah narrates the occasion when brothers, hitherto alienated and violently hostile to each other, overcame the past and embraced each other in forgiveness and love. Can this not happen now between adopted siblings?* Can such a reconnection not come to be within a metaphorically linked, theologically defined family?

Even as I write, I fear that Christian missionaries or, even more insidiously, Jews for Jesus—people who (unlike the redeeming avant-garde of Christianity) believe that Judaism is superseded, and Jews have no right to exist as Jews anymore—will misuse these words. These people, who believe that Christianity has taken over Judaism like some succubus that must now govern the behavior of its host body, seek to abolish the Jewish religion.

---

* Rabbi Naftali Zevi Judah Berlin (1817–1893), one of the leading Rabbis of his generation and head of the classic Volozhin Yeshiva for 40 years, writes in his commentary *Haamek Davar* on Gen. 33:4 ("Esau ran to greet him. He embraced him and, falling on his neck, he kissed him; and they wept.") as follows: "AND THEY WEPT. Both wept. This teaches us that at this moment Jacob was roused to love Esau. So it will be for the future generations: in the moment when the seed of Esau will rouse themselves in the spirit of purification to recognize the seed of Israel and their value, then we [Jews] too will rouse ourselves to recognize Esau for his is our brother . . . ." Genesis with the commentary called *Haamek Davar* (Jerusalem: Vaad Ha Yeshivot, 1970, p. 245) I thank Rabbi Yechiel Eckstein for this reference.

Messianic Jews are even more abusive in that they use Jewish rituals and symbols as masks for a supersessionist Christianity in order to facilitate Jewish abandonment of Judaism. Such people could distort my argument that Jews and Christians are one people and use it to recruit Jews for Christianity. But one cannot be a Jew and a Christian at once. The decision that believers must choose one or the other was made in the first four centuries of the Common Era, and I believe that this separation into two distinct covenantal communities was the will of God. Efforts to utilize the close relationship of the two faiths to switch Jews more readily to Christianity represent a continuation of an historical abuse—using Christian religious experience to annihilate Jewish religious existence. Such efforts delegitimate Christianity.

N.B.: I have heard that there are now forgery-proof checks, treated so that if anyone tries to alter the signature, there is a widespread chemical reaction, which causes all the writing on the check to blur and vanish. How I wish that this book could be printed with special ink that would disappear should anyone exploit these words of reconciliation to undermine Judaism's distinctive existence (or even read these words with such malicious intent). To put it another way, these words reflect an act of trust in good Christians to oppose and prevent such approaches. Sincere Christians must be on guard to protect the brother whom their traditions have hurt. They must insist that all Christians finally honor the deeper truth in Jesus' statement: There are many mansions in my Father's house.

Let me also at this time express the same prayer and place a parallel covenantal anathema on any traditionalist Jews who may try to distort these writings to allege falsely that these words dilute Judaism's independence or collapse the distinctions between Judaism and Christianity. Such actions would constitute bearing false witness. Similarly, any attempts to use this search for theological reconnection to justify indifferentism or religious syncretism are malicious, trivializing distortions of the desire to find and do God's will. Any attempts to utilize these teachings to enable intermarriage and/or validate assimilation are misreadings, betrayals of religious integrity and of the divine intention to call into being two parallel covenantal communities working side by side to bring God's Kingdom.

Toward a New Understanding: Wrestling with God and with People

While the new relationship between Judaism and Christianity may start with Jewish affirmation of a familial connection to Christians, it should lead Jews and Christians alike to recognize the common roots as well as the joint and parallel missions of the two religions. In their separate faith, Christians are nurtured by the mother's milk of Sinai's covenant and Mosaic teachings. Admittedly, Christians often interpret Hebrew Scripture differently. They reinterpret theology and spiritualize or negate various injunctions of Israelite law in light of their own religious experiences, and practice fewer elements of the Torah than do Jews. Still, they attribute a once and ongoing (albeit not equivalent) holiness to the foundational texts of the Jewish tradition. In the final analysis, Christians seek to realize the broadest biblical promises—spiritual, relational, and material blessings—and build the fully redeemed world for which Judaism stands. Christian witness confirms the validity of Judaism's testimony as well.

Once the veil of hatred is lifted from between the two faiths, it becomes clear that Judaism has a fundamental stake in Christianity's achievement. As Maimonides suggested, Christianity's success brings Judaism's end goals closer; Christians advance an outcome on which Judaism has staked its credibility and truth. Even though Christians have shifted the balance of the Judaic religion, incorporated new mechanisms of worship, and introduced new channels of Divine Presence (which, in some cases, are unacceptable to Jews), these clashing claims should not obscure the common interest between the two. Once it is understood that the two religions are intended to function side by side, those changes that differentiate them from each other must be judged as differing tactical steps taken to reach out to the world. Their disagreements should be labeled "controversies for the sake of heaven," which, therefore, leave a permanent positive result.[7] Or, perhaps one may borrow the terminology of the Rabbinic midrash. There is a controversy that leads to the repair of the world and to filling it with life (which is constructive) and there is a controversy that only brings chaos to the world (which is destructive).[8] It is time to turn the controversy between Judaism and Christianity into a force for *tikun olam*.

In rethinking the relationship of Judaism and Christianity, much of the theological speculation has focused on whether the two religions represent two covenants or one. It is time to suggest that both come to fulfill one covenant—the Noahide. In their further development, both religions grow out of one and the same covenant, the Abrahamic/Sinaitic, but by the will of God they have branched into two parallel covenants to reach out to humanity in all its diversity of culture and religious need. Nevertheless, the members of the two faith communities remain part of one people, the people of Israel, the people that wrestle with God and humans to bring them closer to each other; thus they narrow the chasm between the ideal world that God seeks to bring into being and the real world.

Being part of one people has moral consequences, at least in Judaic tradition. Extending help to humanity legitimately starts with the members of one's own family and people. Therefore, the two communities owe special help to each other. One feels special rejoicing in the achievement of fellow citizens. Therefore, Jews who always yearned for a universal redeemer and who accept little of Jesus' message should nevertheless appreciate Jesus' service as a spiritual messiah to gentiles; he is not a false messiah, but a would-be redeemer for the nations.

Members of a single people feel special responsibility when other members are in danger. At the present time, a massive wave of anti-Semitism is sweeping through the Muslim world, driven by anger at Islam's failure to modernize and further inflamed by the Israeli-Palestinian struggle. This phenomenon is not unlike the tide of hatred that flowed through Christendom during the Middle Ages. Some of the images disseminated today (such as the libel that Jews use gentile blood in their ritual foods and *The Protocols of the Elders of Zion*, a purported insidious Jewish plot to control the world) are derived from old-time Christian demonizations or secularized versions thereof. Many of the thirteen million Jews facing one billion Muslims—including a small violent terrorist Muslim minority—feel endangered and lonely. As brothers, Christians can sympathize, offer solidarity, and defend; as sisters, Christians can testify to Muslims and urge them to avoid repeating Christianity's past errors and sins, pointing out how the stain of these behaviors troubles Christians today. This situation offers Christians the opportunity to make amends for the anti-Jewish sins that they have repudiated at last in this century.

As I write, there are millions of Christians suffering oppression and discrimination, even violence, in a host of countries around the world (some, but not all, in the same Muslim countries that are the scene of anti-Semitism). Jews have the opportunity to work for the freedom and well-being of these Christians, much as they have done, over the past 50 years, for the threatened members of their Jewish family. Thus they can practice an important form of *imitatio Dei* toward Christians and others. "I [God] am with him [the sufferer] in distress. I will rescue him and treat him with dignity" (Ps. 91:15—my translation). Says Maimonides: "All of [the people of] Israel and *those attached to them* are like brothers, as it is written: You are children to the Lord your God (Deut. 14:1). And if a brother will not have compassion for his brother, then who will?"[9] Indeed, Maimonides insists that such compassion is a defining characteristic of a member of the people of Israel.[10]

So what is the mission of the multibranched people of Israel in this time? What does it mean today to wrestle with God and humans to bring them closer to each other? Judaism and Christianity must wrestle with God to reveal how to grow closer in loving affirmation of each other's dignity and mission and thus enable them to overcome the pattern of authoritative past traditions and divine revelations that set each faith at the other's throat. Each community must wrestle with God to bring both Torah and Gospel closer to the human condition, to transmit the ideals in a manner less punitive and condemning of humanity. Rather, they and God must interpret the instruction in a manner more magnetic and capable of drawing out the best in people out of freedom and choice, until all is perfected. Each community must cry out to God against a world order that is marked by hunger, deprivation, cruelty, and innocent suffering; each must press for a divine delegation of strength to move the world toward redemption, now.

Each faith must wrestle with humanity to draw closer to God and each other, to recognize the image of God in the other and respond lovingly on a greater scale than ever before. Both faiths must struggle to push away the use of force and the vanity of monopoly and strive to witness voluntarily. They can offer each other moral support as they renounce past privilege and give up the sense of entitlement and superior status. Standing together, the two can more effectively combat aggressive secularism and scientific materialism. Linked to each other, the two can more easily acknowledge the dignity of secularists and their contribution to shaping a better world. The secular movements that knew their own limitations have played a positive role in placing constructive limits on religion. Now all groups can interact and affirmatively balance society and culture to maximize human betterment. Perhaps the spiritual comfort that the two communities can give each other can empower them to give the other religionists and secularists their due without surrendering the two religions' own norms and their distinctive witness to Creation, Covenant, and Redemption.

The two faiths need each other's help to contend effectively with rampant materialism and reactionary terrorism. The two must realize that the more they overcome the demons of the past, the more they become God's witnesses, channels of divine blessing for a suffering humanity, couriers of redemption. Yet Jews and Christians must recognize that the two faiths together cannot accomplish the full task. Once they admit this truth, they can respect other faiths as well. Then wherever people call out in the name of the Lord, there God will come and bless them all.

If Judaism and Christianity rise above past degradation and enable themselves and each other, then they prove that faithfulness to God can inspire heroic love and forgiveness. Thus these two faiths can give unique testimony to the power of life and love to overcome death. This teaching is central to their covenantal affirmations; it is exemplified in their histories. The force of their proclamations will be even more overwhelming if they can connect to each other and thus prove that the "love [which] is stronger than death" is even more powerful than the "jealousy which is harder than *She'ol* [the realm of death]" (Song 8:6).

The love that flows from recognizing the other as an image of God may start inside one people, but it evokes response from all who come in contact with it. Then the gathering love can flow and overflow through the hidden channels and links that connect all humans to each other. The wrestling through the night will be followed by the rise of a sun of healing and a word of mutual blessing. Then those who have gone before—God and the humans who began this journey—can join with God and all who walk this way today and with those yet unborn who will take up the task to complete *tikun olam.* When Jacob and his brother become Israel, a moment of redemption is at hand. This is our time and our mission. Walk this way, and, someday, blessed humanity will cry out: This is the day that God (and humans) has made. Let us rejoice and be glad to be in it (Ps. 118:24—my translation).

Notes

1. Philip Birnbaum, *Daily Prayer Book* (New York: Hebrew Publishing Company, 1992), p. 73; my translation; italics added.

2. Joseph B. Soloveitchik, *Lonely Man of Faith* (Northvale, NJ: Jason Aronson , 1997), p. 28.

3. Babylonian Talmud, *Sukkah* 52b.

4. For a comparison to Caro's views, see the more complex, more positive attitudes toward sexuality in Caro's peers, the circle of mystics of Safed grouped around Isaac Luria, as portrayed in Lawrence Fine, *Physician of the Soul, Healer of the Cosmos: Isaac Luria's Kabbalistic Fellowship* (Palo Alto: Stanford University Press, 2004).

5. Weinberg letter reprinted in Marc Shapiro, "Scholars and Friends: Rabbi Jehiel Jacob Weinberg and Professor Samuel Atlas," in *Torah U-Madda Journal,* vol. 7 (1997), p. 118.

6. See on this Irving Greenberg, *The Ethics of Jewish Power* (New York: CLAL, 1982); reprinted in R. R. Reuther and M. Ellis, *Beyond Occupation: American, Jewish, Christian and Palestinian Voices of Peace* (Boston: Beacon Press, 1990), pp. 22–64.

7. *Ethics of the Fathers* (Pirke Avot) chap. 5, par. 17.

8. *Genesis Rabbah*, chap. 4, sec. 6.

9. Maimonides, *Mishneh Torah*, Hilkhot Matnot Aneeyim, chap. 10, halacha 2—italics added.

10. Ibid.

Part Two

LOOKING
BACK

The New Encounter of
Judaism and Christianity

We are now in the opening stages of a new encounter of Judaism and Christianity. The dynamic force driving the new dialogue has thus far come from outside the religious traditions. It has been supplied by what I would call the universalization of culture. This means the extraordinary capacity of modern culture to communicate, i.e., the extraordinary openness of the cultural medium in which we live. It has thrown us together and by exposure and involvement has made us part of each other's consciousness. Who could have imagined years ago that straitlaced middle-class people would appropriate the world of bohemia or the homosexual, or that of the underbelly of society through literature and mass media? Who could have foreseen that the agony of Vietnamese or Biafran children would be seared into the minds and hearts of Americans by a medium such as television? This empathetic encounter forces us to see the reality of the other person. In biblical terms, one might call it the expansion of human consciousness to recognize the image of God in the other person. The "image of God" is defined in Jewish tradition as the equality, uniqueness, and the preciousness of the other person. Such a recognition makes a demand on me. The act of identification means that I will experience the sorrow and the need of the other. Historically, humans have lived in communities that created internal mediums in which they experienced the reality of their own group. The outgroup frequently had only abstract or caricatured existence. But the direct and genuine encounter now overwhelms these stereotypes and abstractions, making the other flesh of my flesh. The empathetic discovery of the other person leads inevitably to discovery of the other's culture, values, and religion. As I identify with the other, that which is precious to the other becomes precious to me—not least because it has produced him or her.

The first people to recognize the situation were the lay people who, living together and thrown together, discovered each other. Up until now, it has been the fate of theologians and religious leaders to be most sheltered, to be living within the internal medium of the faith, and therefore to be the last to discover the other.

The last one in sometimes does have a special gift to bring to the situation. He may have a sense of perspective—if she can comprehend the successes and failures of those who have gone before. And if this person is insightful and farseeing, he may be capable of discerning the new situation in overall gestalt and what new possibilities have been opened up. To appreciate all that is possible in the new situation, we would do well to go back at least briefly to the initial encounter of the Jewish and Christian communities and see what options of relationship and self-understanding were taken and what options were not. It may give us insights into the options that may face us today, particularly if we can grasp what new factors and forces are present in today's encounter. This may help us avoid errors that could abort the new encounter—in fulfillment of the old dictum that those who ignore history are condemned to relive it.

The original encounter of Jews and Christians took place at the very birth of Christianity some two millennia ago. If I might simplify and view the situation in somewhat Jewish or even secular terms, the following happened. A group of Jews decided to go to the world with the good news of a certain basic understanding of the human condition and fate—an understanding that they shared with the Jewish community. The basic news was: In this rather darkling and cruel world, a world in which empirical or existential experience all too often seems to confirm humankind's aloneness in an alien or hostile universe, nevertheless, humankind is not alone. There is a God who loves humans and treasures them. This points to the preciousness of humankind and its ultimate redemption. Not that Jews or Christians could be oblivious to the evidence of humankind's slavery or worthlessness or its abandonment—Job or Ecclesiastes are proof enough of that. But in the face of this evidence, it was the claim of Judaism and again of Christianity that we have a fundamental turning situation or orientation moment that promises that evil, slavery, and death are the deviations from the norm and they will be overcome. In Judaism, it is the Exodus event and the history of God's relationship to his people; for Christians it was the Christ event, which confirms that, contrary to the present situation, the ultimate reality is the preciousness of humanity and that humankind will be redeemed.

106

In electing the course of going to the gentiles, the Christian community came to break with a certain aspect of Jewish tradition. It was the claim of the tradition that this illumination cannot be imparted or implanted by faith alone. If it is to be believed in and realized in the lives of humans, it must involve and permeate the entire way of life. Judaism encased or formulated its fundamental perception of human dignity in a *halakhah*—law, as it is commonly referred to in Christian circles—although it is more accurately described as the Way. (*Halakhah* may be literally translated from the verb *"haloch,"* to walk; i.e., it is the walking or the way.) This is an attempt to take every action of love and orient it toward the central vision of humanity and God. On a deeper level, the tacit claim is that only in a certain kind of cultural matrix, and only with a certain kind of discipline and memory, can humans come to love consistently such a commitment. The Way and its actions served to root in life the faith and the commitment. Moreover, it hoped to avoid the danger of affirmations that were not concretized in life. The insight of the role of deeds is one of the fundamental stresses of the Jewish tradition. It was the ultimate conclusion of the Christian community that the redeeming action of faith would express itself in life rather than necessarily requiring the specific disciplines of the Way.

Since the world needed consolation and good news, it would be fruitless as well as irrelevant to reargue that question. However, the question may be relevant in judging the success of Christianity in its mission. Insofar as this consolation for all people is humankind's true patrimony and destiny, we might agree that going to the world was necessary and fruitful. But at this critical juncture, due to many factors, the Christian community elected to define its covenant not as a second covenant for the world—not even as a (complementary) covenant for the gentiles—but as a New Covenant. To be more specific, it was defined as a new covenant that thereby superceded or fulfilled the old. Undoubtedly some of the force for this option came from the destruction of Jerusalem, which must have seemed to many Christians as historical confirmation (i.e., an act of God in history) that the Jewish social system had indeed come to an end. Some of the push for this option must have derived from the very closeness and rootedness of the community in Judaism, which did not permit it to leave Judaism without actively denying that which was close enough to continue to represent a claim upon it. Perhaps it was the fact that Christianity spread so quickly among the gentiles and so little among the Jews that sealed its fate. (There is of course the possibility that indeed it was the New that supercedes the Old. But this option I take not to be valid in light of the history of Judaism from that day to this day, as well as in light of my own faith commitments and reading of the promises of God in Scripture.) It is

107

my suspicion that this decision and all its implications were not fully perceived by those who took it. But it proved to be a tragic turning point that foreclosed the possibility of a genuine encounter between Jews and Christians for a rather long period of time.

The fatal aspect of this self-definition is that it made the continuation of Judaism a problem theologically. Indeed, by implication, it could suggest that the existence of the Jewish covenant becomes a direct blow at the validity of the covenant of Christ. If it was claimed the blindness and hardheartedness of the Jews accounts for the rejection of Jesus, then a living Judaism, manifestly alive and religiously creative, would undercut the notion of blindness and suggest that maybe Jews saw correctly. Since Judaism is intrinsically linked to the Jewish people and its destiny, then the existence of the Jew becomes a problem, too. Given the political triumph of Christianity and its wide spread and the consequent imbalance of force between the two communities, use of power became the irresistible temptation to resolve the problem.

Of course, Judaism could be denied its life by stereotype and caricature. Its petrifaction, soulless legalism, etc., are all Christian ways of saying that it is "dead," i.e., its existence need not be taken seriously, and therefore the notion of supercession (and the validity) of the new covenant is upheld. Since the life and existence of the Jew, however, was bound to break through such stereotypes, the conversion of the Jew becomes the next necessary step to resolve the anxiety of the conflict and contradiction implied by Christian self-definition. This failing, the most tragic further alternative suggests itself: For the mob or the ecclesiastical agitator, it is the physical destruction of Jews; for the Papacy, it is all too often the physical continuation of the Jews, but in a degraded enough state to testify to God's rejection of their covenant. This analysis, of course, is too logical and neat and does not do justice to the multitude of economic and social factors that play a crucial role in crystallizing hateful attitudes into violent acts. But the portrait is, I think, close enough to the psychological dynamics of the two faiths and communities to tell an essential truth. It has been estimated that more than six million Jews died during the course of various persecutions through the Middle Ages—comparable to the very figure that makes us stand aghast at the demonism unleashed in modern times.

It must be understood that the Jewish community stereotyped in turn. Given the same imbalance of power and the temptation and attraction of joining the majority, it could not afford the luxury of appreciating Christianity. It was hard enough to remain faithful to Judaism (and millions undoubtedly yielded to various pressures and left Jewry and Judaism) even when Christianity was alien, forbidding, and viewed as intellectually or religiously outrageous. People who would allow themselves to see its beauty and magnificence would likely be swept away by it.

The inability to redress the political balance meant that Jews could not recognize Christianity's spiritual appeal either. Throughout this period, then, Christianity is seen within the Jewish community in caricature or stereotype. In the Middle Ages, it even takes the form of crude attempts to impugn the paternity of Jesus—as a way of dismissing the entire claim associated with him. Of course, the very intensity of the attack can again be seen as a reflection of the need to minimize the appeal. There was, therefore, a tacit kind of consensus to have no real encounter on the part of the two communities. Christians would fear that it might undermine the claims of the New Covenant; Jews would be concerned lest they be pulled into the orbit of the Christian faith. Perhaps the most surprising thing about the relationships in these centuries is how much real contact and even fructifying influences managed to break through these barriers, and the deep psychological identity needs that they met.

I believe that this option taken had tragic effects not only for Jews but for Christians and for the success of Christianity. Implicit in this stress is a devaluation of Judaism and therefore of its emphases. The central theme of the *halakhah* is the sanctification of the everyday. Activities such as eating, sexual relations, and business activity are directed to God and sacralized by the mitzvot (commandments). These very acts ensure that a positive value will be placed on such activities, and a great stress on redemption of the here and now will be emphasized. It is not that closeness to Judaism could have guaranteed Christianity's retention of these emphases—or of the prophetic centrality of social justice. But the distance from Jews and Judaism opens Christianity to greater influence of Hellenistic viewpoints. At the least, it prevents a dialogic witness and reminder of the importance of these concerns. The result is a significantly greater incorporation of notions of the conflict of the body and the spirit or the rejection of this world. This weakened the impact of Christianity on the life of its people and of Western society. Distancing from the Hebrew prophets was a significant factor tempting Christians to render unto Caesar that which was Caesar's; tempting it to be concerned for the soul to the neglect of the body. Alienation from Hebrew faith encouraged Christianity to conceive the sacred as the antithesis of the secular and as a realm set aside from life. This particular tendency toward otherworldliness is now commonly recognized as a major component of modern humans' revolt against religion for the sake of affirming the needs of humankind in this world. Providing the theology of passivity to the deprivations of humanity in the here and now in effect made Christianity all too often guilty of collaboration with and even undergirding of an unhappy status quo. It is not accident that the felt need for the rediscovery of the secular has led to the great revival of concern and interest in Old Testament studies. They serve as source for images of concern and sacrality in the realm of the secular. Yet the living testimony to these emphases was denied to Christianity during the period when it was most tempted to resort to asceticism and other worldly spirituality.

Perhaps the worst legacy of this self-understanding was the built-in hostility to Judaism and the Jew that it engendered. The teaching of contempt is a psychological outgrowth of such a relationship and self-definition. This theology thus tended to legitimate the continuation of hate within the very covenant whose fundamental message was love. The very radicalness of the demand of love would evoke resistance and difficulty in fulfillment of the call. The provision of a kind of "privileged sanctuary" within the heart of the community practically guaranteed that hatred would survive and flourish despite and within the gospel of love. There is a sad and ironic comment of the Rabbi of Kotzk, one of the later masters of the Hasidic movement. Satan fought Hasidism bitterly in its inception, for he feared its capacity to renew religious commitment and to overcome his actions. When he saw that he could not stop its spread, he wisely decided to join it. Thus he found sanctuary within the movement that threatened to destroy him, and he destroyed it. The provision of a recognized outlet for hatred represented a shelter for it and a constant focal point of infection of hate for the entire body religious. Within the framework of the covenant, one could deceive one's self that the devil's work was the will of God. This exception generated hostile, morally compromising behavior patterns in Christian life and resulted in a great failure to eliminate the sources of evil and readiness to hate within the culture. That after 1,900 years of Christian nurture, Western man and woman were capable of the demonism we have witnessed in our time challenges the very adequacy of Christianity as civilizing influence and moral pedagogue to Western man and woman. This is not the least of the prices paid for this supercessionist definition of Christian covenant.

The pattern of mutual denial and unresponsiveness could not change as long as the power relationship was unchanged and as long as the consequent spiritual closedness to each other persisted. But since the advent of the Modern Era, the growth of national states and secular power spelled doom for political Christendom. The separation of church and state and the growth of secular citizenship meant that the sword was no longer available to Christianity. The temptation of power was removed from the church. In all fairness, there is no guarantee that Judaism would have acted differently had it had the power—unless it be that it did not define its validity by the invalidity of other faiths, not even of Christianity. But Judaism could not coerce all along even if it wanted to do so. The removal of this power from Christianity meant that Jews could relax as well. And the new living together and social contact meant that soon the Jew and the Christian would see each other as living in vital communities.

Arthur A. Cohen, a Jewish theologian, has told the story of how he, a child raised in a fairly secular home with little religious depth, came in contact with Mortimer J. Adler and the Catholic group at the University of Chicago. Cohen had deep religious feelings that had found no outlet in Judaism as it was marginally and in attenuated form available in his home. For the first time in his life, he was exposed to the magnificent sweep and philosophic complexity and attraction of Christianity. Cohen seriously considered conversion. He decided not to convert but to become a religious Jew. Obviously, Arthur Cohen could not treat Christianity theologically as did Jews of previous generations and far different encounters. What Arthur Cohen did on the sophisticated theological level was done by the Jew and the Christian in the local neighborhood. Sometimes great theologians were as influenced by such social contacts as were the simplest of laymen. Krister Stendhal has spoken of how his rediscovery of the Hebrew prophetic vision followed an encounter with secular Jews animated by passion for social justice. Although these Jews rejected the prophets' religious way, still Stendhal acknowledged that he had never realized that Jews could be such a vital force for social justice. Suddenly he felt that he must take the Hebrew prophetic vision seriously again.

Whatever the faults of shallowness and conventionality of the early days of Brotherhood Weeks,[1] they wrought more finely than they thought. The laymen's intuition grasped what theologians were not yet ready or capable of explaining: the ongoing vitality and validity of the other's covenant. This attitude opened up new lines of concern and communication. But as long as this view remains the layman's, the new possibilities are conditional affirmations only. Any turn of the historical or social situation could undercut this new respect and allow the revival of the old triumphalism or contempt. This breakthrough of the laity is one of the options that theologians, then, can and must explore. This is particularly promising since the removal of the old angle of vision could lead to greater recognition of facets of Judaism downplayed in the old constellation of Christian theological designs.

A second factor leading to the new encounter is the secularization of culture. The vitality of secularism and its intellectual and visionary assault on established religions has placed all religious groups under great pressure. The very feeling of slippage leads to an instinctive turning to other religious groups for reassurance—a kind of huddling together for comfort. There is an enormous amount of rethinking, theological restructuring, and new adjustments to the new culture to be undertaken. It is far from clear which will be the most fruitful approaches to these tasks, or whether the process will not undermine the religious tradition. Each group's experience and solutions with this task become of potential value and significance to the other. Thus Martin Buber's response becomes exceedingly useful to many Protestant and Catholic theologians, just as Will Herberg draws upon Reinhold Niebuhr, and Joseph Soloveitchik draws upon Otto and Kierkegaard. A positive contact with a person in another tradition reopens relationship to his or her whole tradition, potentially.

A crucial new factor in the contemporary encounter is the event of the Holocaust of European Jewry. The Holocaust is a very ambiguous force in this situation. It divides and unites. Perhaps it divides more than it unites, but, nevertheless, it forces a new encounter. The Holocaust is an event of such magnitude that it clearly ranks with the fundamental experiences of Jewish history, such as the Exodus or the destruction of the Temple. Its theological influence has been restricted up to now by the numbness of the Jewish community and the terrible incommensurability of the event. But its impact is growing with every year. On the one hand, the Holocaust divides because it stands in Jews' eyes as a kind of demonic culmination of certain Christian teachings that made it possible. Christians legitimately may argue that other causes were involved and that modern secular or pagan forms led the anti-Semitic attack in this century. But the Jew experiences the history of the church's injection of anti-Semitism into the bloodstream of European culture. The Jew experiences the direct correlation between fundamentalist, particularist Christianity and the survival rate of Jews under the Nazis. Put simply: The key variable related to the survival of Jews was neither Jewish resistance nor Nazi efficiency. The key variable was the attitude of the local non-Jewish population. Did the local population resist, condemn genocide, hide Jews, or even merely disapprove strongly, the Jewish survival rate went up. The rule of thumb is that the more deeply Catholic or fundamentalist Orthodox or Protestant the population, i.e., the more particularist and unmodernized the form of Christianity present, the lower the Jewish survival rate. Eighty to 90 percent of the Jews of Poland and the Ukraine were murdered, but only 40 percent in secularized or sophisticated Catholic France, and a minute fraction in highly secularized Denmark. Adjust for the differential German use of terror in the East against the local population, for the easy availability of shelter in Sweden for Denmark's Jews, etc., and the starkness of the key variable still testifies. Then, too, the silence of the Christian church haunts the dialogue situation. Without denying the many acts of individual courage and speaking out by the relatively few, protests (for the most part, mild and indirect) by church official figures were rare; basic silence is the overwhelming fact.

If these were the only facts of the Holocaust, then, of course, there would be no dialogue possible. But the Holocaust has had another impact. It has elicited a very significant reaction of repentance and responsibility in the Christian community—or, at least, parts of it. Interestingly enough, here again the reaction is greater today than 20 years ago. Turn to the Darmstadt statement on the Jews in 1948, written in Germany three years after the Holocaust by German theologians who presumably, at that time, should have been full of shame and regret. The statement labels Jewish suffering as God's punishment for continued rejection of Christ. "The fate of the Jews is a silent sermon, reminding us that God will not allow Himself to be mocked. It is a warning to us, and an admonition to the Jews to be converted to Him, who is their sole hope of salvation" (World Council of Churches, "The Relationship of the Church to the Jewish People", pp. 49–50). This from the midst of the people that had conceived and executed the Final Solution.

Compare to this view the guidelines issued by the National Conference of Catholic Bishops for implementing Vatican II's statement on the Jews, and one can sense the growing power of this reaction. This is a profoundly cleansing response. Recognition of guilt and self-criticism is the first step to spiritual health and testifies to the renewed moral vitality of the people involved. (The prophetic denunciation of Israel is thus one of the most remarkable tributes to the spiritual grandeur of a people, i.e., so great were they that they produced people capable of utter dissatisfaction with the status quo who blamed their own people and not others. This fact has been neatly reversed by traditional Christian polemics that used the denunciations to prove Israel's unworthiness.) Insofar as Christian acceptance of guilt due to the Holocaust leads to a rethinking of the relationship to Jews and Judaism, it moves further to renew the vitality of Christian confession and elicits a positive response from Jews. To mourn together has long been a powerful uniting bond in the fellowship of humanity.

On the Jewish side, the Holocaust has a paradoxical effect as well. In the writings of opponents of Jewish-Christian dialogue, it is a major barrier to an encounter. Steven Schwarzschild, editor of *Judaism,* in opposing dialogue has written plain and simple: It is too soon. One cannot have conversations while the blood of six million is still warm. And there is no question that at dialogues the Holocaust has frequently divided Jew and Christian and even interrupted communication. And yet, on the other hand, to put it crudely, there is the fear of a repetition of the Holocaust that drives the Jew to seek out the gentile in the hope of establishing a new personal relationship that could act to prevent a recurrence. With the notable exception of Abraham Joshua Heschel, there is little doubt that the leadership and initiative for dialogue from the Jewish side in the post–World War II period came from Jewish defense organizations rather than theological bodies. The agencies knew that unchanged Christian attitudes could support and nourish anti-Semitic attitudes and actions, and that this was literally a matter of life and death for Jews. That defense agencies should take the lead in theological dialogue testifies in its own way to the tragic history of this relationship. As such, this sponsorship might well be at least as much an embarrassment to Christians as to Jews.

Beyond the reaction of defense, however, is the fundamental Jewish tradition that the proper and necessary response to tragedy is the affirmation of the frail bonds of humanness and responsibility that still hold. A number of Jewish theologians have pointed out that the people, Israel, has survived not so much by winning in history—it has more often lost—but by responding to death and destruction with redoubled life-building and affirmation. "On the day the Temple was destroyed, the Messiah was born," says the Talmud. The mourner who has just experienced the tragedy and absurdity of death is asked to recite as a memorial prayer, the *Kaddish*—a plea for the establishment of the Kingdom of God in our time. Moreover, the witness of dehumanization and the cheapness of human life that is given by Auschwitz must overwhelm the testimony of the faith of Israel in God's love and man's worth—unless some powerful impulse of healing and love is expressed to redress the balance. One might cite the biblical account of the aftermath of the Flood. The first commandment to Noah after he comes out of the ark is that the human being is made in the image of God, and that one who spills mortal blood commits *the* great crime and will be held accountable. The widespread destruction of human life implies its worthlessness and must be immediately contradicted by a renewed affirmation and practice upholding its value. Such healing demands a new outreach to all people, whatever the history of the past. At least two Jewish theologians, Emil Fackenheim and Zalman Schachter, in specific response to the Holocaust, have called for a new Jewish theology of the gentile and of Christianity with greater stress on responsibility and greater appreciation of the religious life of Christianity and its relationship to God.

Another great event of our time in Jewish history is the rebirth of the State of Israel. It, too, introduces a new factor in the encounter, and one that seems destined to play a larger role in the future. Of course, the crisis of June 1967 and the widespread Jewish feeling that official Christian circles failed to respond appropriately to the threat of renewed genocide in Israel has focused attention on the Jewish state in current Jewish-Christian dialogue. That crisis only dramatizes the underlying issue in the relationship posed by the rebirth of the state. The emergence of a new Jewish commonwealth in the land of Israel fundamentally challenges some of the images that grew out of the first encounter. Part and parcel of the notion of the new covenant replacing the old is the conclusion that exile is the punishment for the rejection of Christ. The eternal wandering of the Jew has been repeatedly interpreted as the Jew's destiny until he accepts Christianity. This was Cardinal Merry de Val's reaction to Theodor Herzl, the founder of modern political Zionism, when he came to the Vatican for help in obtaining the Holy Land. One may speculate as to what extent the continued Vatican refusal to recognize officially the existence of the State of Israel represents not merely concern for Arab Christians but this particular theological hang-up. The emergence of the state by giving flesh to certain prophetic passages in the Hebrew Bible is a direct challenge to the notion that the prophecies are to be allegorized and applied to "Israel of the Spirit" instead of "Israel of the flesh."

Perhaps the reestablishment of the physical community of Israel in a physical and political state may inspire new reflection on the religious significance of a physical people and their actual existence. The capacity to reestablish a state after 2,000 years of exile, in its own way, testifies to the vitality and life of the Jewish tradition that inspired this restoration and of the Jewish people that carried this out. It certainly strikes at the image of petrifaction or the claim that Judaism comes to an end with the birth of Christianity. Last but not least, the existence of Israel has escalated the moral dilemma of the classical relationship of Judaism and Christianity to unbearable levels. If the only solution to Jewish existence is that the Jews be converted or that they disappear physically, then the establishment of the state makes the conversion much less likely. The other alternative cannot take place without a major new episode of genocide. This is to say that Christianity would be "upheld" only by a successful holocaust in which it would be implicated of at least tacit cooperation. (Compare A. Roy Eckardt's essay on silence of the churches in June 1967, the epilogue in his book *Elder and Younger Brothers*.) Coming on the heels of the Holocaust in Europe, this is a burden that few people of conscience—and, a fortiori, the powerful revival of the Christian conscience—are able or willing to bear. Indeed, such an event would spell the destruction of Christianity's last moral capital in a modern culture that already is deeply critical of its record on moral and human questions. And so the existence of the State of Israel is a goad to a new Christian relationship to Jews even as it begins to rebuild the biological, and even spiritual, security of the seed of Abraham.

We have, then, a most paradoxical situation in this emerging new encounter between Judaism and Christianity. On the surface, both religions are faced with serious threats to their viability and existence. They are on the defensive rather than in a moment of preparation for a vast expansion. Judaism is still bloody and deeply crippled from its recent experiences and even short of people to participate in dialogue. Christianity is under the pressure of sins of the past vis-à-vis Judaism. Yet surface appearances notwithstanding, there are many more possibilities of positive interaction and mutual enrichment in the new situation than were present or were explored in the first encounter. And the particularly vital new element in the current dialogue is the entry into it of the traditional groups and the theologians who are the "last in" to the situation. As long as the motives are defense or conversion (and on the official level, these two motives are still quite strong), the fruitfulness of the dialogue is likely to be primarily institutional and limited. And as long as (in the early days) the encounter was between the indifferent or the excessively modernized with the excessively modernized, the religious possibilities were at best ambiguous.

When people come together out of religious commitment and not to find the secularism that they have in common, the new possibility is fundamental religious and theological enlightenment of each other. If there is the courage and security to confront each other in all our particularity, contradiction, and uniqueness, the two traditions can significantly enhance or deepen themes and strands in each other that should be augmented or developed in the present moment. The truth is that every religion has many positions along the spectrum and many possible options of response to the moment that it does not explore fully. The other tradition may indeed have explored the alternate way. Seeing it in the other's life may make it more meaningful or more possible in my own framework. Not infrequently the new appreciation of the alternate model may lead to the repositioning of the elements in my own total religious response.

For Christians the new encounter offers the possibility of a fuller recovery of the biblical, this-worldly thrust of religious faith. It would mean a greater stress on the claims of social justice and on sacralizing the secular ("secularizing the sacred" in current Christian theology). This is a dimension that Christians are seeking to recover, and there are many areas where the *halakhah* and the constellation of Jewish tradition have kept and intensified the centrality of these concerns. There are many practical techniques as well that can serve as models for response to be learned. I believe that the sense of the peoplehood of the believing community is another area that has been axiomatic in Jewish tradition that will be increasingly important in Christian self-understanding. This last will be connected to the question of exile.

One of the most difficult trials facing Christianity is the fact that having been a majority religion for most of its life, it is now entering into its own diaspora: the exile of Christianity in the secular world. There are many problems of living in exile. Sometimes it distorts the personality as one seeks self-protection. Sometimes the need for identity may lead to isolation or to hostility and even hatred for the world that surrounds. But there is an even more subtle problem in coming to grips with being a minority in exile in the world. Sometimes the response's motive force is a desire to escape from or evade the fact of being in exile. This can lead to such a great desire to be with the world that one surrenders one's own unique insights.

The Jewish experience of living in exile, of being in the world yet not totally of it, could significantly strengthen Christianity at this moment. This is necessary lest Christianity, in its legitimate desire to recognize and join in that which is good and significant in contemporary secular culture, also forget that it still has a prophetic and critical role to play even in this world. It would be all too easy for Christians to confuse their own position with the liberal or even with the radical movements. I find frequently a strong tendency in all too many liberal Christians to identify simplistically with the new left or with the Third World—as if the underdog is automatically righteous. To identify totally with the world, however, is to betray the dialectic of religious living. It is to surrender the duty to unite, in one commitment, total immersion in the immanent with the complete awareness of the transcendent.

It is interesting to note how a secular theologian such as Harvey Cox has tried to balance his paean to the secular city with a new stress on this need to dissociate and play a critical role within it. Jewish theologians who were fresh from Auschwitz and from a century and a half of excessive identification with the world found it difficult to fall into one-sided readings, i.e., Cox's identification with the world in the first place. Only as it maintains its capacity for dialectical religious living can Christianity play its role of fullest significance for the world.

Another area of potential insight to Christianity is of particular promise for Catholics. As Catholicism moves toward the pole of personal participation (as against the stress on the sacramental dimension of religion), it could gain illumination from the Jewish experience. The destruction of the Temple turned Judaism by force majeure, as it were, from the primacy of its sacramental and grace options to a deep exploration of religion as a way of life and toward the stress on personal participation, the internalization of religious values, and the "priesthood of the laity." (Sometimes history is strangely beneficent in destroying something that would not have voluntarily been given up—but that once destroyed frees us to explore even more fruitful possibilities.) In Judaism's experience, Catholics can find a response to a similar experience (the modern situation is undermining the sacramental). Judaism contains a case study in all the options that arise at the moment of destruction (including the groups that deny that the destruction has taken place and urge that no adaptation be made) and possibly even a chance to see what mistakes were made that might be avoided. Of course, all

117

analogies are of limited value, but there is enough similarity to offer much sound insight.

For Jews, too, the new encounter offers extraordinary opportunities for religious illumination, not only in a new understanding of Christianity but in the internal development of Judaism itself as well. For one, it may help overcome the equivalent hostility-cancer in Jewry. To the extent that the pressure of the past has legitimated an antagonism or stereotyping of the gentile, and to the extent that this has become an important dimension of Jewish identification and Jewish self-definition, the death of this impulse through contact may lead to the forced option of a Judaism of voluntary choice and love. This would end the tragic distortion of the Jew's identity being partly the definition: I am against the other. Similarly, in a kind of dialectical mirror to the Catholic experience, Judaism may come to revalue and recover some of its own sacramental dimensions. The development of the Rabbinic tradition has shifted the center of equilibrium of Jewish religious life away from this concern so that the role of God's grace is often relatively neglected. A more subtle balance of grace and personal responsibility can emerge from exposure to the theme of grace in the other.

Perhaps the most striking Jewish repositioning may take place in the dialectic of particularism and universalism. Built into the covenant with Abraham's seed is a particularist pole that lies in exquisite balance with the vision of God's universal love in many prophetic and Rabbinic sources. In the course of the ghetto experience, the equilibrium point was inevitably pushed toward the pole of particularity and parochialism. One may hope that out of the dialogue will come a new Christian appreciation of the particular. I am profoundly convinced that such new appreciation is a desperate necessity if the modern mass culture is not to destroy the variety and legitimacy of humanness. However, I am equally certain that the classic dialectical balance in Judaism of concern for all humankind, of seeing Judaism as something responsible for the world, that seeks to speak to the world at large must be recovered in all its range. This may be one of the gifts of dialogue and modern life to Judaism.

A general religious principle can be derived from the examples of mutual illuminations that I have given, and it is relevant to the value of dialogue. It has been all too easy—even cheap—to set up Law-Gospel antinomies and suggest that Law is intrinsically likely to end up in legalism and petrifaction. (The equivalent Jewish stereotype is that Gospel ends up in vague assertion, abstraction, and behavioral hypocrisy.) The fundamental spiritual and psychological reality is that no religious way or option is automatically preserved from decay or loss of meaning. Whatever the religious style, people and communities tend to go stale after a while, particularly if that "while" encompasses centuries or whole spans of civilizations. What is needed for spiritual freshness is not so much one path or the other, but a capacity for alternation or at least for correction in light of the alternate emphasis. This is done by periodic renewal movements from within, but they can be triggered and/or influenced by openness to communities and traditions exploring different ways or in different stages of cycles. One is struck by the fact that the great vitality of Catholicism today is, in part, the result of the past century and a half of withdrawal and parochialism. Behind the walls thrown up by the siege mentality, great reservoirs of spiritual energy built up. Now that the energy is released, it is generating great forces at a time when the groups first integrated into the modern world seem somewhat spent, or at least, waiting for a new religious impulse.

Within the Orthodox Jewish community, those who seek renewal are often challenged for seeking to do things or explore options previously done primarily by Reform and Conservative Judaism. To which my own personal response has been that this is also a time when the two modernizing movements seek to recover the traditional ways—because each group instinctively seeks to explore the polarity that it has neglected relatively, because in this alternation lies freshness and power.

Dialogue may offer the benefits of alternation in the opportunity to seriously encounter other traditions that explore in their emphasis the dimensions that are more muted in my own tradition. This makes possible a subtler balance and blending of religious options all along (instead of polar swings), which could make each tradition more capable of meeting the needs of the wide variety of human temperaments and individual differences found within its communicants. This is certainly an exciting possibility for traditions that include many elements that are, in effect, polar explorations of common phenomena.

There is another crucial issue and possibility in the new encounter. It is the possibility of true pluralism, i.e., a love pluralism of passionate people, not the tolerance of apathy. Modernists often claim that secular culture has achieved this true pluralism. And one of the standard secularist dismissals of religion contrasts this acceptance with the long and bloody history of religious wars. I believe that this modern complacency is far from justified. The reason we no longer have religious wars is not so much that modern people are so pluralist, but that they no longer care so passionately about religion.* The religions that modern people believe in—Marxism, nationalism, capitalism, et al.—they still kill for, and on a scale that makes the picayune achievements of

---

*This was written in 1968. Since 9/11/2001, we have been taught that people who care passionately about religion are back and they are prepared to terrorize without limit and kill without mercy.

the Thirty Years' War or any of the great religious wars seem very old-fash-ioned indeed. Therefore, the contemporary world desperately needs models of living together out of love despite, and because of, passionately held commit-ments. The difficulty is that it has few if any such models. If religionists can be inspired by their commitments to such an achievement, this would truly re-store the capacity for witness of religion in the world today.

Up to now, however, all religious traditions (including the secular ones) have preserved themselves by setting up exclusive communities with inter-nal mediums, which defined themselves vis-à-vis the outside and built up strong in-group feelings. Christians, because they were usually a majority in the Western countries, often obscured from themselves that they were en-gaged in the process of setting up (new) Israel vs. gentile dichotomies as much as Jews were. The conscious and unconscious management of infor-mation flow and social contact made this technique effective and viable. The needs for the psychic rewards provided by in-group identity and reinforce-ment gave these groups strength and dynamism. But the openness, perme-ability, and dissemination of outside images that are characteristic of modern culture are collapsing this support for religion.

I would venture that the main cause of the decline of religion in the mod-ern world has not been the decline of faith. There are more Jews studying Torah full-time today than at any time in Jewish history, just as there are more Christians willing to give their life to work for Christ in the most selfless way than at any time in history. But there has been a tremendous desertion by the fellow-travelers, i.e., the bulk of people who were religious because it was the community pattern or that of the in-group, or because they found rewarding the psychic gains in believing that their faith was better than the other. As modern culture has suffused the community with images of the greatness of the other and with the persuasiveness and beauty of the alterna-tive ways, older systems have collapsed. Moral codes that were dependent on such in-group psychic rewards and reinforcements have proven particularly vulnerable. As long as the proverbial Victorian novel or seminary catechetics courses monopolistically claim that pleasures of the flesh led to degradation and unhappiness, as long as the fallen woman (or the girl who kisses boys on the first date) went directly down the road to dissolution and the gutter, such moral systems could persist, backed by community pressures. Pick up the newspapers and films today and one discovers immediately that the swingers are having a rather good time of it. (They are probably romanticized in the portrayal.) The result is the growing collapse of the old affirmations. One of the unfortunate results of the old setup was that the other moral options were not available or serious options. Therefore, there was no real competition to meet. All too often this meant that there was no incentive to make the established morality meaningful or enjoyable. This lack meant that traditional morality was more vulnerable than it had to be once the open situation came into being. It may be that this need to make morality enjoyable or meaningful is the challenge of this moment to moralists.

The great question for us is: Can we create a community that is committed enough to live in an open situation? My own community (the Orthodox Jewish community) is full of predictions that the Catholic Church is not long for this world, and that it will dissolve into secular culture. These predictions are ideological rationalizations, of course. They justify not trying the same renewal experiment, which is what the group is afraid to do. The reassurance to status quo is the claim that once a religious group yields its inner community sanctions and management of the information flow, it will not be able to maintain itself. This is, indeed, a real possibility that I am sure many Catholics have noted; some with anticipation, some with fear. Given the unprecedented nature of this effort, dialogue may play its most constructive role. Can we genuinely create a Judaism and a Christianity free of in-group distortions and rewards? We will never know until we try. Insofar as Judaism has been caricatured within the Christian community, the Christian need not experience Christianity in all its depth and beauty in order to remain a Christian. If he or she can dismiss Judaism as legalism or tribalism or petrifaction, there is no serious alternative to match. Insofar as a Jew could dismiss Christianity as ascetic or otherworldly, he or she need not confront the question of the validity and significance of living in his or her own tradition in its grandeur.

Whether, indeed, the religious communities are prepared to give up the easy sanctions of human distortions and develop a faith that is so open to God that it does not need the in-group payoffs is a big question mark. If religions cannot do this, then their future appears dim indeed. The culture will become more pervasive and the mass media can reach deeper and deeper into the groups with alternate images and models of living. Apparently films do affect people even more deeply than books and identify them with the other, *pace* Marshall McLuhan. The key to religious survival and to variety and plural cultural trends in an increasingly homogenized world depends on the creative solution of this challenge. The only way religions can raise people in this open manner and the only way they can develop a new vocabulary and imagery that does not distort the other is by speaking constantly and by raising people constantly in the presence of the other. It may take centuries to develop the new vocabularies and images, and they will only be created if the new encounter is open, frank, and loving.

To attempt this experiment will be to become involved in fundamental theological rethinking and changes within our own traditions. I do not believe that Christianity can seriously do this without a profound shift in its understanding of the relationships of the two covenants—Jewish and Christian. It will have to come to the recognition that God's promises are not lightly given and are not forfeited. Even as they were given by God's love rather than humankind's merit, so they are not lost by humans' lack of merit—if indeed they did lack merit. This would mean a new Christian self-understanding that would base its validity on its own moral and religious life—not on the death or insufficiency of others. Nor will Judaism be exempt from self-consideration. The great searching point there will undoubtedly be the gentile-Jewish dichotomy that characterizes the Jewish way and life, and which can too easily flip from legitimate particularity to egocentricity and insensitivity to the fullness and claims of the other. These reconsiderations will not be quid pro quos but the fruit of the discovery and love of the other. And the range of rethinking and new language development is more staggering than may be apparent. There are thousands of areas where the simple use of words is so loaded and distorting. The word *Pharisee* is a negatively loaded word in Christian terminology; it is one of the great words of Jewish tradition. The Law-Gospel dichotomy, the God of Love and God of Wrath, and the universalism-particularism negative contrast are only surface examples of how widespread the problem is. And as the distortions are removed, the danger of being swept up into the other becomes great. Yet, if successful, the enterprise offers the possibility of pure service of God.

This open faith is dependent on a trust in God so complete that I do not demand an advance pledge that I am right and the other is wrong. The new situation requires a willingness to live under the judgment of God without the easy assurances of guaranteed righteousness and salvation. In a world where people are learning first hand the universal problems of humanity and consequently feel an urgent need to heal them, perhaps the new encounter can give us the possibility of Jew and Christian—and all people—working side by side in this encounter until the end of days.

Let me add: There are indeed people who are willing to live side by side until the end of days who do so because they are fully confident that the Messiah, when he comes, will confirm their rightness all along. Of course, it is a step forward to live together until that time. But even here, we may underrate the love and wonder of the Lord. I have often thought of this as a kind of nice truism. Let us wait until the Messiah comes. Then we can ask him if this is his first coming or his second. Each of us could look forward to a final confirmation. Perhaps I was a bit too narrow in my trust in God with this initial conception. After entering the dialogue, I wrote a short story in which the Messiah comes at the end of days. Jews and Christians march out to greet him and establish his reign. Finally they ask if this is his first or second coming—to which the

Messiah smiles and replies: "No comment.". . . Perhaps we will then truly realize that it was worth it all along for the kind of life we lived along the way.

Notes

1. A popular program in the early days of interfaith activity was called Brotherhood Week. Frequently the Week involved lay people interactions, often marked by a get-to-know-your-neighbor, or let-us-say-nice-things-about-each-other's-religion emphasis. Sometimes, literally, it was the brotherhood, e.g., Men's Club of the synagogues and churches that got together. Typically, there were very limited liturgical encounters or theologial conversations in those programs [IG—2004].

New Revelations and
New Patterns

 ## THE RELATIONSHIP OF JUDAISM AND
CHRISTIANITY: THE IMPACT OF HISTORY

Judaism experiences revelation in the events of its history, as well as in its commandments. Much of the Five Books of Moses consists of instructions about how to live in the light of the Exodus. This pattern continued in later history as commandments and holidays were added by the Rabbis in response to later historical "revelatory" events such as Purim and Hanukkah. In turn, Christianity grows in the bosom of Judaism, seeing itself as the historical unfolding of the biblical covenant. In the words of *Nostra Aetate:*

> As this Sacred Synod searches into the mystery of the Church, it recalls the spiritual bond linking the people of the New Covenant with Abraham's stock.
> For the Church of Christ acknowledges that, according to the mystery of God's saving design, the beginnings of her faith and her election are already found among the patriarchs, Moses and the prophets (*Nostra Aetate*, Section 4, Par. 1–2).[1]

A statement in Romans (9:4–5) spells out even further that the foundation stone on which Christianity is built is the covenantal election of the original Israel: "Theirs [the Jews'] is the sonship and the glory and the covenants and the law and the worship and the promises, theirs are the patriarchs and from them is the Christ according to the flesh" (ibid.). This passage reminds us that initially Jesus could only be recognized as revelation by Jews operating out of Jewish categories of expectation and promise. His first followers shared the Jewish model of a covenant entered into through God's mighty acts in history. They accepted the principle that revelation is not finished and can be affected by later events in that salvation history. Because history is open, because humans have freedom even to disobey God, and because God is neither fixed image nor possession, new events in history may illuminate the covenant or unfold new dimensions of covenant living. Christianity is the wager of faith of the original Jewish Christians that Christ's life was authentic revelation, validated by existing Jewish norms.

Then Jesus' death made clear that he could not or would not fulfill the original expectations. This had to be seen as proof that he was a false messiah or as new revelation of the character of messianic salvation. Because the phenomenology of Jesus' revelatory power was so real to them, the faithful disciples did not yield even to the shock of the Crucifixion. The disciples were in a Jewish thinking mode in their perception that this tragedy did not end their revelation but rather shed new light on the nature of messianic salvation.[2] Thus their acceptance of the Resurrection as a further event confirming the new covenant was deeply Jewish in its logic, even though it shifted their religious focus from the Temple and ongoing Jewish worship and channels of atonement[3] to Jesus, and even though its long-term effect was to separate them from the bulk of Jewry, which rejected their experience and thinking.

The Christian Interpretation

The rootedness of the first followers of Jesus in Jewish salvation history and the shared norms of validation made his nonacceptance by other Jews especially problematic and troubling. The fact of common expectation made the ongoing, mainstream Jewish hope for other salvation threatening to the validity of Christianity. It had to be accounted for in the context of the shared fundamental that the Jewish people possessed authentic and original covenant, as well as messianic hope. Given the disciples' conviction that they had experienced true revelation, they were unwilling to deny the phenomenology of salvation they had experienced. The group of Jews following Jesus, therefore, moved to interpret the Jewish rejection as blindness, obduracy, and hardness of heart. These were all the more damning qualities for appearing in a group already blessed with illumination. In the words quoted in *Nostra Aetate*, "Jerusalem did not recognize the time of her visitation."[4]

The destruction of the Temple and the failed Bar Kokhba rebellion of 132–135 confirmed this view. Although the mainstream of Jews did not accept their conclusion, the Hebrew Christians were "thinking Jewish" when they interpreted these events of destruction as being normative events with a religious message. These events confirmed the analysis—or even originated the analysis—that the old channel of salvation was stopped up and that a new channel was the valid one. It followed that a new people of God had been born. From there to the punishment and rejection theory of Jewish exile is not a big jump. Ironically enough, every step of this development followed Jewish models and categories, even if the net result was a repudiation of Judaism. The consequent insistence on the finality of Christ and the revelation in his life meant that Jews were condemned unless they saw the light. To someone like Paul who cared passionately about Jews, this reversal of destiny gave great anguish—enough for him to insist that they would ultimately see the light and be saved. The condemnation caused much less pain to gentile Christians, and they could view it with equanimity or relish—or with a righteous sense of true faith triumphant.[5]

The Jewish Interpretation

By the same token, the Jewish community, faithful to Israel's covenant, could hardly be indifferent to messianic claims or possible divine revelation. The community showed its openness to messianic hope repeatedly before and after Jesus.[6] Jeremiah's words suggesting further illumination in history were always before its eyes. "Behold, the days will come, says the LORD, it shall no more be said: 'As God lives, who brought up the children of Israel from the land of Egypt' but: 'As God lives, who brought up the children of Israel from the land of the North, and from all the countries whither He had driven them . . .'" (Jer. 16:14–15; 23:7–8). Unhappily, each and every messiah to whom the Jews opened up ultimately disappointed and could not bring final redemption. Rather than losing hope or yielding to despair, the bulk of Jews—or at least the saving remnant of Jews—continued to rely on God and the divine promises, and to hope again.

Faithful to its covenant and trusting God's promises, Israel had to search its own heart and life when confronted with messianic claims for Jesus as well as the later development—the announcement that Judaism, the original covenant, was over. In the experience of the destruction of the Temple and the crisis of faith which followed, Jews came to the same conclusion that Christians did in response to the Crucifixion: Their faith was not destroyed or shown to be false. They were being called to new forms of service and understanding while continuing on the way to the final salvation of the world.[7] Finding its religious life vital, the presence of God real, and its trust in God's promises unbroken, the Jewish people could only conclude, sadly, that again a group of faithful Jews had responded in hope, only to discover (again) that the time had not yet come for fulfillment. As in the other cases, some Jews were too loyal to the new messianic revelation to surrender it. Most Jews were faithful both to God as the source who could and would yet generate redemption, and to reality, which yet proclaimed its resistance to that process.[8] They felt no need to cling to the new experience, since they were confident that God could and would bring true redemption in its time or when they were worthy.

True, this false messiah was spectacularly successful in the world. Among some Jews, this fact alone evoked some special recognition or status for Christianity as a religion that had spread hope and knowledge of God and covenant throughout the world and thus brought final redemption closer.[9] Still, Christianity was intrinsically contradictory to Judaism's validity, precisely because of the shared assumptions. Therefore, faithfulness to covenant made contradicting Christianity religiously necessary and affirmative. The record of brutality and Jewish suffering brought on or contributed to by Christianity made it that much clearer that here was a false messianism, one that might be dismissed by some as having lapsed into idolatry.[10]

The Modern Interpretation

For almost 1,900 years, there was hardly any other interpretive option available to believing Jews or Christians. This typology (either supercession or falsity) is intrinsic in the central affirmations of both religions, due particularly to shared roots and assumptions. The movement away from these models started initially among Jews or Christians who had lost faith in the authority of shared roots or the credibility of religious claims. They could use humanist and tolerance categories to change relationships. The liberal embarrassment at past hatred and prejudice combined with the regret and shock of the climax of the Holocaust to set the stage for *Nostra Aetate*.[11]

The direction and content of *Nostra Aetate* were a vector of opposing forces. There was openness to fresh understanding of revelation in the Catholic Church, and there were those who believed this opened the door to a positive new understanding of Judaism. On the other hand, the church was still profoundly rooted in its classic heritage; its trust in the adequacy and fullness of its own religious life was still relatively unshaken, and it had strong institutional interests that resisted change. The perception of faithfulness to the magisterium combined with fear of undermining the faith of the masses to keep the declaration on the Jews fairly conservative. The understandable result was *Nostra Aetate*, Section Four, an admixture of elements out of the rethinking, tolerance, and traditional models. It sought to create new esteem and to open new options in Jewish-Christian relations, as in the deploring of anti-Semitism and the ambiguous but pregnant citation that "He [God] does not repent of the gifts He makes nor of the calls He issues" (Rom. 11:28–29). [12] Still, as a document faithful to the finality of Christian revelation, *Nostra Aetate* was driven to come down on the side of the old traditional model of the relationship. This accounted for such affirmations as "Jerusalem did not recognize the time of her visitation;" that Christ made "Jew and Gentile . . . one in Himself"; that the authorities of the Jews and those who followed them had pressed for the death of Christ; and that most ambiguous sentence of all, "Although the Church is the new people of God, the Jews should not be presented as repudiated or cursed by God, as if such views followed from the Holy Scriptures."[13]

It was widely recognized in 1965 that all these ambiguities and ambivalences would have to be worked out in further development and that the final significance of *Nostra Aetate* would depend on the fruit it bore, e.g., on the direction the Catholic Church would take in explicating and developing its conflicted and conflicting views.

Since *Nostra Aetate,* the atmosphere of warm expectation and romance surrounding dialogue has cooled, as the radical hopes of the 1960s have been followed by the realism, disillusion, and sobriety of the 1970s. The Jewish perception of inadequate response by Christians to the crisis of the State of Israel's existence in 1967 and (somewhat less so) in 1973 has had a chilling effect. Jewish preoccupation with internal needs and Israeli survival and Catholic wrestling with internal trends unleashed by Vatican II have been limiting factors. Still, dialogue has continued, and new areas have opened up; individual Christians have gone far in their new understanding of Judaism and its role in the divine economy of salvation. A comparison of the working document on Jewish-Christian relations ("Reflections and Suggestions from the Application of the Directives of *Nostra Aetate* 4," circulated on December 16, 1969) with the actual "Guidelines and Suggestions for Implementing the Conciliar Declaration, '*Nostra Aetate*' (n. 4)," issued on December 1, 1974,[14] shows there have been further improvements. However, internal resistance blocked potential theological great leaps forward at the institutional level.

The working document included important breakthroughs: recognition of the present and living reality of the Jews, who were given a Torah by God, within it a word that "endures forever," "an unquenchable source of life and prayer, in a tradition that has not ceased to enrich itself through the centuries." Similarly, it recognized that "fidelity to the covenant was linked to the land" and thus connected directly to the existence of the State of Israel.

It affirmed that "the Old Testament should not be understood exclusively in reference to the New nor reduced to an allegorical significance."[15] By contrast, the promulgated guidelines omitted both the land and Israel and the Jewish Torah that endures forever.[16] The document hedges its acknowledgment that the history of Judaism did not end with the destruction of the Temple with the insertion that the importance and meaning of Jewish tradition was "deeply affected by the coming of Christ."[17] Gone also is the simplicity of statement that "Jesus . . . was a Jew," agreeing more than disagreeing with the Judaism of his time, and a critic from within.[18] Instead, there is "Jesus . . . born of the Jewish people," bearing a new gospel message, perfecting the old, which is "manifest in the New."[19]

Such theological hedging is not merely the result of political give-and-take in the church structures. It is intrinsic to the historically elaborated structure of the relationship of Judaism and Christianity. As long as the finality of Christian (and Jewish) experience of revelation is affirmed and dated to the opening round of their encounter and Christian formation, the coherence of Christian revelation, seen integrally, is in tension with the affirmations of Judaism's continuing integrity. Indeed, any positive affirmations vis-à-vis Judaism remain subject to repeal by any resurgent Christian assertion of doctrinal adequacy or any proclamation that, in its transcendence, Christianity should not be dominated or reshaped by modern categories.

NEW REVELATION AND NEW PATTERNS

However, there has been a major development in the past decade: the crystallization of the awareness among many Jews and some others that this is a period of renewed revelation within Judaism. Aaron's staff has blossomed again, or, if you will, the olive tree has brought forth extraordinary and unexpected branches.[20]

In this generation, two events have occurred of a magnitude that stamps them as major normative events in Jewish history. They are orientating events—pointing beyond themselves as models for living in the light of God's concern and working for the day when all humanity will live in a perfected world. They are the event of Holocaust—unparalleled tragedy and destruction, towering over the other great tragic watershed of 1,900 years ago, the destruction of the Second Temple—and the event of the rebirth of Israel—the experience of redemption as has not been experienced by Jews on this scale since the Exodus. Following the classic paradigm of salvation history, these events illumine and fundamentally reinterpret the meaning and significance of the past 1,900 years and the constellation of Judaism and Christianity.[21]

For Jews, reinterpretation of past canon in the light of further history is a well-traveled road. But this approach should be applied to Christianity as well, for this process can liberate it from the legacy of hatred and contempt for Judaism. This is a legitimate move, for in the words of Vatican II Council's Dogmatic Constitution:

> In His goodness and wisdom, God chose to reveal Himself and to make known to us the hidden purpose of His will . . . This plan of revelation is realized by deeds and words having an inner unity. The deeds wrought by God in the history of salvation manifest and confirm the teaching and realities signified by the words, while the words proclaim the deeds and clarify the mystery contained in them (Dogmatic Constitution of Divine Revelation, Chapter 1, Section 2).[22]

What then is the message projected by these new revelations? The Holocaust is a most radical contradiction of the fundamental statements of human value and divine concern in both religions.[23] The successful carrying out of the Holocaust and the response of Jews and Christians during this event are profoundly revelatory. For Christianity, the Holocaust reveals the demonic consequences and hateful potential present in its traditional picture of Judaism and the Jews, i.e., "the teaching of contempt" tradition. Notwithstanding the argument that Nazi anti-Semitism is pagan, to the extent that the "teaching of contempt" furnished an occasion or presented stereotypes that brought the Nazis to focus on the Jews as scapegoats in the first place, or created a residue of anti-Semitism in Europe that affected local populations' attitudes toward the Jews, or enabled some Christians to feel they were doing God's work in helping or in not stopping the killing of Jews—then Christianity is deeply implicated in the Holocaust.[24] This precedes the issue of church silence or actual complicity.[25]

Since the teaching of contempt goes straight back to the Gospel accounts, the Holocaust's fierce flames really reveal the privileged sanctuary of hate allowed to exist at the very heart of and in fundamental contradiction to the gospel of love that is the New Testament's true role and goal. The cancer is so deep that it is questionable whether anything less than full confession and direct confrontation with even the most sacred sources can overcome it. This is not said triumphalistically, but in reverence of Christianity. Repentance is a sign of life and greatness of soul. Those who deny are tempted thereby into repetition.[26]

There is further revelation that is perhaps even more problematic. Much of the church's efforts and protests were for Jewish converts to Christianity and against forced divorces and other violations of Christian canons in the execution of the Holocaust—rather than against the principle. The picture of a totally silent Vatican is too simplistic. Nevertheless, it turns out that so many of the protests were in defense of non-Aryan Christians. Despite knowledge of the dreadful atrocities going on, the lines and structures of human responsibility were narrowly drawn, apparently because of excessive emphasis on the significance of Christian belief as *the* category of solidarity and due to the placing of the Jews outside the pale. Thus, the German bishops and confessional or conscience Protestants who spoke a clear word against the Nazi euthanasia policy did not speak such a word against the mass slaughter of Jews.[27] The late protests on behalf of Jewish *converts* in Poland and Hungary in 1943 and 1944 must be seen in the context of the terrible scenes of burning children alive and mass gassings known in exact detail by reports substantiated and forwarded to the Vatican by the Papal Nuncio.[28]

To put it cruelly and unfairly (because only in this way is the issue illuminated), one can translate the language of protest this way. If children believe in Jesus Christ as Savior and Word Incarnate, they should not be burned alive. If they do not believe in Jesus Christ as Savior and Word Incarnate, it is not *so* bad that Christians ought to risk speaking out. Nothing could be further from the message of Jesus Christ; nothing could make atheism more religiously and morally attractive an alternative. In short, the Holocaust reveals that the redemption and revelation of Christianity is inescapably contradicted by the constellation of its classic understanding of Judaism. It must choose between them. The conviction of the ongoing validity of Christianity demands that an alternative understanding exist. This conviction grows in part out of the testimony of true Christians who risked their lives and gave their all to save victims, and who resisted Nazism and went to their own Calvary out of concern for the crucified Jew. Unfortunately, they were a small minority.

In the same spirit, they do wrong who justify the silence of the church or the Pope by prudential arguments, claiming that declarations would not have helped, or that, by Nazi fiat, Jews were outside the "flock" that a bishop might serve. If to be a Christian is to be willing to take up the cross to testify, there was hardly ever a more appropriate time to risk crucifixion than when children were being burned alive to economize on the one-half cent's worth of gas it cost to kill them. Besides, such arguments are an injustice to the actual record of the church. In Bulgaria, in France, and (at a late date) in Rumania, church intervention preceded those governments' ceasing collaboration and refusing to honor commitments already made to deport Jews. In two of the three countries that never agreed to deport their Jews (Finland, Denmark, and Italy), the dominant church denounced racialism or anti-Semitism publicly even before the war. In Hungary, in July 1944, protests by the Vatican, among others, halted the deportations, but only after two-thirds of the Jews had been shipped out.[29] As Dr. Helen Fein says in her major study of Jewish survival in the Holocaust, "Church protest proved to be the single element present in every instance in which state collaboration [with Nazi genocide] was arrested. . . ." On the other hand, successful segregation of the Jews is the most direct cause of Jewish victimization; segregation was most likely to occur in states in which the dominant church had failed to repudiate racial ideology.[30] The challenge is the extent to which theological categories and church interests dominate and suppress moral response because of the attitudes toward Jews that grew out of the conviction of the unique, universal validity of Christianity.

Another issue illumined in the Holocaust is the classic "Israel of the Flesh" *vs.* "Israel of the Spirit" dichotomy. After all, is not "Israel of the Spirit" a more universal, more committed category? Yet, when absolute power arose and claimed to be God, then Israel's existence was antithetical to its own. "Israel of the Flesh" gives testimony by its mere existence and therefore was "objectively" an enemy of the totalitarian state. By the same token, neither commitment to secularism, atheism, or any other religion— nor even joining Christianity—could remove the intrinsic status of being Jewish and being forced to stand and testify. This testimony, voluntarily given or not, turns out to be the secret significance of "Israel of the Flesh." A Jew's life is on the line, and therefore every kind of Jew gives testimony at all times.

"Israel of the Spirit" testifies against the same idolatry and evil. Indeed, there were sincere Christians who stood up for their principles, who were recognized as threats and were sent to concentration camps. However, "Israel of the Spirit" had the choice of being silent; with this measure of collaboration, it could live safely and at ease. Not surprisingly, the vast majority chose to be safe. As Franklin Littell put it, when paganism is persecuting, Christians "can homogenize and become mere gentiles again; while the Jews, believing or secularized, remain representatives of another history, another providence."[31] And lest there be any question or hesitation about saying "Jesus was a Jew," let the Holocaust test speak. Were Jesus and his mother alive in Europe in the 1940s, they would have been sent to Auschwitz.

The Holocaust suggests that Christians (and Jews) have glamorized modern culture and underestimated evil. It suggests that, from now on, one of the keys to testimony in the face of the enormously powerful forces available to evil will be to have given hostages, to be on the line because one is inextricably implicated in this fate. The creation of a forced option should be one of the goals of moral pedagogy after the Holocaust. This is the meaning of "chosenness" in Jewish faith.

The Christian analogy to this experience would be a surrender of the often self-deceiving universalist rhetoric of the church and a new conception of the church as the people of God—a distinct community of faith with some visible identification—that must testify to the world. There is a corollary to such a model; some strategy of designation and delineation is needed that will identify this people. This is somewhat in tension with tendencies to formulate either a "religionless" Christianity or, at best, one less separated from the world. I believe there is merit in *both* poles of the tension. There may be a possible reconciliation of both needs through the choice of subtle forms of identification. Such a move will expose the church to persecution or worse from future rivals or tyrants, but this same step paves the way to an honest particularism that can recognize the existence of other peoples of God without surrendering its own absolute commitment or the command of its Lord. Thus, Christianity could live and testify in a truly pluralist world while preserving the ultimacy of its message.

The Holocaust profoundly reorients Jewish understanding as well. It reveals that Jews have not appreciated Christianity enough. This is a reflection of the general Jewish tendency to underestimate Christianity's redemptive contribution to the world, due to the bad experience Jews have had with it. Anger at Christian mistreatment has obscured the dialectical behaviors stimulated by the importance of Judaism in Christianity's worldview. Feeling both jealousy and awe, Christians persecuted, but also kept alive and protected, Jews.[32] Even persecuting Christians gave Jews the option of converting, rather than styling the Jew as intrinsically demonic and beyond the right to exist. Rebuking the widespread, almost stereotyped Jewish identification with secular, liberal modernity and against Christianity,[33] the Holocaust suggests that modern values created a milieu as dangerous as—more dangerous than—Christianity at its worst. Indeed, Jews have a vested interest in Christianity's existence. Russia, the society of secularism triumphant, has demonstrated again that secular absolutism is just as dangerous to Judaism as is an abusive Christianity, unchecked.[34]

The Holocaust warns of the danger of solidarity weaknesses in Jews and Judaism. These were exploited by the Nazis to divide and conquer Jews. It calls for a major strengthening of the human and ethical solidarity resources of Jewish tradition to stop another Holocaust from happening—and to ensure that if others be the victims, Jews will not be indifferent or apathetic by dint of prejudice. To achieve this state of moral responsibility will require Jewish self-criticism and self-development and removal of every negative image of gentiles or Christians or, for that matter, of women or other minorities.

For both religions, the Holocaust breaks the old secular-religious dichotomy. Who is the atheist? When the Einsatzgruppen in Simferopol,

Crimea, could get up extra early on Christmas morning in 1942, to finish shooting the Jews before the others awakened—so as not to disturb the spirit of the holiday, some making it back in time for mass;[35] when Heinrich Himmler could demand belief in God of his SS men so they would not be like the atheistic Marxists;[36] when Jean-Paul Sartre, fountainhead of atheism, could break with his Arab allies in 1967, refusing to allow another Holocaust, though the Pope remained silent; when the Satmar Rabbi's followers negotiated with terrorists: Then the invisible church or synagogue has become a moral necessity. In these circumstances, secularity should be seen as the mask for those who give up the advantage of acknowledged faith (e.g., the church will try to save you in the Holocaust), because at such a time such advantages are blasphemous. Fear of God is defined biblically as inability to hurt—or unswerving reverence and care for—the image of God.[37]

Never again should official badge or professed religious belief allow murderers to escape condemnation and excommunication or allow victims to be excluded from the circle of humanity. Surrendering religious exclusivism or triumphalism is a crucial moral step.

Here the dialectic of the Holocaust makes its appearance again. It reveals that in pure secularity humans appoint themselves God and thereby become the devil. It warns that glorification of human autonomy can evoke the nemesis of human idolatry; that in the amassing of science, technology, and efficiency lies the potential for mass killing, so that simple affirmation of human autonomy and human might is no longer morally tenable. This liberates Jews and Christians to be in tension with, as well as to celebrate, the secular city.

For both religions, the Holocaust reveals a fundamental shift in the ethics of power. The overwhelming force on the side of the murderers corrupted the murderers and frequently broke or added to the torment of the victims. The total absence of any check led to such phenomena as boredom, desire for variety in killing, playing with and tormenting the victims, and suppression of goodwill, since all the pressures and sanctions were toward being crueler to the victims. Moreover, the Nazi ability to exercise infinitely gradated power over the victims broke many people, leading them to sacrifice their most beloved family and precious values. As a result, self-sacrifice and spiritual demonstration were obscured or suppressed. Witness this scene from the summer of 1944 at Auschwitz, portrayed by Tadeusz Borowski, a Polish inmate.

> They go, they vanish. Men, women and children. Some of them know. Here is a woman—she walks quickly, but tries to appear calm. A small child with a pink cherub's face runs after her and, unable to keep up, stretches out his little arms and cries: "Mama! Mama!"
>
> "Pick up your child, woman!"

"It's not mine, sir, not mine!" she shouts hysterically and runs on, covering her face with her hands. She wants to hide, she wants to reach those who will not ride the trucks, those who will go on foot, those who will stay alive. She is young, healthy, good-looking, she wants to live. But the child runs after her, wailing loudly: "Mama, Mama, don't leave me!"

"It's not mine, not mine, no!"

Andrei, a sailor from Sevastopol, grabs hold of her. His eyes are glassy from vodka and the heat. With one powerful blow he knocks her off her feet, then, as she falls, takes her by the hair and pulls her up again. His face twitches with rage.

"Ah, you bloody Jewess! So you're running from your own child; I'll show you, you whore!" His huge hand chokes her, he lifts her in the air and heaves her on to the truck like a heavy sack of grain.

"Here! And take this with you, bitch!" and he throws the child at her feet.

"*Gut gemacht*, good work. That's the way to deal with degenerate mothers," says the S.S. man standing at the foot of the truck.

"*Gut, gut, Russki.*"[38]

Out of this comes the realization that there has been a horrible misunderstanding of the symbol of the Crucifixion. Surely, it is clear now that the point of the Gospel account is the cry: "My God, my God, why have you forsaken me?" Never again should anyone be exposed to such one-sided power on the side of evil, for in such extremes not only does evil triumph, but the suffering servant now breaks and betrays herself. Here is fundamental reorientation away from traditional Christian and medieval Jewish glorification of suffering passivity.

In the explanation of Rabbi Menachem Ziemba, who died in the Warsaw ghetto: Sanctification of the Divine Name manifests itself in varied ways, at the end of the eleventh century or in the middle of the twentieth century. In the past, during religious persecutions, Jews were required by the law to give up their lives even for the least essential practice. In the present, *halakhah* (Jewish law) demands that Jews fight and resist to the very end with unequalled determination and valor for the sake of the sanctification of the Divine Name.[39]

Out of the Holocaust experience comes the demand for redistribution of power. This accounts for the urgency with which Jews proclaimed the State of Israel after the Holocaust, and for the overwhelming worldwide shift of Jewry toward Zionism. Only the transfer of power to potential victims—power enough to defend themselves—can correct the new balance of power. This is the subterranean source of the enormous proliferation of liberation movements worldwide. This poses a challenge to Judaism and Christianity—to overcome those moral traditions that praise renunciation and suspicion of power and glorify defeat.

Here again the Holocaust gives us dialectical revelations: One should not romanticize the moral stature of the victims. The ability to use force is the ability to hurt; the tendency to give unlimited moral validity to erstwhile victims is false to the dialectic and encourages the worst tendencies in such movements. One must support a moral balance of power and dialectical checks on force as well as an unceasing reconciliation and resolution of conflicts. Thus the right and the need for Israel to exist, to protect past and potential victims of genocide, is corrected by concern for refugees. This concern intensifies morally as the threat to Israel's existence recedes, but we should never let concern for refugees become cover for genocide.

To work in real power situations requires one to eschew merely prophetic stances. Prophets can rely on spiritual power and make absolute demands for righteousness. Governments have obligations to protect people. This will involve calling upon the halakhic resources of the Jewish tradition to judge specific situations and to reconcile conflicting claims and shifting facts. It means linking ultimate ends and proximate means in a continuing process. It cannot be done without some involvement, guilt, partial failures, etc. How can this be done without religion's blessing bloody arms or supporting an exploiting status quo? Dialectically it should be added that usually participation in the world leads to selling out to the status quo, unless one is refreshed by exposure to prophetic norms. Each religion will need the other's norms, strengths, and criticisms to save it from failing this challenge and to correct it along the way.

If the calling is to overcome crucifixion and prevent it from happening, then religious concern must focus on resurrection. The religious policy implication of this theme is to explore the sacred dimensions of affluence and celebration. The focus on redemption/resurrection draws attention to the other revelatory event, the redemption that has taken place in this generation—the rebirth of the State of Israel. As difficult to absorb in its own way and, like the Holocaust, a scandal to many traditional Jewish and Christian categories, it is an inescapable part of Jewish historical experience in our time. And while it is a continuation and outgrowth of certain responses to the Holocaust, it is at the same time a dialectical contradiction to many of its implications. As I have written elsewhere:

> If the experience of Auschwitz argues that we are cut off from God and hope and the covenant may be destroyed, then the experience of Jerusalem affirms that God's promises are faithful and His people live on. Burning children speak of the absence of all value, human and divine; the rehabilitation of one-half million Holocaust survivors in Israel speaks of the reclamation of tremendous human dignity and value. If Treblinka makes human hope an illusion, then the Western Wall asserts that dreams are more real than forces and facts. Israel's

faith in the god of History demands that an unprecedented event of destruction
be matched by an unprecedented act of redemption, and this has happened.[40]

This statement must not obscure the moral danger and profound ambiguity of a secular state carrying a religious message. One must be alert to the recalcitrance of the real to receive the ideal, the mixing of good and evil components in the real world, the danger of idolatry, the exhaustion of living in the tension of ideals and realities, and the "Gott mit uns" tendency that could easily sell out God for idols. Not the least part of our hesitation is the actual cost in suffering, Arab and Jewish, that Israel's birth has entailed. Hence Israel's revelation is a very modern one—flawed, partial, and real.[41] The moral danger is inescapable; the task is to become involved, to sustain the tension, to move beyond the easy stereotypes of law and gospel, to correct faults, and to minimize evil. It will take all the "Christian" testimony of the evil in human nature and all the "Jewish" testimony that the Messiah is not yet come to keep this secular revelation from degenerating into idolatry. It will take the fullest spiritual maturity of Jew and Christian to appreciate Israel in the real world it inhabits, and to protect it from the real dangers that its isolation poses to its very existence.

The Talmud tells that, after the destruction, God's might is shown in divine restraint from violating human freedom by intervening and preventing the evil, but divine awesomeness is shown in that the people of God still exist.[42] This revelation summons humankind to secularity, to create and rehabilitate the divine image in a human community. This is the ultimate testimony—perhaps the only credible one—that can speak of God in a world of burning children. And it summons humans to co-responsibility with God, that this fragile redemption be preserved and nourished.

It is a highly significant indication of the continuing operation of God's spirit in the church that it instinctively moved in its renewal in a number of these directions even before it saw the significance of these revelatory events. Articulating and recognizing these signs will sharpen and deepen renewal and release powerful forces of the selfless love of God, open to all. *Nostra Aetate* was written with awareness of the Holocaust and of Israel, but as yet the revelatory significance was not grasped, even by the Jews. Hence, the document temporizes on the brink. The stakes now are considerably higher.

If Christianity finds the strength to admit the reappearance of revelation in our time, at one stroke this undercuts the entire structure of the "teaching of contempt" tradition. For the bringing forth of revelation truly affirms that God does not repent of giving gifts. Such a Christian recognition restores God's gift of Christ to gentiles as an act of love and of broadening the covenant rather than an act of cruelty that spiritually and physically destroys the original chosen people. It removes the shelter of legitimated hatred and allows Christianity to confront the evil in human hearts with the unqualified challenge of the command of love.

Nor does the recognition undercut the validity of the Gospel message. The further revelation clarifies Paul's affirmation that Jewish rejection of Christ paves the way for gentile acceptance into the covenant. By a further act of grace, the past claim of supercession is found to be a Christian way of stating that the ultimate and valid experience of redemption is operating—but now this way of stating that claim is no longer needed. It is a way that must be rejected, given its evil effects. The later revelation illuminates the earlier, giving the new interpretive key, i.e., God's unbroken promises. It is another case of what the Dogmatic Constitution, cited above, calls "clearer understanding . . . enjoyed after they had been instructed by the [further] events."[43] (In that case, Christians subsequently navigate by the star of Christ's risen life; in our case, they allow themselves to be oriented by further revelation in history.) Henceforth, for Christians, confirmation of the unfailing nature of the first covenant confirms the credibility and power of the second covenant.

The reappearance of revelation is an enormous gift in an age when secularism and scientism have all but undercut the sources and credibility of covenant faith, when Holocaust and history have all but overcome hope. The most powerful confirmation of religious hope is that crucifixion and resurrection have occurred in this generation—in the flesh of the covenanted people.[44] This development spells liberation from the tyranny of modern categories—a restoration of the old religious role of fighting idolatry. At the same time, the admission of the significance of secularity in this revelation gives great impetus to the Christian search for renewal in this world and for the appropriate understanding of divinity made incarnate in human context. It releases Christianity from timeless spirituality to find its word incarnate in the temporal lives of humans. If Judaism finds the strength and feeling to admit revelation in this time, then it too has the prospect of renewed hope and divine presence—much needed in an age in which secularity has shriveled many of the roots of faith.

Paradoxically enough, the security of its own confirmation, the restoration of the land, and the covenantal sign release Judaism to ponder anew the significance of Christianity. It may well be that in its medieval state of powerlessness, Israel, gnawed at by the contrast of hope and reality, could only push Christianity away—or, diplomatically, argue that the righteous of the gentiles have a share in the world to come or that they have the Noahide covenant to live by. Given the axiom that Christian validity means Jewish invalidity, the people Israel could only trust the phenomenology of its vital religious life and the reliability of God's promises and reject Christianity's claims. Confirmed now in its resumed redemption, shaken by the Holocaust's challenge not to put down others, Judaism can no longer give comfortable answers. It must explore the possibility that the covenant grafted onto its narrative is a way whereby God has called gentiles to God. Of course, this invokes the principle "by their fruits, you shall know them." When Jesus' messianism led to hatred, exclusion, and pogrom, Jews could only judge that it was a false hope. If it now leads to responsibility, *mitgefuhl,* sharing of risk, and love, then its phenomenology becomes radically different. Suffice it to say—without irony—Christians have an extraordinary opportunity in this age: of showing the power of love and concern for Jews and the embattled beginnings of Jewish redemption, the State of Israel. Such a demonstration would give new seriousness among Jews to Christianity's own perception that it is a vehicle of divine presence and redemption in the world.

One of the gifts of such new possibilities is an end to easy Jewish identification of liberation with secularity and liberalism, and a much greater Jewish sense of pluralism, of Christianity as a moral/religious balance wheel, and of the need to preserve these values in a fast homogenizing world. Such rethinking would lead to a new sense of the preciousness of "parochial" education and of the need to husband resources of particular traditions, an area American Jewry has been slow and remiss in understanding—a mark of the continuing tyranny of easy modernity.

There is, of course, enormous Christian resistance to recognizing further revelation. After all, even Judaism and "observant" Jews have not yet given this revelation the centrality and response it deserves. Christian resistance is rooted in that fidelity to Jesus that emphasizes the finality of Christ as revelation. In the words of the Dogmatic Constitution on Divine Revelation: "We now await no further new public revelation before the glorious manifestation of our Lord Jesus Christ."[45] The key word is "await." Sometimes revelation comes when it is not awaited. To rule out new revelation absolutely because the church possesses revelation already would be to stand guilty of just the failure with which it (unjustly) charged Judaism and the Jews almost 2,000 years ago. To rule out another revelation out of pride and importance in one's own revelation would be an egregious error. It would really be an attempt to preserve the church's triumphalism—since, clearly, the further revelation does not necessarily undercut the church's basic experience.

Rather, the church should appeal to the words of the Schema on Ecumenism:

> Every renewal of the Church essentially consists in an increase of fidelity to her own calling . . . Christ summons the church as she goes her pilgrim way to that continual reformation of which she always has need insofar as she is an institution of men here on earth. Therefore, if the influence of events or of the times

139

has led to deficiencies in conduct, in church discipline, or even in formulation of doctrine . . . [these] should be appropriately rectified at the proper moment . . . There can be no ecumenism worthy of the name without a change of heart.[46]

Thus the paradox: Fear of new patterns bespeaks fear of the Christian capacity to sustain growth and catharsis. Confession of Christian guilt and affirmation of revelation is the statement of Christian hope unbroken.

It may seem incredible to speak of hope in a generation of holocaust and in a world where humans starve; where the survivors of the Holocaust, isolated, are constantly threatened with a repetition; where oil-purchased votes yield constant condemnations and assaults on the legitimacy of this fragile experience of redemption. Yet, this is the ultimate testimony of Judaism and Christianity: hope—to affirm life and its ultimate redemption.

The Christians who see the implications of the Holocaust and Israel are a prophetic leaven in the church who give hope that the church can be reborn, purged of its hatred, and rededicated to its mission of hope and its message of redemption to come from the world. True, the number of such Christians is still small—sometimes this fact evokes despair—but surely the number is no smaller than the band of 12 who started the faith 1,900 years ago. To some Christians, such admissions risk the death of Christianity. Actually, the reluctance to admit Israel's existence represents the temptation to create a situation where another genocide can solve the Jewish problem. But such a genocide could only destroy Christianity's final moral capital. True, for Christians to take up the new revelation is practically an invitation to be crucified. It is to confront the Gospel—and to admit that no one owns God's love. For 2,000 years, Christianity has taught that death to pride and triumphalism is rebirth to love and life. One hopes it has the resources to show this truth in its own life again.

For Jews, too, the unqualified confrontation with Christianity, without a priori dismissal, is a most painful prospect. For the Jews to accept the revelation of the Holocaust and Israel is to challenge existing denominational lines and to open up to fellow Jews and the world in a new, painful, risky, yet exhilarating way.

This, then, is a moment of messianic promise. In this generation, which has seen the ultimate triumph of absurd death and meaninglessness, can come a mighty rebirth in Judaism and Christianity, so that another book of God's revelation may yet come out of this experience. "They that hope in God shall renew their strength," whatever their disappointments. If the risk is taken, later generations will tell how 4,000 years after Exodus and 2,000 years after Calvary, Jews and Christians renounced the guarantees and triumphalism. They faced ultimate death, worked together, and overcame death with renewed life and extreme hatred with love, which is the Divine

Presence in our midst. Truly, if this can be done, Judaism and Christianity are peerless redeeming models for the world, and this is a messianic moment.

Notes

1. In Walter J. Abbott, ed., *The Documents of Vatican II* (New York: Guild Press, 1968), pp. 664–665.
2. This was the Jewish response to the destruction of the First Temple and later the Second Temple. See Salo W. Baron, *A Social and Religious History of the Jews* (Philadelphia: Jewish Publication Society, 1952), vol. 1, chap. 5; vol. w, chap. 10, 11. See also I. Greenberg, "Judaism and History: Historical Events and Religious Change," in *Ancient Roots and Modern Beginnings*, ed. Jerry V. Diller (New York: Bloch Publishing, 1978).
3. Cf. in Jacob Neusner, *Early Rabbinic Judaism* (Leiden: E. J. Brill, 1975), "Emergent Rabbinic Judaism in a Time of Crisis: Four Responses to the Destruction of the Second Temple," pp. 34–49, especially pp. 41–43.
4. Abbott, *Documents*, p. 64.
5. Contrast Paul in Romans 9–11 with the church's tradition. See on this Rosemary Ruether's *Faith and Fratricide* (New York: Seabury Press, 1974), pp. 53 ff., chap. 2.
6. See on this Gershom Scholem, *The Messianic Idea in Judaism* (New York: Schocken, 1971), and his *Sabbatai Sevi* (Princeton: Princeton University Press, 1973).
7. See on this my "Crossroads of Destiny: Responses to the Destruction of the Temple" (New York: n.p., 1975).
8. See Jacob Taubes, "The Issue between Judaism and Christianity," *Commentary*, vol. 16 (December 1953), pp. 525–533, especially pp. 531 ff.
9. See Jacob Katz, *Exclusiveness and Tolerance* (Oxford University Press, 1961), especially chap. 9, 10.
10. Katz, *Exclusiveness and Tolerance*, pp. 87, 89 ff.
11. Irving Greenberg, "The New Encounter of Judaism and Christianity," *Barat Review*, vol. 3, no. 2 (June/September 1968), pp. 113–125.
12. Abbott, *Documents*, pp. 664, 666–668.
13. Ibid., pp. 664, 666.
14. Fr. Cornelius Rijk (then director of the Holy See's office for Catholic-Jewish Relations), Fr. Edward Flannery (then executive secretary of the U.S. Bishops' Secretariat for Catholic Jewish Relations), Abbot Leo Rudloff, O.S.B., of Jerusalem (consultant of the Vatican Secretariat for Promoting Christian Unity), Fr. Theodore de Kruyt (a consultant on the unity secretariat), and Fr. S. LeDeault, "Reflections and Suggestions for the Application of the Directive of 'NOSTRA AETATE,' 4," text issued by Press Dept., U.S. Catholic conference, December 16, 1969; Commission for Religious Relations with the Jews, "Guidelines and Suggestions for Implementing the Conciliar Declaration 'Nostra Aetate' (n. 4)," (Rome, December 1, 1974).
15. Rijk, et al., *Reflections*, pp. 2–3.
16. Commission, *Guidelines*, pp. 1–2.
17. Ibid., p. 5.

18. Rijk, *Reflections,* p. 4.

19. *Guidelines,* p. 5.

20. These words are said with great diffidence. These are the most solemn and serious affirmations that can be made. The official Jewish religious sectors and authorities were, by and large, just as unprepared for this as were most people. However, in 1956, Rabbi Joseph B. Soloveitchik in an address, "Kol Dodi Dofek," proclaimed the reestablishment of the State of Israel to be a new (albeit hidden) revelation. Reprinted in Joseph B. Soloveitchik, *Divrei Hagut Ve-ha'arakha,* (Jerusalem: Department for Torah Education and Culture in the Diaspora of the World Zionist Organization, 1982).

21. My use of the word "revelation" in the rest of this section means that the event—like all revelations—leads to reorientation of the believers and is not merely an additional datum or nuance of understanding. See on this Paul M. van Buren's review of my essay cited below in *Journal of American Academy of Religion,* vol. 45, no. 4, p. 493.

22. Par. 1 in Abbott, *Documents,* p. 112.

23. See Irving Greenberg, "Cloud of Smoke, Pillar of Fire: Judaism, Christianity and Modernity after the Holocaust," in *Auschwitz: Beginning of a New Era?* ed. Eva Fleischner (New York: KTAV, 1977), pp. 1–55.

24. Ibid. See also A. Roy Eckardt, *Elder and Younger Brothers* (New York: Scribners, 1967), introduction and part I; and Franklin H. Littell, *The Crucifixion of the Jews* (New York, 1975).

25. Cf. such behavior as the Vatican's reaction to Vichy France's law of June 2, 1941, isolating the Jews and depriving them of their rights, that "in principle there is nothing in these measures which the Holy See would find to criticize," in Saul Friedlander, *Pius XII and the Third Reich: A Documentation* (New York: Knopf, 1966), p. 97; or Archbishop Grober's pastoral letter in Germany in March 1941, indicating that "the self-imposed curse, 'His blood be upon us and our children,' had come true terribly, until the present time, until today," quoted in Gunther Lewy, *The Catholic Church and Nazi Germany* (New York: McGraw Hill, 1964), p. 294; or the Vatican's help to thousands of German war criminals to escape after the war—including Franz Stangel, commander of Treblinka, mass murderer of over a million Jews!—in Gitta Sereny, *Into That Darkness* (London: Andre Deutsch, 1974), pp. 289–323. On all this, see Helen Fein, *Accounting for Genocide: National Responses and Jewish Victimization during the Holocaust* (New York: Free Press, 1979), especially pp. 64–120. This outstanding study is now fundamental to any discussion of the relationship of Christian anti-Semitism to the Holocaust. In a nutshell, Fein's work shows that the alienation from the other or the presence of categories of understanding that allow the victim to be isolated by the Nazis is the key to Nazi success in genocide. For a magisterial study of the background of this issue in Germany, see Uriel Tal, *Christians and Jews in Germany* (New York: Cornell University Press, 1975).

26. Cf. Greenberg, "Cloud of Smoke," pp. 20ff.

27. Cf. Lewy, *Catholic Church,* chap. 9–11; John S. Conway, *The Nazi Persecution of the Churches* (New York: Basic Books, 1968), pp. 261–283. See also the as-yet-unpublished but very important Wolfgang Gerlach, "Zwischen Kreuz und Davidstern: Bekennede Kirche in ihrer Stellung zum Judentum in Dritten Reich" (unpub. dissertation, University of Hamburg, 1970).

28. In her testimony at the Nuremburg trial, a Polish guard, S. Smaglewskaya, revealed that in the summer of 1944, Jewish children were ordered to be burned alive to economize on the gas used for mass murder. "Their screams could be heard back at the camp," she reported, in *Trial of the Major War Criminal before the International Military Tribunal* (Nuremburg, 1947–1949), vol. 8, pp. 319–320.

29. Cf. Fein, *Accounting for Genocide*, p. 67; see also chap. 4.

30. Cf. ibid., chap. 3.

31. Franklin H. Littell, *The German Phoenix: Men and Movements in the Church in Germany* (Garden City, NY: 1960), p. 217. On the conflict of Nazism as a religion with Judaism and Jews, see Uriel Tal's very important essay, "Religious and Anti-Religious Roots of Anti-Semitism," Leo Baeck Memorial Lecture 14 (New York: Leo Baeck Institute, n.d.).

32. Yosef Yerushalmi, "Response to Rosemary Ruether," in Fleischner, *Auschwitz*, pp. 97 ff.

33. On Jewish modernity, see Milton Himmelfarb, *The Jews of Modernity* (Philadelphia: Jewish Publication Society, 1973), especially pp. 154–157, 158, 178; and Charles Liebman, *The Ambivalent American Jew* (Philadelphia: Jewish Publication Society, 1973).

34. See Himmelfarb, *Jews*, pp. 283–296; and Greenberg, "Cloud of Smoke," pp. 14 ff.

35. *Trials of War Criminals before the Nuremburg Military Tribunals, under Control Council Law No. 10*, vol. 4 (The Einsatzgruppen Cases), U.S. *v.* Otto Ohlendorf, et al. (Washington, DC: U.S. Government Printing Office, 1952), pp. 500–503 and 215 ff.; cf. also p. 309.

36. Quoted in Roger Manvoll, *S.S. and Gestapo* (New York: Ballantine, 1969), p. 109.

37. Cf. Greenberg, "Cloud of Smoke," pp. 45 ff.; also "A Hymn to Secularists," dialogue of Irving Greenberg and Leonard Fein at the General Assembly, Chicago, November 15, 1974, cassette distributed by the Council of Jewish Federations and Welfare Funds, New York, 1975.

38. Tadeusz Borowski, *This Way to the Gas, Ladies and Gentlemen* (New York, 1967), p. 87. Borowski's work is formally "fiction." It is actually memoir and its accuracy is verified by many personal witnesses.

39. Quoted by H.T. Zimels, "The Echo of the Nazi Holocaust in Rabbinic Literature" (n.p., 1975), pp. 63–64. Ziemba was killed by the Nazis on April 24, 1943. Initially, in August 1942, he opposed armed resistance. See also the reflection on the loss of significance of martyrdom in Lawrence Langer, *The Holocaust and the Literary Imagination* (New Haven: Yale University Press, 1975), chap. 1.

40. Greenberg, "Cloud of Smoke," p. 32.

41. Cf. Irving Greenberg, *A Guide to Purim* (New York: National Jewish Conference Center, 1978), pp. 11–13. Cf. Jon Levenson, "The Scroll of Esther in Ecumenical Perspective," *Journal of Ecumenical Studies* 13 (Summer 1976): pp. 440–452.

42. Babylonian Talmud, *Yoma* 69b.

43. "Dogmatic Constitution on Divine Revelation" in Abbott, *Documents*, p. 124.

44. Some Christians have dared to develop the Holocaust/ Israel tie in the model of crucifixion/redemption. I use this analogy with great trepidation. One must beware of its past associations and possible misuse. Thus, for some Christians, the Holocaust is co-opted to reinforce the crucifixion as credible Christian symbol (Moltmann). There is also the danger of dignifying the Nazi Final Solution as a necessary step on the way to salvation. Such a glorification can be avoided if the

crucifixion is addressed through Holocaust categories as total degradation and as a model of what should *not* be tolerated or allowed to happen rather than as redemptive suffering (see above). Cf. on this, A. Roy Eckardt, "Christian Responses to the Endlosung," *Religion in Life* 47 (Spring 1978),pp. 33–45.

45. "Dogmatic Constitution on Divine Revelation," in Abbott, *Documents*, p. 113.
46. "Decree on Ecumenism," ibid., pp. 350–351.

Toward an Organic Model
of the Relationship

This essay does not focus on the Holocaust, but in part it is a response to the Holocaust. In the light of the Holocaust, the willingness to confront, to criticize, and to correct is the ultimate test of the validity and the vitality of faith. One might say that the religion that is most able to correct itself is the one that will prove itself to be most true. Those who claim they have the whole truth and nothing but the truth and there is nothing to correct thereby prove how false and how ineffective their religious viewpoint is. The most powerful proof of the vitality and the ongoing relevance of Christianity is the work of people like Alice and Roy Eckardt, whose fundamental critique of Christianity is surely one of the most sustained and devastating moral analyses in its history. But their work, and that of others like them (e.g., Paul van Buren, Rosemary Ruether, and Eva Fleischner), is both healing and affirming of Christianity.

In that spirit, this exploration is an attempt to ask Jews and Jewish thinkers to focus not only on Christian failure and the Christian tradition of the teaching of contempt. "The Holocaust cannot be used for triumphalism. Its moral challenge must also be applied to Jews."[1] Let us ask ourselves whether it is possible for Judaism to have a more affirmative model of Christianity, one that appreciates Christian spiritual life in all its manifest power. If for no other reason, let this be done because if we take the other's spiritual life less seriously, we run the great risk of taking the biological life less seriously, too. It was the Christian theological negativism and stereotyping of Judaism that created that moral trap into which all too many Christians fell during the Holocaust. At the least, it encouraged relative indifference to the fate of the

145

other. In the light of the Holocaust, Jews have to ask themselves: Is there anything in Jewish tradition or the Jewish perception of other religions like Christianity that could lead to some indifference to the fate of others?

After the Holocaust, a model of the relationship of Judaism and Christianity ideally should enable one to affirm the fullness of the faith-claims of the other, not just offer tolerance. It is important to avoid a kind of affirmation of the other that is patronizing. Take Martin Buber, our master and teacher. In Buber's book *Two Types of Faith* and other writings on Christianity, one is fascinated by the incredible openness (which profoundly affected me). Martin Buber speaks of "my brother Jesus." (The daring and the power of that statement! I could never use that term.) Yet in Buber's approach, Jesus' true religion is the subterranean religion that runs through Judaism also. The Christianity that Buber loves turns out to be suspiciously like the Judaism that Buber loves. That religion, theologically misled by Paul, turns into the Christianity we all know. Now, Buber in his own way was a remarkable pioneer. But is that ultimately the message (i.e., that Christianity is a wonderful religion when it fits [our] Jewish ideas)? Should not Jewish theology seek to be open to Christian self-understanding, including the remarkable, unbelievable claims of Resurrection, Incarnation, etc.? Can one, as a Jew, take these claims seriously without giving up one's Jewishness? Up to now, the agreed response is that if you take such claims seriously, there is nothing further to be as a Jew. This is why Jews who are serious Jews have rejected these claims in the past.

This essay seeks to articulate a model that would allow for the Christian possibility without yielding the firm conviction that Judaism is a covenant faith, true and valid in history. I believe that Judaism has never been superseded, and that its work is yet unfinished. We need a model that would allow both sides to respect the full nature of the other in all its faith-claims. (One must recognize that there is a whole range of Christian self-understanding and a whole range of Jewish self-understanding, from the most secular to the most fundamentalist. Ideally, a model should allow room for that range of understanding, and still not exclude the fullness of the faith-claims of the other.) Last, but not least, the model is willing to affirm the profound inner relationship between the two religions, and to recognize and admit how much closer they are to each other than either has been able to say without denying the other. Up to now, the affirmation that the two religions are profoundly close was made by Christians who claimed that Christianity grows organically out of Judaism in the *course of superseding Judaism.* To the extent that there have been Christians who have affirmed Judaism as valid, they have had (to a certain extent) to overemphasize Jewish differentiation in order to make space for Jewish existence.

To the extent that there were Jews willing to see Christianity as a valid religion, they also tended to stress the differences, in order to protect Judaism. This model will seek to reduce the gaps without denying the authenticity of the other.

THE SCRIPTURAL MODEL

Judaism is a religion of redemption. The fundamental teaching of Judaism is that because this world is rooted in an infinite source of life and goodness, which we call God, life within it is growing, increasing, and perfecting. Life is developing to become more and more like God. The ultimate achievement so far is the human being. The human being is so much like God as to be described as in the image of God. As life develops, it becomes more and more dignified. Human life is of infinite value, equal, and unique. Judaism claims that this process of development will continue until life's fullest possibilities will be realized, i.e., until life proliferates, unfolds its capacities, extends, and finally overcomes death.

If that is not incredible enough, Judaism makes a further claim. The world that we live in, in the realm of the history of humans, is where this perfection will come. There is another realm; Rabbinic Judaism affirms a world to come. But this promised perfection of life will be achieved in the realm in which the five senses can see and measure, in the realm of history. Sickness will be overcome; poverty and oppression will be overcome; death will be overcome. The political, economic, and social structures will be restructured to support and nurture the perfection of life.

Finally, Judaism says that if God is good and God is a source of infinite life and infinite goodness, no one should have died in the first place. To perfect the world, it would not be enough to overcome death prospectively. Judaism goes on to say that there will be resurrection. All those who have died will come to life. Then all will know that everything about God is true. Note that faith is not a fairy tale. If all that is promised does not happen, then the whole Torah is an illusion, a fable. This affirmation is part of the courage and daring of Judaism. It sets the test of its truth not in another world that cannot be measured, and not in a world from which there are no travelers who have returned with firsthand reports. Judaism insists that redemption is going to happen in this world, where you can see it and measure it—and if it does not happen, then the religion is revealed to be an illusion.

This vision of Judaism was set in motion by a great event in Jewish history: the Exodus. Exodus points to a future goal in that it promises that not only Jews will reach the Promised Land of freedom and equality, but all people. By its own definition, then, Judaism is a religion that is open to further events in history. Or to put it another way, Judaism has built into its own self-understanding that it must generate future messianic moments. And the central revealed metaphor that guides this process from the beginning is covenant. The covenant is between God and Israel. God could do it alone. But the achievement of total perfection of the world will take place as the result of the efforts of both partners. Although the promised perfection seems beyond human capacity, the two partners between them can achieve it. In principle, the Divine respects human free will. Therefore, this final perfection cannot simply be given by God *or* brought on by human effort only.

The covenant is the motor of the process of getting to the final redemption. The covenant is Israel's commitment not to stop short of perfection. It is the pledge to testify, to teach the world, and to witness to other human beings. The covenantal process is the answer to the question: What do I do now to perfect the world? The answer is: Work it step-by-step. Use an army to reduce the possibility of war. If one has to fight, one should kill as few people as possible. A commitment to achieve perfection step-by-step means that the model of perfection itself unfolds in history.

To summarize: Judaism is a religion of redemption and perfection, rooted in history, operating through a covenant, illuminated by history, and open to further events of revelation that will clarify its message, with an implied pedagogical model of the relationship of God and humans in which God will help the humans unfold, but will not force them to be free.

JUDAISM AND CHRISTIANITY

In light of all this, to be a faithful Jew is to look forward to further events of revelation and redemption beyond the Exodus—events that will illuminate the covenantal way and guide it forward. When should one most look forward to these kinds of events? In time of great despair and setbacks. That is the time to anticipate the Messiah. To those committed to the triumph of life, goodness, and justice, the moment of great injustice is the time to look forward even more to messianic redemption. When evil reigns supreme, the true balance and direction of history has been disturbed. The only event that can correct such imbalance is a major redemptive move on the other side.

The logic of covenantal redemption explains why Judaism, in fact, generated Christianity. One might argue that generating Christianity is a necessary sign of Judaism's vitality. It is a sign that the dynamics of the covenant are operating. If Judaism did not generate messianic expectations, and did not generate a messiah, it would be a sign that it was dead. As long as Jewry is generating messiahs, it is faithful to its own calling. If Judaism does not generate messiahs—at least until the final Messiah does come and straighten out the whole world—then there is something wrong.

(In writing about the Holocaust, I once wrote that I was ashamed of the fact that, in this generation, there was not at least a false messiah. A false messiah would show that the Jews were truly living up to their vocation, which is to hope and expect the Messiah, particularly in such tragic times. If one hopes for the Messiah and a false one shows up—well, it is regrettable but at least one has tried. Not to generate even a false messiah is a sign that people are complacent; they have either lost hope or do not care.)

The later event that illuminates the earlier event and guides us to its fulfillment is the messianic moment. This is why I believe the early Christians were thinking like faithful Jews when they recognized Jesus. Like good, faithful Jews, they were looking for a redeemer, particularly in a difficult century. Lo and behold! They recognized his arrival. That is a very faithful response of a Jew—to recognize that the Messiah has arrived, and to respond.*

The early Christians were equally faithful, and equally acting out of loyalty to their Jewish understanding, when they responded to a further event, one they had not anticipated at all: namely, the Messiah's death.

Caution: Whenever one responds to a new event, in the belief that this event illuminates the original event, there is a risk. On the one hand, the response shows faithfulness. On the other hand, there are great dangers. One risk is to give your trust and faith to a false messiah—the new arrival may turn out not to be the true Messiah. There is a further risk that the new developments may lead to a transformation of the original ideas. Then, out of trying to be faithful to the new experience, one may find oneself in some way leaving behind or betraying the original commitments. Which then are true: the old ideas or the new ones? Or both? The answer, of course, is that there is no guarantee in advance. Wait until it is all clarified and it will be too late. One must respond right now. Faith response is a wager of one's own life, out of faithfulness.

Consider the Jewish *Sitz im Leben* of those faithful Jewish Christians responding to the charismatic redeemer in their midst. Here was this man whom they experienced as their redeemer. He was shockingly killed. It was a terrible, degrading death. Equally shocking was that the Messiah was supposed to bring the final perfection: peace, dignity, prosperity, and independence. Instead of doing all this, this messiah died miserably, and according to some reports, even in despair and self-denial.

---

* Although to this day, every such accepted messiah has failed to fulfill Jewish hopes.

Now, as faithful Jews (they still were not Christians), how ought they to have responded to his death? Should they have said, "He was a false messiah?" Should they have betrayed their original insight that this person was a redeemer? Or should they have thought, "Maybe this death is another event that illuminates the meaning of the previous event?" Maybe the Crucifixion is not a refutation of Jesus' being the Messiah, but rather a clarification of the nature of redemption. Up to now, they thought that the Messiah would straighten out the political and economic world because that was the mental image of what it meant to perfect the world. But if I as an early Christian knew this was the Messiah but he did not bring worldly liberation, I had an alternative to yielding faith. The alternative was to say that the death is teaching a lesson. The lesson is that true redemption is not in this world. The kingdom of God is within you. Faith leads to a world of spiritual perfection; even though I am a slave, I am free in Christ.

The Christians responded faithfully, but later history suggests they made a hermeneutical error. To put it another way: In retrospect, it was a mistake to say that the explanation of the Crucifixion is that the redemption is beyond history. That judgment generated a fundamental continuing problem of Christianity. In its faithfulness to its vision of Christ come—pitted against the shocking reality of a world of suffering and evil and poverty—Christianity is continually tempted to answer: "This vale of tears is not the real world. The world of suffering and oppression does not matter. It is trivial or secondary. The world that really counts is the spiritual world. That is where you can be born again—and free right now." But this finding betrays the fundamental claim of Judaism that life itself and not only afterlife will be perfected.

As they struggled with the meaning of their faithfulness to Jesus, Christians went on to make a second error, when the destruction of the temple came a generation later. But this second error was again the outgrowth of a response of faith to a great historical event, i.e., another paradigmatic, authentic act of a religious Jew. In the light of the destruction, Jewish and gentile Christians concluded that they had misunderstood. They thought that Jesus was the fulfillment of the Jewish promises within the bounds of Jewish life and hope going on as before. But if the Jews do not accept Jesus, even after their temple is destroyed, is this not a proof that God has in fact rejected them? And using the same hermeneutical model, would not gentile Christians conclude that the acceptance of Christianity in the world proves that Jesus came not to continue the old and the original covenant, but rather to bring a new covenant to humanity? And since the Jews failed to understand, have they not forfeited the promise? In short, the classic Christian interpretation that Christianity has superseded Judaism is an understandable hermeneutic, rooted in Jewish models of interpretation and capable of being derived out of faithfulness to past Jewish modes of thinking. The paradox is that although Jewish thinking was involved in arriving at this conclusion, the conclusion itself was devastating for future Jewish-Christian relations. In effect, the response to the destruction created a model of relationship in which the mere existence of the Jews is a problem for Christianity. The obvious temptation—continually given in to—was to solve the problem by getting rid of the Jews.

There were and are three classic Christian ways of removing the Jewish problem. One was to insist that the Jews were not really alive: Judaism was a fossilized religion; Jews are children of the devil; they are dead, but the devil is pumping them up, etc. This is the way of caricature and dismissal, of stereotypes of legalism and *spät Judentum.* In taking this tack, Christians did not deal with the possibility that God was keeping the Jews alive because God wanted their testimony to go on until the world itself was redeemed. The second way was to convert Jews to become Christians so there would be no problem. However, by and large, the Jews declined to yield their witness. The third way, if the other two did not work, was to kill the Jews; then there was no contradiction between Jewish existence and Christianity anymore.

The supersessionist interpretation continually tempted Christianity into being neither the gospel of love it wanted to be nor the outgrowth of Judaism seeking to reach out and realize Israel's messianic dream that it could have been. Christianity was continually led to become an otherworldly, triumphalist religion that put its own mother down; it spit into the well from which it drank.

The Rabbis and the Jews had a similar problem from the other side. After all, they sensed the profound continuity from Judaism into Christianity. The hermeneutical language that the Rabbis applied to Hebrew Scriptures is paralleled by many of the Christian claims. What made the situation worse, or more difficult, was that Christianity triumphed. Christianity became a world religion, far greater in its numbers than Judaism. How can one account for that, if one believes that Judaism is true and the Messiah has not come yet? In Jewish terms, could there be more clear proof of Christian claims than the fact that it triumphed in history?

The Jews, too, handled the problem by a series of responses. First, the Christian victory was not really a victory: "Look how evil the world is even after Jesus' career." This is the bedrock of Jewish response to Christianity, but it does not deal with the possibility that the nature of redemption is being redefined, widened, or partially realized.

Second, Christianity is neither a gospel of love nor God's message, because look how cruel Christians are to Jews. Far from bringing redemption,

Christianity has brought a whole new sum of evil and cruelty into the world. That is the best proof that Christianity is not a true religion.

Third, Christians claim to supersede Jewry. Christians themselves say that if Christianity is true faith, then Judaism does not exist or has no right to exist. But Jewry knows that it is alive and vital. Obviously, Christianity must be false. If your truth means that I am not valid, but I know my own validity, then you must be false.

The fourth Jewish response was that Christianity triumphed among the gentiles. No Jew would fall for that fairy tale of a virgin mother. If you were pregnant from someone else, what would you tell your husband? This is fundamentally how medieval Jews handled Christianity. Joseph was a fool enough to believe. With one Jew, you never can tell. But the Jews as a whole would not buy it. That a whole world would buy it proves that gentile heads can be filled with anything. This understanding bred contempt for gentiles rather than appreciation for their joining in the work of achieving total redemption, i.e., both worldly and spiritual. Of course, the contempt was earned and reinforced by Christian mistreatment of Jews.

Christians were tempted to step out of history because the Messiah had come already and the ongoing suffering was a problem, so the answer was that history did not matter. Jews were also tempted to step out of history, because in that arena, Christianity had won—to which the Jewish answer was that what happened in history was now unimportant. Christianity had triumphed—temporarily. When the final redemption comes, all these huge statues and towers will come crashing down, and humanity will know the truth. Jewry, this small pitiful people that had no political clout, has really been the heart of the world. All the rest has been just a big, flashy show, up front—temporarily. Therefore, Judaism also stepped out of history to wait for its final redemption.

The one thing the Rabbis would give Christianity, then, is that Jesus was a messiah—a false messiah. This negative view conceded very little. Jesus was not the only false messiah in Jewish history; he was neither the first nor the last. In the seventeenth century, Shabbetai Zevi, one of the great false messiahs of Jewish history, swept the Jewish world. The Jews are still looking for a messiah. So, if a few Jews followed Jesus, it proved nothing. The Rabbis concluded that Christianity was an alien growth, developed by those who followed a false messiah.

The Rabbis perhaps erred here. Understandably, they did not do greater justice to Jesus because they were surrounded by an enemy (i.e., Christians) one hundred times larger than Jewry, aggressively proselytizing and persecuting the Jews in the name of Jesus' claims. Out of defensiveness, the Rabbis confused a "failed" messiah (which is what Jesus was) and a false messiah. A false messiah is one who has the wrong values, i.e., one who would teach that death will triumph, that people should oppress each other, that God hates us, or that sin and crime are the proper way. In the eighteenth century, a putative Jewish messiah named Jacob Frank ended up teaching his people that out of sin comes redemption; therefore, one must sin. Such is a false messiah.

A failed messiah is one who has the right values and upholds the covenant, but does not attain the final goal. In the first century, 130–135, Bar Kokhba, the great Jewish freedom fighter who led a revolt against Rome that temporarily drove Rome out of Jerusalem, sought to free the land. He was hailed by Rabbi Akiva and many great rabbis as the Messiah. His rebellion was crushed; it did not bring that final step of redemption. It turned out that he was a failed messiah. But Akiva did not repudiate him. Since when is worldly success a criterion of ultimate validity in Judaism?

Calling Jesus a failed messiah is in itself a term of irony. In the Jewish tradition, failure is a most ambiguous term. Abraham was a "failure." He dreamt of converting the whole world to Judaism. He ended up barely having one child carrying on the tradition. Even that child he almost lost.

Moses was a "failure." He dreamt of taking the slaves, making them into a free people and bringing them to the Promised Land. They were hopeless slaves; they died slaves in the desert, and neither they nor Moses ever reached the Promised Land.

Jeremiah was a "failure." He tried to convince the Jewish people that the temple would be destroyed unless they stopped their morally and politically wrong policies; he tried to convince them to be ethically responsible, to free their slaves, and not to fight Babylonia. No one listened.

All these "failures" are at the heart of divine and Jewish achievements. This concept of a "failed" but true messiah is found in a Rabbinic tradition of the Messiah ben Joseph. The Messiah ben David (son of David) is the one who brings the final restoration. In the Messiah ben Joseph idea, you have a messiah who comes and fails—indeed is put to death—but paves the way for the final redemption.

In fact, Christians also sensed that Jesus did not exhaust the achievements of the final Messiah. Despite Christian claims that Jesus was a total success (the proof being that redemption has been achieved; it is of the otherworldly kind), even Christians spoke of the Second Coming. The concept of the Second Coming, in a way, is a tacit admission that if at first you don't succeed, try, try again.

One might argue then that both sides claimed—and denied—more than was necessary in order to protect their own truth against the counterclaims of the other. Both sides were too close to recognize each other, and too close and too conflicted to come to grips with each other's existence as valid in its own right. Both faiths stepped out of history to protect their own position, i.e., Christians denying anything revelatory further can happen in history because Christ is the final revelation, Jews denying any further revelation in history because Judaism is a covenant that cannot be revoked.

There was even more theological fallout to these moves. Religion tended to abandon the world to Caesar or to mammon. Religion all too often ended up as an opiate of the masses, i.e., promising people fulfillment in the great by-and-by if they accept suffering and the world as it is. In a way, each group was defining the sacred out of history into another realm.

Placing the sacred beyond history protected faith from refutation and disappointment, but the cost was high. It is not surprising then that each faith tended to generate movements from time to time that sought to redress the balance or that sought to bring the "missing" part of redemption into being. What was defined as "missing" grew out of the interaction of tradition, local culture, and the historical condition of the group. Since the concept of redemption can be pushed toward a spiritual realization or a worldly one, both religions developed parallel responses along a spectrum of positions within each faith. These developments further complicated the relations between the two faiths even as they ensured greater overlap and parallelism between them.

In retrospect, a key moment of division came in the differential response of the two groups to the destruction of the Second Temple. The Christians reacted to the destruction as the best proof that the Jews had forfeited their covenant. If the main vehicle and channel of Jewish relationship to God has been cut off and destroyed, is this not decisive proof that God has rejected Jews? In fact, the Jewish Christians left Jerusalem before the final destruction, thus, as the Jews saw it, abandoning the Jewish people. Christians assumed that Jewry had no future and went off to make their own religion, their own faith, their own home, and their own future.

The Christians were wrong. Judaism did not disappear, and the Jews did not disintegrate. The Rabbis encountered a crisis equal to the early Christians' experience of the Crucifixion, i.e., being cut off from the channel of revelation and connection to God, with the question gnawing at their faith: Why did evil triumph in this world? The same questions that Christians raised, Jews understood, too. Does the destruction mean that the Jews are finished? Does it mean the covenant is finished? The Rabbis responded with faith in the covenant and trust in God and the goal. The Rabbis answered, as the prophets before them, that the destruction was punishment for sins, and therefore a mark of divine concern—not rejection. The most fundamental insight of the Rabbis was: Why did God not vanquish the Romans, even as God had destroyed the Egyptians? The Rabbis concluded that God had "pulled back," but

154

not to abandon Jews and not to withdraw from this world because of some weakening of concern. Instead of splitting the Red Sea again, God was calling the people of Israel to participate more fully in the covenant. Instead of winning the war for the Jews, God was instructing the Jews to participate in redemption themselves. The Jews failed to do so adequately. They engaged in civil war and fought each other instead of the Romans. Since they had timed and conducted their rebellion wrongly, the Jewish failure was the Jewish failure, not God's rejection. The lesson of the destruction was not that God had abandoned Israel, but that God was deliberately hiding in order to evoke a greater response, and a greater participation in the covenantal way.

This "hiding" can be seen as a kind of "secularization" process. In the Temple, the manifest God showed overwhelming power. In the old Temple, God was so manifest that holiness was especially "concentrated" in Jerusalem. If one went into the Temple without the proper purification ritual, it was like walking into a nuclear reactor without shielding, i.e., one would inescapably die. The synagogue is a place one can enter with milder preparation and far less risk. The Divine is present but its power is "shielded."

In "hiding," the Divine was calling on Israel to discern the Divine, which was hidden but present *everywhere*. The manifest God is visible in Jerusalem; the hidden God can be found everywhere. One need not literally go to Jerusalem to pray. One can pray anywhere in the world. The synagogue, which was a secondary institution before the destruction, became a central institution afterward. In the Temple, God spoke either directly, or through the breastplate, or through the prophet. The synagogue is the place where you go to speak and pray—when God no longer speaks to you.

The deepest paradox of the Rabbis' teaching was that the more God is hidden, the more God is present. The difference is that in the good old days one did not have to look; the divine illumination lit up the world. Now, one must look. If one looks more deeply, one will see God everywhere. But to see God everywhere, one must understand. The key to religious understanding is learning. The Jewish people, in biblical times an ignorant peasantry, awed by sacramental, revelatory experiences in the Temple, were trained by the Rabbis to learn and study. Now that God no longer speaks directly, how would one know what God wants? The answer is to go to the synagogue; there one does not see God visibly, but one prays and asks God for guidance. Go ask a rabbi: "What does God want from me?" and the rabbi answers, "I do not have direct access. I will study the record of God's past revelation. I will study the precedents for the situation and give you my best judgment as to what God wants right now." Note that the human agent takes a much more active part in discerning God's will, but the answer is much less certain at the end of the process. Whenever one asks a question, rabbis disagree.

When there is human participation, there is disagreement, but the contradictory views are both valid because both have applied human judgment to the classic sources in a good-faith attempt to know what God wants.

In the triumph of the Rabbis, there was an incredible transformation of Judaism. The manifest, sacramental religion of the Bible was succeeded by the internalized, participatory, more "laical" faith of the Rabbinic period. Indeed, the Rabbis came to the conclusion that they had lived through events comparable almost to a reacceptance of the covenant. Even as Christians responded to their great religious experiences by proclaiming their record to be a New Covenant, Jews responded to theirs by affirming a *renewal* of the covenant.

In short, to reverse a classic Christian explanation of the relationship of Judaism and Christianity, I would argue that both Judaism and Christianity are outgrowths of and continuous with the biblical covenant; that indeed Christianity is closer to the biblical world, but not in the triumphalist way that Christianity has always claimed. Rather, Christianity is a commentary on the original Exodus, in which the later event—the Christ event—is a manifest, "biblically" miraculous event. God becomes incarnate and self-validating through miracles. Obviously, many Jews will argue that closing the biblically portrayed gap between the human and the Divine, between the real and the ideal, by incarnation is idolatrous or at least against the grain of the biblical way. But even if incarnation is contradictory to some biblical principles, the model itself is operating out of classic biblical modes—the need to achieve redemption, the desire to close the gap between the human and Divine that includes divine initiatives, etc. Thus, one can argue that incarnation is improbable and violative of other given biblical principles or that it is unnecessary in light of the continuing career of the Jewish people. But one can hardly rule out the option totally, particularly if it was intended for gentiles and not intended for Jews. This approach grants Christianity legitimate roots in the biblical tradition, but also locks it into a biblical mode of theological action.

By contrast, Judaism went into a second stage, continuous but developed out of the biblical mode. In this stage, God is more hidden and Judaism is more worldly. In this stage, the human matures and the covenantal model leads to greater responsibility for human beings. I personally consider the rabbinic to be a more mature mode of religion. However, I would also affirm that the sacramental mode (Christianity) was most appropriate for gentiles, then as this was the first step of gentile covenantal relationship with God. Jews were in that same mode in their first stage, also. The choice of this mode bespeaks the divine pedagogy of love, which approaches people where they are and, only after they have grown into the covenant, leads them to new levels of relationship. Nor does my analysis foreclose the possibility that sacramental Christianity is in fact an extended form of biblical religion, i.e., one in which God is even *more* manifest and present.

N.B.: The foregoing model of the relationship of Judaism and Christianity to each other and to biblical faith is offered with great diffidence. The statement that Christianity is closer to the biblical mode can be misused to reassert the old Christian claim that Christianity is the true outgrowth of the biblical covenant and that Judaism is cut off from its roots. Moreover, the model opens great vistas of Christian legitimacy in Jewish eyes without any guarantee that the ongoing Christian denial of Jewish validity will be stopped. My affirmations, then, may feed Christian triumphalism and supersessionism. I acknowledge the risk, but I think it is worth the risk to overcome the dismissals and divisiveness that weaken the role of both religions. I turn to Christians in trust and love and depend on them to prevent triumphalist abuses. Failure to prevent such abuses would only prove that Christianity is not a valid hermeneutic on the biblical covenant. It would suggest that the sum of woe brought into the world by Christianity will go on and on, undermining its claim to be a legitimate major step forward on the road to redemption.

By the same token, many Christians will find the concept that God called Jewry to a new level of relationship in the covenant a denial of their own belief in Christ as the ultimate event. I do not underestimate the challenge in giving up the monopoly claims or in recognizing Judaism as a form of independently valid relationship to God. Yet this model offers the affirmation of the fullest possibilities of Christ—from God Incarnate to prophet or Messiah or teacher—but freed at last of the incubus of hatred and monopolistic claims of owning God. For this model to work, Jews as well as Christians will have to have faith in the sufficiency of God's capacity to offer love enough for everyone and that the Lord who is the *Makom*/Place, who is "the ground of all existence," has many messengers.

THE NEW ERA: AFTER MODERNITY IN THE LIGHT OF THE HOLOCAUST AND THE REBIRTH OF ISRAEL

The history that both religions denied in order to claim their own absolute validity came back to haunt them. In the modern period, the revolt of humans against oppression, suffering, and inequality led to an enormous growth of secularism and rejection of religion. Both Christianity and Judaism lost serious ground to popular revolts in the name of the very goals they were pledged to achieve in the first place. Both faiths were forced back into history by the overwhelming weight of modern culture and scholarship that continually dug at their claimed foundations, i.e., transcendent extrahistorical truth. Modern scholarship insisted that the denial of history is false. Revelation is in history. To deny that, one must ignore or contradict archaeology, anthropology, sociology, philosophy, and history. Religions that deny their history are judged to be false and nonfactual by the standards of modern culture. Reluctantly but inexorably, both religions have been forced to confront their own historicity.

An event of great historical magnitude has now gone beyond modernity in pushing faith back into the maelstrom of history. In the Holocaust, Jews discovered they had no choice but to go back into history. If they did not take power, they would be dead. The only way to prevent a recurrence was for Jews to go to their land, establish a state and protect themselves, and to take responsibility so that the covenant people could be kept alive. In this generation, the Jewish people—secular as well as religious—took responsibility for its fate, and for the fate of the divine covenant with Jewry. This is the meaning, not always recognized, of the reestablishment of the State of Israel.

Christians also have been forced back into history by the impact of this event. Those faithful Christians realized that the evil portrait of Judaism, the whole attempt to assure Christian triumphalism, had become a source of the teaching of contempt and had convicted Christianity or implicated it in a genocide in the face of which it was indifferent or silent. The Holocaust forced Jews and Christians to see that the attempt to protect faith against history was an error, and that both religions can have no credibility in a world in which evil can totally triumph. I have argued that the true lesson of the Crucifixion has been misunderstood by Christians because of their past triumphalism. In the light of the Holocaust, one would argue that the true lesson of the Crucifixion is that if God in person came down on earth in human flesh and was put on the cross and crucified, then God would be broken. God would be so exhausted by the agony that God would end up losing faith, and saying, "My God, my God, why have you forsaken me?" If God could not survive the cross, then surely no human can be expected to. So the overwhelming call for both religions is to stop the Crucifixion, not to glorify it. Just as Jews, in response, took up arms and took up the power of the state, so Christians are called simultaneously to purge themselves of the hatred that made them indifferent to others and to take up the responsibility of working in the world to bring perfection. This is the common challenge of both faiths; they can ill afford to go on focusing on each other as *the* enemy.

There is another possible implication. Destruction of the Temple meant that God was more hidden. Therefore, one had to look for God in the more "secular" area. Living after the Holocaust, the greatest destruction of all time in Jewish history, one would have to say that God is even more hidden. Therefore, the sacred is even more present in every "secular" area. Building a better world, freeing the slaves, curing sickness, and taking responsibility for the kind of economic perfection that is needed to make this a world of true human dignity—all these activities pose as secular. But in the profoundest sort of way, these activities are where God is most present. When God is most hidden, God is present everywhere. If when God was hidden after the destruction of the Temple, one could find God in the synagogue, then when God is hidden after Auschwitz, one must find God in the street, in the hospital, and in the bar. And that responsibility of holy secularity is the responsibility of all human beings.

Similarly, apply the Rabbis' analysis of why God did not stop the Romans to the question of why God did not stop the Holocaust. The question is *not* "where was God during the Holocaust?" God was where God should have been during the Holocaust. God was with God's people—suffering, starving, and being gassed and burnt alive. Where else would God be, when God's people are being treated that way?

The real question is: What was God's message when God did not stop the Holocaust? God is calling humans to take full responsibility for the achievement of the covenant. It is their obligation to take up arms against evil and to stop it.

The implication of this model is that Judaism is entering a third stage, or at least a new level of covenantal development. This is the ultimate logic of covenant: If God wants humans to grow to a final perfection, then the ultimate logic of covenant is for humans to take full responsibility. Taking full responsibility does not imply a human arrogance that dismisses God, or the human arrogance that says more human power is automatically good. "Covenantal commitment" implies the humility of knowing that the human is not God. The human is like God, but is ultimately called by God to be the partner. This requires the modesty of recognizing that one is a creature as well as a creator. Using this covenantal understanding, one can perceive God as the Presence everywhere—suffering, sharing, participating, and calling. However, trust in God or awareness of God is necessary but not sufficient for living out faith. The awareness moderates the use of power; trust curbs power ethically. But the theological consequence is that without taking power, and without getting involved in history, one is religiously irresponsible. To pray to God as a substitute for taking power is blasphemous.

The new human responsibility level implies that the events of our lifetime are revelatory. Therefore, one has to incorporate those events into religion and into our understanding. If we are to be true partners with God, and if we have full responsibility, then we are morally responsible for our own traditions. If there is anything in our own traditions that demeans, or denies, or degrades somebody else, then one cannot answer that it is the Word of God and so be it. One must answer: It is my responsibility. God has given me a call to take responsibility. Even if that means one must argue with God or confront God, that also is a responsibility. If, indeed, God said that only a male can stand in for God, then someone who is faithful to God would have to argue with God: "It is not right—woman is also your creature, in your image." If God declared the Jews blind and hateful, to be treated as pariahs, then one must confront God and call God back to the universal love that God has revealed to humanity.

This is a time of major transformation in which the past experiences on the road to perfection are reinterpreted in light of the events of our lifetime for both religions. I believe we are living in an age of the Jewish reacceptance of the covenant. The re-creation of Israel is the classic covenantal symbol. If you want to know if there is a God in the world and is there still hope, if you want to know whether there is still a promise of redemption, then the Bible says one goes back to Israel and makes the streets of Jerusalem resound with the laughter of children and the sounds of brides and grooms dancing (see Jer. 33:10). That is what is happening in Jerusalem right now. This is true notwithstanding all the political, economic, and moral flaws of the new earthly Jerusalem. The flaws, the tragic conflicts with Arabs, and the difficulties are all part of the fundamental proof that here we have the hidden Presence. This moment of revelation is fully human; this moment of redemption is humanly fully responsible in the presence of God.

One might suggest that the Holocaust has its primary impact on Judaism. Nevertheless, as a Jewish theologian, I suggest that Christianity also cannot be untouched by the event. At the least, I believe that Christianity will have to enter its second stage. If we follow the Rabbis' model, this stage will be marked by greater "worldliness" in holiness. The role of the laity would shift from being relatively passive followers in a sacramental religion to full (or fuller) participation. It can be argued that Protestantism had made these moves centuries ago. But, according to this model, both Protestantism and Catholicism must invite more direct, active relationship between the believer and God. Both must avoid the situation in which leaving the decisive connection to Jesus results in greater moral passivity. In this stage, Christianity would make the move from being out of history to taking power, i.e., taking part in the struggle to exercise power to advance redemption. The religious message would be not accepting inequality but demanding its correction. The movement is toward learning and understanding as against hierarchy and mystery. Christians—as Jews—will recover the true role of Israel/Jacob who struggles with God and with people, for the sake of God and of humanity.

Unless this shift toward wrestling with God takes place, those Christians who seek to correct Christianity vis-à-vis Judaism will be blocked by the fact that within the New Testament itself are hateful images of Jews. Therefore, humans must take full responsibility for repairing the breach, but not out of arrogance or idolatry. It must be done without making God into the convenient one who says what one wants to hear. Out of the fullest responsibility to its covenant partner, Christianity can undergo the renewal that I believe it must undertake.

The unfinished agenda of the Jewish-Christian dialogue is the recognition of the profound interrelationship between both. Each faith community experiencing the love of God and the chosenness of God was tempted into saying: I am the only one chosen. There was a human failure to see that there is enough love in God to choose again and again and again. Both faiths in renewal may yet apply this insight not just to each other, but to religions not yet worked into this dialogue. Humans are called in this generation to renew the covenant—a renewal that will demand openness to each other, learning from each other, and a respect for the distinctiveness of the ongoing validity of each other. Such openness puts no religious claim beyond possibility, but places the completion of total redemption at the center of the agenda.

Judaism as a religion of redemption believes that in ages of great destruction, one must summon up an even greater response of life and of re-creation. Nothing less than a messianic moment could possibly begin to correct the balance of the world after Auschwitz. This is a generation called to an overwhelming renewal of life, a renewal built on such love and such power that it would truly restore the image of God to every human being in the world.

Notes

1. See my "Cloud of Smoke, Pillar of Fire: Judaism, Christianity, and Modernity after the Holocaust," in *Auschwitz: Beginning of a New Era?* ed. Eva Fleischner (New York: KTAV, 1977), pp. 20–22.

The Respective Roles of the Two Faiths in the Strategy of Redemption

From the time that Judaism and Christianity grew together, matured into separate religions, and separated, until today, the two have had one central message in common: the triumph of life. Both affirm that this is a world grounded in (or created by) God, an infinite source of life, goodness, and power. Life is growing and becoming more and more like the God who is its ground. The human being has the qualities of life—freedom, consciousness, relatedness, and power—that are the fundamental qualities of God. Because human life possesses these qualities at a level that no other life has, it is the highest form of life and has attained the dignity of being "in the image of God." (True, major branches of Christianity teach that the image of God has been defaced by humanity's original sin. This doctrine means not that the godlike capacities have been lost, but rather that there is an innate tendency to use them for evil.)

As defined by the Talmud, by dint of being in the image of God, each human life has the innate dignity of infinite value, equality, and uniqueness. The task of religion is to uphold the sacredness of the image of God and to nurture its further growth in each human being. Not the least way in which this is accomplished is by relating the human—as individuals and in community—to the God who loves and confirms the human.

With the help of God and the leadership of the religious faithful, the process of perfecting life will go on until the triumph of life takes place. The world itself will be restructured to respect and treat properly the life that is in the image of God. The ultimate result will be victory over death as well as over all those forces of degradation of life that exist in the world.

To realize this tradition of the victory of life and the fulfillment of life's "image of God" potential, humanity would have to overcome poverty, hunger, war, oppression, sickness, and even death itself. These worldly goals—as dramatic and even improbable as they may appear—are the necessary infrastructure for the attainment of the ultimate fulfillment. According to both Judaism and Christianity, overcoming the enemies of life will pave the way to the fullest realization of the relationship between God and humanity. In the climax of material, relational, and spiritual wholeness, the fullest depth of life's capacity will be reached.

By contrast, hungry, starving, oppressed people cannot realize the supreme potential of their life force, or even the fullest development of relationship and love. While it is true that the poor or the suffering may relate to God out of their agony even more than the affluent and the wealthy, they turn to God from a place of weakness or suffering. The Jewish dream is that humans establish ultimate relationships—with God and fellow human beings—out of strength and freedom.

ILLUSION, HOPE, AND COVENANT

Judaism and Christianity both promise that this vision of perfection, which appears so far from the present reality, will nevertheless come to be. Taken by itself, such a vision sounds in all candor like a fantasy—like an escapist illusion. Indeed, much of modern culture has developed from the growing human conviction that this "fairy tale" is not worth waiting for and that one can and should do something in the present to improve conditions. But neither religion offers itself as a fairy tale; nor is either content to remain a vision. Neither religion claims that the promised land, the final stage of history, is already a fact. The vision of each is most accurately described as a hope.

Why is a hope different from an illusion or an escape? Hope is a dream that is committed to the discipline of becoming a fact. Illusions and fantasies do better when one does not try to carry them out. Dreams are often so disappointing when realized that one prefers to cling to the dream rather than risk disillusion. A hope commits itself either to become a fact or to renounce itself and to confess not merely failure but falsity. Thus both religions have staked their truth and their truth claims on making their vision into a fact. Both religions have backed this hope by a commitment to make it happen. The covenant is the pledge to work to realize the dream. This decisive move—the transcendent and the immanent reaching out toward each other—unites the two religions. This unlimited partnership of the Divine and the human is the ultimate dimension of religious calling in both traditions.

COVENANT AS DIVINE COMMITMENT TO A HUMAN PROCESS

From the divine perspective, the covenant is nothing less than God's promise that the goal is worthy and will be realized, that humans will be accompanied all the way, and that God will provide an ongoing model of how to be human. The divine initiative elicits a matching response—a human promise to persevere and work until the goal is reached. Both religions teach that the people of Israel, the covenantal people (however each faith defines that), are pledged not only to work but also to teach and to model how to be human to the rest of humanity.

There is yet another dimension implied in covenant. Attaining the infinite goals of this vision appears to be beyond finite human capacity. The needed accomplishments appear to be so transcendent and so remarkable that in a sense only God can accomplish them. Nevertheless, says the Bible, God has made a commitment that the final result will not be imposed; it will not be granted by divine fiat. The state of perfection will be accomplished on and through a human scale only. The central point of the covenant process itself is that despite having all the power to do what God chooses, God has chosen to make the divinely desired outcome dependent on *human* capacities and efforts.

The Bible witnesses that God voluntarily limited God's self. God calls humans into partnership out of love and respect for them. But people do not function in the abstract; they function in the context of other people. They create institutions. They organize themselves in groups to carry out their mission. They function with hierarchies or with "rules of the game." They create committees. This process, too, is affirmed by the divine pledge.

The very fact that God chose to work through committees already shows the ultimate risk taken by the Divine! The limitations, frustrations, and betrayals—even the surprises and acts that exceed divine expectations—are all implicitly factored into the covenantal process accepted and affirmed by God. The risk is indissolubly attached to the repeatedly renewed divine commitment to work with the people of God and other human messengers within the human context. Both religions testify that no matter what disappointments and anguish have followed, God has remained committed to working through human agency. This means that redemption will take place through humans who are rooted in the natural order. The people of God seek roots in their land, grow attached to their own homeland, identify with particular heroes, relate to a particular family, and create a particular community. Thus redemption takes place within the matrix of human history.

The commitment to covenant also means that redemption will take place at a human pace. It has taken the twentieth century with its revolutionary experiences to make us realize the depth and subtlety of that biblical point. The covenantal dream is revolutionary, but the pace is incremental. Revolutions, if they are to be carried out both humanely and properly, take place on an evolutionary time scale. Human rarely go more than one step at a time voluntarily. Attempts to force them to go faster—even when the goal is perfection—typically run into normal human resistance to radical change. All too often, those who seek to bring about perfection in one stroke become impatient and oppressive. They decide to eliminate the opposition that is holding up the final breakthrough. Soon a new oppression has been established for the sake of redemption.

The great temptation that saviors—divine and human—always are attracted to is to redeem people against their will, i.e., to force the other to be free. This way too often ends up being oppressive because it leads the redeemer to slip into the deepest form of contempt for the very beings that the savior seeks to redeem. The contempt grows out of the gap between humans as they are and as the redeemer wants them to be. Thus the logic of redemption corrupts the logic of love itself. By contrast, the divine faithfulness to the principle of working through human agency at a human pace grows out of divine humility and is a statement of profound respect for the human. The acceptance of human limitations is an ultimate act of divine love.

Another implication of this human dimension in the covenant is that God uses human models to bring out the humanness of humans. Moses, David, Rebecca, and other biblical figures are all too human models. Christianity's affirmation of Incarnation adds to the Hebrew biblical statement the claim that God so wanted to be a part of the covenantal process that God literally took on human form in order to play another crucial role in the process. If this concept is not carefully controlled, it can undermine the very goal it seeks to advance, viz., the perfection of humans. Triumphalist interpretations of the Incarnation that use it to demean Judaism (i.e., that claim that this is a higher revelation, one beyond the grasp of Judaism's religious categories) tend to devalue the human role in the covenant. Thereby, they destroy the object (human dignity and completion) for whose sake God undertook the whole covenantal process!

Giving up the supercessionist interpretations of the Incarnation would constitute a Christian recovery of respect for humanity and of the divine respect for humanity.

For this reason, the Christian tradition, in its wisest forms, resisted attempts to make Jesus into a purely divine being. It insisted on his ultimate retention of humanness—even though this created great philosophical problems and paradoxes. The dynamic tension is never resolved because human feelings of adequacy to cope with reality vary from culture to culture. To put it bluntly, whenever humans feel helpless or despair, they are more likely to hope and expect that a divinely sent redeemer (or, according to the Christian claim, that God "in person") will bring redemption. In cultures, such as modernity, where the sense of human power grows, the focus on Jesus' humanity grows.

From this perspective, one difference between the two religions can be stated thus: Whereas Jewish tradition affirms that the final goals can be attained under the leadership of a human avant-garde, Christianity adds the claim that God became the human model that leads humans into the final state. Thus Christianity also concedes that only a human model can bring out the fullness of humanity. Once the triumphalist distortion is removed, Christians can begin to recognize that the incarnation model is profoundly Jewish, albeit rejected by Judaism. Jews can begin to recognize that the incarnation concept should not be dismissed as some bizarre import from Hellenistic culture but viewed as an extension of the use of human exemplars to evoke maximum covenantal behavior. It is not that Jews and Christians will accept each other's views on this issue, but they can come to realize that both positions grow out of strategies for achieving the goals of the covenant held in common.

Divine models alone cannot bring out the fullness of humanity because the Divine is too great, too overwhelming, and too much beyond human experience. When one encounters somebody so great that one cannot dream of being that way, the experience brings out a feeling of insufficiency and guilt. This may lead people to abandon trying to grow altogether. By contrast, seeing a fellow human being performing at a level beyond one's own current standard brings out the realization that it is possible to do the same. This enlarges one's own potential. For this very reason, Christianity, despite its affirmation of Incarnation, remains committed to the use of human models to evoke the response of others. And Judaism a fortiori insists on human paradigms.

In an early stage of my own personal religious development, I was struggling with my Jewish heritage and some of the ethical dilemmas and self-criticism generated by encounter with the Holocaust. I hesitated, with great inner conflict, and asked myself whether to question or wrestle with inherited traditional positions. No one wants to be an outsider, and I was especially hesitant because I was deeply rooted in my tradition and I love it. At this critical juncture, I received crucial guidance from Christian thinkers. I saw profoundly Christian thinkers, deeply rooted in their tradition, challenging its inherited traditional positions on Judaism. The model of Christian candor, of Christian self-criticism and integrity in wrestling with inherited norms attributed to the divine source, such as can be seen in the work of thinkers such as Roy Eckardt and Paul van Buren, evoked in me the belief and then the capacity that I could grow and develop beyond my own past behavior. If they, as Christians, could hold themselves to the standard of patriarch Jacob, who became Israel by struggling with God and humans, perhaps I as a Jew could do it within my own tradition as well.

 ## FROM GENERATION TO GENERATION: HOPE AND COVENANT

The goal of perfection is "unreal" when it is stated as if it were already true or to be achieved at once. If we understand from the covenantal model that the final outcome will be accomplished humanly, we recognize that the goal is reached gradually, one generation at a time. We will take it as far as we can go and then we will pass it on to our children. If we pass it on properly and the next generation takes up the task, and the next generation after that, then ultimately, albeit step-by-step, redemption is transformed from being a fantasy into a realizable dream. If we persist, if we achieve some piece of the final perfection in every generation and yet never settle for that partial accomplishment, then we can go on to perfection itself. This is the incredible tenacity and power of the covenantal commitment.

As long as there is family life or a community (that can pass the vision on to other generations, even if I personally have no children), then this dream becomes steadily more achievable. When Abraham started, what were the chances of overcoming death? The average life expectancy in the Middle East in Abraham's time is estimated to have been no more than 20 to 30 years of life. Now, a mere 3,500 years later, the average life expectancy in America, at least, is close to 80 years old. If we can triple the human lifespan every 3,500 years, to achieve total triumph over death should not be all that difficult! The key is to think in terms of eons, not just in terms of one lifetime. The self-directed narcissism of modern life encourages the belief that life ends with one's own life. If we think in terms of the incredible human capacity to pass on the covenant, our chances of final realization are much better than superficial appearances imply.

THE PARADOX AND DIALECTICS OF COVENANT

In accepting human agency and human partnership, God has taken on extraordinary risks. Humans can only hear so much. The greatest of teachers cannot go more than a little beyond his or her students' capacity without losing them. Therefore, the divine word must be self-limited to the extent of human capacity—or perhaps a little beyond. This raises the risk that humans will hear selectively only what they want to hear, i.e., only part of the word of God. Humans may lose sight of the goal. Thus humans in the very process of carrying out a mission can subvert it.

Along the covenantal way, a community is needed to rear and educate children and to pass on the covenant from generation to generation. But what about the natural tendency of communities to treasure only their own members? The message of universal love in the covenant of redemption can easily be turned inward onto the community and lead to a rejection of others. Such inwardness can turn a gospel of love into a rationalization of hatred, persecution, and murder. It can turn a religion that seeks redemption into a family business, conscious only of the need to take care of one's own immediate relatives.

There are many dialectical tensions built into the covenantal structure. There is grace, the divine role in the partnership, and the extraordinary initiative of God's love. Yet, the counterpart is the centrality of humans and the fullest participation of the human in the process. When they focus on the aspect of grace, both individuals and communities find it difficult to explore the limits and potential of human participation in covenant. Similarly, if one focuses on continuity in the covenant, it is difficult to plumb the depths of change and transformation in history. If, on the other hand, there is a community that is particularly quick to understand the role of transformation or change, it finds it difficult to adjust to the ongoing validity of tradition. Humans cannot keep the covenantal tensions in perfect balance. The key to upholding the totality of covenant and the fullest realization of the goal is that there be multiple communities working on many roads toward perfection—and that there be mutual criticism to keep standards high. Perhaps this is why the divine strategy utilized at least two covenantal communities. Even with Christianity and Judaism both in the world, neither religion has succeeded in bringing the final redemption to its fullest flowering.

Seen from this perspective—dare one say from the perspective of a divine strategy of redemption rather than from within the communities embedded in historical experience and needs?—both religions have more in common than they have been able to admit to themselves. Although they are independently valid faiths, they differ so fundamentally that the traditional record is dominated by bitter conflict. Yet both Judaism and Christianity share the totality of their dreams and the flawed finiteness of their methods. In each religion the dream is revolutionary, but it is embedded in a community and a tradition that work realistically for ultimate realization.

Both Judaism and Christianity dream of total transformation while remaining willing to accept the finitude and limitations of humans and go one step at a time. Both groups have persisted in preaching their messages despite their difficulties and historical suffering. And despite the terrible history of their relationship, each has witnessed to God and the human covenantal mission in its own way. For what often seems an eternity, both have hoped and waited, and both have transmitted the divine message and worked for the final redemption.

RESPONSES TO THE HOLOCAUST

In our lifetime, we have lived through the greatest assault in history on this vision of hope and on the covenantal way. The Holocaust was not only a triumph of death. It was the denial of all value to life. It is one thing to kill six million people—a devastating blow to the dreams of life's triumph. But there is a far more radical denial in the Holocaust. Consider the fact that Nazi operatives calculated in 1942 that if they worked the average Jewish prisoner to death over a period of nine months, the profit per person was 1,631 RM (Reichsmarks) on the average. The profit margin was enhanced by lowering the daily amount of food and by collecting the gold teeth and utilizing the bones and ashes of the cremated prisoners. It is one thing to kill people; it is another thing to number them and turn them into ciphers while they are still alive. That constitutes an active denial of the infinite value and uniqueness of the human.

It is one thing to kill people, but it is another thing to turn them into filth that stinks of excrement. It is one thing to kill Jews, but it is another to cut the asphyxiating gas supply per chamber load in half in 1944 to save money. That decision meant that it took twice as long to die in agony. By 1944, the Nazis had reached the ultimate efficiency. It cost less than one-half penny per person to gas the Jews in 1944. Then it was decided to throw Jewish children alive into the crematorium to save that one-half cent. Such decisions go beyond murder. They are theological decisions, affirmations of anti-values. They deny the image of God. They testify that life is worthless.

Such a successful mass murder and denial of the value of life poses the most radical question. As Richard Rubenstein argued, in such a setting the only messiah is death. Not the triumph of life but the triumph of death is the most accurate description of human history. In the perspective of Auschwitz, there is no hope. In Auschwitz, the whole covenantal way, with all of its remarkable accomplishments and with all of its wonderful contributions to human history, is revealed as an illusion.* This is the reality that Jews and Christians have lived through in our lifetime. It is the response to that reality that we must focus on now.

How did the two religious communities react to this total assault, this decisive victory for death? The more we reflect upon this response the more we realize the wisdom of the Divine: to depend on humans after all. Surely one of the great religious moments in history has been revealed in the human response to this overwhelming experience of death.

POWER AND THE RETURN TO HISTORY

Both religions responded in fundamental faithfulness to the covenant. They decided to go back into history and to face the challenge. For Jews, this meant the commitment to take power in order to protect and restore the value of life. Jews could not depend on waiting for the Messiah or on God's grace. They had to reassert the value of life by taking power. To restore the image of God in the individual Jew, they had to create a society, and an army, and a political structure that could truly uphold the infinite value of the human. Jews had to build a structure that promised that if in the future a Jew was excluded and isolated as a target for murder or for hunger or for death, there would be an Israeli paratrooper to come into Entebbe, or a Mossad agent who would sneak into Sudan or Ethiopia to take people out of starvation and oppression to life again. Jews knew that in order to take power and to renew the covenant of hope, they had to settle in the land that incarnated the biblical promise of restoration and renewal of the covenant. They had to overcome death with life, which is to say that they had to have children. The overwhelming majority of Jews did not despair of the Messiah, as Rubenstein's logic suggested they should. Rather, they despaired of waiting for the Messiah.

---

* I do not mean that both religions have identical problems with the Holocaust. This experience of hopelessness strikes a double blow at Christianity. In addition to the crisis of the unredeemed world that Jews confront, Christianity must confront the fact that it is implicated in creating the context of hatred that made Auschwitz possible. Nevertheless, the central crisis for both grows out of the shattered paradigm of the triumph of life.

Since they could not just wait, they decided that they had to take action to bring the Messiah.

Among Christians, similar responses have taken place, although not as universally. Among Christians, too, the overwhelming response has been a renewed commitment to redeem the world. The growth of the theology of liberation, with all the problematics it raises, is an affirmation of commitment not to accept life as it is, but to bring closer the final redemption. Christian self-critique and Christianity's commitment to become a gospel of love after serving as a source of hatred of Jews for 2,000 years bespeaks an extraordinary restoration of the purity of the covenant. The Christian search to recapture the human role in the covenant, expressed so powerfully in Vatican II, is an attempt to restore to the church a partially lost dimension of the role of the people of God and of community in history. Such affirmations of life and hope ought to be celebrated by Jews no less than Christians.

Both religions have made the commitment to take power in order to attempt to restore the credibility of the covenant. To take power in our time is a serious enterprise. To take power is to become more like God—that capability of *imitatio Dei* is also part of the ultimate vision. Henceforth, religion can no longer be seen as just a matter of spirituality. Taking power is an imitation of God, just as love is an ultimate connectedness with God, and just as consciousness is an identification with the Divine. All these qualities are characteristics of God.

When humans develop genetic engineering or nuclear power, they are taking on aspects of the power of God. When humans exercise democracy and freedom, they are imitating the capacity and humanity of God. Any assumption of divine power raises the possibility of idolatry, the risk of making partial human power absolute and using it without limit. Such an idolatrous attitude is evident when people turn nuclear power into world destruction, or genetic engineering into human manipulation. Such abuses turn freedom into license and anarchy, and art into violent pornography. A thousand other abuses are possible under freedom. Since the commitment to take power increases the moral risk for all humanity, one must intensify the demand for covenantal limits, for mutual criticism, and for multiple models. In short, we are more deeply drawn to the need for more than one covenantal community.

THE ETHICS OF POWER AFTER THE HOLOCAUST

The greatest challenge facing both religions today is how to handle the return into history. For Jews, the first step is to develop sufficient power for life. Israel is threatened. Israel needs enough power to protect itself. The first task for a people who are used to living in exile and powerlessness and existing on tolerance is to develop enough strength to stay alive. Israel needs enough power to give full dignity to its citizens. Indeed, every nation needs economic and political power if it is to give full dignity to its citizens. The need to develop adequate force is not yet sufficiently appreciated in the religious communities. Religions still remain nervous that human power will inevitably lead to competition with God's power. But first, they must learn that the true task is to be like God, i.e., to develop power. This effort leads directly to the second challenge: making sure that power is brought within a covenantal framework so that it is used appropriately.

Both religions face the urgent need to develop an ethic of power. Power does corrupt. Therefore, humanity is always in need of great help to avoid the cancerous corruption that grows as power grows exponentially. For example, Israel needs help to make sure that its citizens participate fully, that it not abuse its Arabs, and that it will not lose sight of its own humanity in defending itself against those who would kill it. That is why both Israel and other communities need all the ethical resources that religion can bring to them.

To prevent power from becoming abusive, both communities need to draw on any other source in society beyond religion that can help them. Jews must learn how to handle openness and freedom so that the process will not lead to assimilation or to disappearance. Jews need to learn how to use the freedom that they now possess wisely rather than to use its license to attack each other and delegitimate each other. Such internal abuse is something Jews were hesitant to inflict on each other when they were afraid of gentiles. Today, with comfort, security, and power in their hands, there is a real risk that Jews will split apart into multiple communities at war with one another.

As Jews discover their own power, they will in turn be enabled to discover the gentile, the Christian, as an image of God. Such a discovery can only come because of the dignity and mutual encounter made possible by a democratic society. When Jews were persecuted ghetto dwellers, they knew the gentile only as the inhuman enemy. The human dimension and the fullest religious dignity of Christians can only be uncovered through dialogue. Jews today are struggling with a new dialectic of universalism and particularism. The protection of the particular, which is a paramount concern throughout Jewish history, is being corrected to overcome the hostility of centuries that led to a cultural demeaning of gentiles and of Christianity. General rejection and negative stereotyping was a very normal human reaction. It represents in-group morality and defensiveness in response to Christian oppression and persecution of Jews. In a situation of power and acceptance, however, one cannot allow the same dismissal of the other. In sum, Jews today must learn to strike a balance between Jewish needs, as urgent and as difficult as these are, and Jewish contributions and obligations to the general society. Jews need both to be themselves and to participate alongside others for the sake of the larger vision.

JEWISH-CHRISTIAN DIALOGUE: THE NEXT STAGE

Let us apply these principles to Jewish-Christian dialogue. There can be no Judaism without Jews. Therefore, Christians must stop attempting to grow by spreading among Jews. Beyond merely ending proselytizing activities among Jews, Christians need to go after the anti-Semitism that is the residue of their own teachings. Anti-Semitism is the most ubiquitous, worldwide, permanent moral infection of human history. Sometimes one despairs of overcoming it. It has now spread in its more virulent form into the Arab world. It is being spread worldwide, even in countries where there are no, or hardly any, Jews, such as in Japan; all this by propaganda emanating from European racists, some left-wing universalists, terrorist Muslims, and some Arab countries as well as from marginal fundamentalist Christians.

It is not enough to stop teaching about Jews as "killers of Christ." The deeper challenge is to go back and uproot the very sources of the contagion that continue to pour this virulent infection into humanity's bloodstream. Christians must make sure that the Christian breakthroughs in understanding Judaism are transmitted and taught on the mass level. The morally and theologically remarkable work done by Christians in the dialogue of the last 20 years has one serious weakness. It remains basically the possession of a minority of inspired people. It is not yet understood properly at the mass level and not yet dominant at the upper decision-making levels.

Christians need to learn to take worldly holiness and liberation seriously without slipping into romanticizing the Third World. Usually, that way ends up with the Christians viewing Israel and American Jews negatively. Such a "romantic" Christian worldview is a real possibility in Christian thought today. Christians are used to seeing Jews as the oppressed and as paradigms of powerlessness. Jews have traditionally played such a role in the Christian imagination, as for example in the "wandering Jew" motif in Western literature. What will Christianity do with Jews who have achieved power, as in Israel, or economic success, as in the United States? Will Jews now become the symbol of bourgeois wealth?

All these issues represent valid Jewish concerns after the Holocaust, but it would be self-indulgent for Jews to stop there in the dialogue. As Jews work with Christians, they will discover the ethical power of Christianity, the religious depth of its liturgical life, and the extraordinary effects of its religious models, even the models that are most remote from Jewish perception of the past 1,800 years. In so doing, Jews will begin to discover the positive aspects of Christian "otherness." Jews will have to fight the patronizing tendency to discover Christianity as a wonderful religion only because it is so similar to Judaism. A more searching understanding of Christianity needs to be developed and articulated by the Jewish community today.

TOWARD A JEWISH THEOLOGY OF CHRISTIANITY

Authentic Jews deeply rooted in their own tradition must struggle to do justice to the organic relationship of Judaism and Christianity. Jews must confront the fact that the separation and the career of Christianity, as painful, as bloody, and as ugly as it has been vis-à-vis Judaism, cannot simply be dismissed as a deviation from covenant history. Historically, Jews have been reluctant to admit the possibility of partnership. While there is both risk (that Christian fundamentalists could abuse such recognitions to try to missionize Jews) and resistance (from Jews who fear that the minority's survival is endangered if there is greater openness and respect for the majority culture), this is a time for heroic measures to advance the cause of redemption. This has ever been the proper covenantal response to great setbacks in history.

In light of the Holocaust, Jews must develop a theology of non-Jewish religions that will articulate their full spiritual dignity. One cannot simply treat them as pale reflections of Judaism. A new theology is ethically necessary. As we learned from the Holocaust, when one treats others as having less spiritual dignity than oneself, the temptation is to stand by when they are physically in danger as well. Theological contempt cannot be separated from human responsibility. It is hard enough to risk your life to save somebody you look up to and admire. It is almost impossible to do it for someone you think is intellectually dense or spiritually inferior. The tradition of spiritual contempt led many Christians to abandon Jews in the Holocaust. Jews who have suffered this indignity in the past must strive harder not to be guilty of similar misjudgments. "What is hateful to you, do not do to others." This is the summary of the whole Torah, according to our master Hillel.

Secondly, Jews must develop the ability to recognize the full implications of the truth that the Lord has many messengers. While it is true that Jews have always believed that there is salvation for the individual outside of

Judaism, this generality does not do justice to the full spiritual dignity of others who, after all, live their lives in religious communities, and not just as individuals.

Finally, given human limitations and the corrupting effect of power, only the wide distribution of political, cultural, and theological power can ensure the safety of the world. A moral balance of power is the best guarantor of moral behavior. It follows that Jews need the presence of Christianity and other religions, as religions need the presence of secular movements, to prevent any one group from attaining societal domination that can lead to oppression. Thus, the presence of many spiritual power centers will enable humanity to move toward the creation of the kingdom of God.

Here then are some thoughts from a Jewish perspective on taking Christianity seriously as a religion on its own terms as well as on our own.

EXODUS, MESSIAH, AND RESURRECTION

Both religions grow out of the Exodus. The Exodus is a fundamental event of liberation, which points beyond itself to further redemptions. The prophets understood this clearly. If the dream is the ultimate triumph of life, then the Exodus is not the end. It is the beginning of the process. The test of Judaism's vitality is that it will continue to generate further movements toward messianic redemption. As long as Judaism generates messiahs, one can be certain that it is alive.

When Judaism stops generating messiahs, it is no longer faithful to its own tradition. That does not mean that every messiah is the final one, or even a true one. It does mean that the messianic impulse is a fundamental test of Judaism's own integrity. In that sense, Christianity is not a mere deviation or misunderstanding, but an organic outgrowth of Judaism itself.

Contrary to what most modern Jews think, the statement of Resurrection made by Christianity grows out of authentic Jewish models. In classical Judaism, resurrection is a legitimate hope. Resurrection is the ultimate statement of the triumph of life. Belief in resurrection is at the heart of Rabbinic teaching; the Rabbis placed the affirmation of this belief near the head of the central Jewish prayer.

The early Christians, nurtured by this Jewish hope, decided to follow the Jew whom they had experienced as a messiah. When the other Jews did not accept this conclusion, the Christians were tempted to interpret this rejection as blindness. The Jewish riposte was: "How can you believe in the Messiah when you see the ongoing presence of death and oppression and suffering?" To this Christians answered, "The kingdom of God is within you."

To remove the cognitive dissonance of a world still suffering evil and op-pression, Christians were tempted to remove the worldly dimension from their vision and to insist that in the spiritual dimension redemption had in fact been achieved. In this way, Christians were motivated to put forth a tri-umphalist interpretation of their relationship to Judaism: Judaism was the carnal, first-stage faith; Christianity was the "true" faith because it raised re-demption to the plane of spirit and eternity instead of remaining fixated at the level of the body and temporality. To this spiritual triumphalism, the Jewish response has been that history shows that Jesus was a "false mes-siah" and Christianity is an otherworldly religion that fails to take concrete history into account.

With the perspective of 1,800 years and of the last 50, perhaps it is time to reassess the ancient family quarrel between Jews and Christians. Over the centuries, in situations where Jews were trying simply to survive surrounded by a vast majority that was hostile, they could not step back and take a dif-ferent perspective on the issue. Perhaps it takes the shattering of worlds rep-resented by the Holocaust to allow new thinking. Perhaps it takes the humility of both communities, existing in a modern world in which all indi-vidual religions are dwarfed, to admit this.

Jews today need to look at the issue, not just from the internal commu-nity vantage point, but from the perspective of the hypothetical divine plan. Assume there is a divine strategy for redeeming the world using human agents; assume it is the divine will that Judaism and Christianity are together in the world; assume that both are ways of affirming both "yet" and "not yet" with regard to redemption. Assume both are true but that each needs the other to embody the fullest statement of the covenan-tal goal and process. What one individual cannot say without being hypo-critical or confused, two communities can state as a balance and corrective toward each other.

THE DIALECTICS OF RELIGIOUS CLAIMS*

The covenant's dialectical moves of divine grace and human participa-tion provide an example. In Hebrew Scripture, humans achieve holiness through family and land, within the natural human order. Yet the very emphasis of the covenant on the natural order leads people to naturalize and

---

* This section (and the whole essay) explore how Jewish and Christian religious approaches complement each other and how the two faiths, in sum, provide a more rounded religious strategy than each one separately. The same explanation can, and should, be applied to other re-ligions, but this book deals only with these two religions.

to domesticate—and even to defeat—the divine claims. So the temporally and spatially rooted Jewish religion needs the universal, landless church perspective as a corrective.

The focus on life and appreciation for the family as the context for the covenant is distinctively Jewish. But no religion that is strong in one pole of the dialectic is likely to do full justice to the other aspect. To preserve the balance, Judaism needs a religion determined to explore the fullness of death, to explore what it would mean to break out of the family model and create a universal, self-defined belief group. Judaism has brought humans even more powerfully into participation in the covenant process (compare the passivity of the biblical temple pilgrim with the activity of the Rabbinic Jewish individuals praying in the synagogue); it needs a counterpart religion that is prepared to explore the element of grace and transcendence in a more central way. Each tradition, to be faithful to its own vision, needs the other in order to correct and to exemplify the fullness of the Divine-human interaction. In this perspective, each religion's experience, viz., Jewish covenant peoplehood and Christian faith community, is more than validated. Each faith's organizational form is also recognized as a valid expression of the plenitude of divine love and the comprehensiveness of the human role in the covenant.

One Christian interpretation of the emergence of their faith has been that Jews lost the vision. Why? Because Christians have experienced their own chosenness, so they assumed that Jews have lost theirs. But why? Why is God not capable of communicating to gentiles through sacramental experiences and to Jews through a more natural order? Why insist that new experiences exhaust God's potential? Why insist that any religious experiences, however valid, impugn the competence or quality of the other?

The general Jewish position has been that Jesus was a false messiah. Why? Would it not be more precise to say that a false messiah is one who teaches the wrong values and who turns sin into holiness? A more accurate description, from a Jewish perspective, would be that Jesus was not a "false" but a "failed" messiah. He has not finished the job but his work is not in vain.*

---

* Since the religion in his name persecuted Jews, spread hatred, and degraded Judaism, then the term *false* messiah was well earned. The term *failed* messiah recognizes that for hundreds of millions, Christianity was, and is, a religion of love and consolation, i.e, the right values. Use of the term also presupposes that the religion in his name stops teaching hatred of Jews and becomes a source of healing support for the Jewish people and a purveyor of respect for Judaism. If it continues to nurture stereotypes and hatred of Jews—or if it misuses these more positive views of Christianity in order to missionize Jews—then it proves that Jesus was a false messiah, after all.

Of course, Christians will hesitate to accept this definition—as will Jews, perhaps more so. Christians will be deeply concerned: Is this a dismissal of Jesus? Does this term demean classic Christian affirmations of Jesus' messiahship and the Incarnation? Jews will be concerned: Is this a betrayal of the classic Jewish insistence that the Messiah has not yet come? Does this term breach Judaism's self-respecting boundary that excludes Christian claims?

I believe that none of these fears are warranted. The term "failed messiah" is an example of the kind of theological language we should be seeking to develop in the dialogue, for it allows for a variety of Christian and Jewish self-understandings. Some Christians will translate this term into their view of Jesus as a proleptic messiah. Others will insist on their own traditional understanding of Jesus' messiahship, but will see in the term a divinely willed, much needed spur to believers to confront the fact that the world is not yet perfect and that their task is unfinished. Other Christians who insist on Jesus' trinitarian status will hear the phrase "failed messiah" as a reminder that God's self-presentation is deeply humble, not triumphalist. God is identified with the weak and the defeated, and with the power of persuasion by model rather than victory by intimidation. Some Jews will read this term as a description of Jesus' actual role in Jewish history; others will understand it as an affirmation of the Jewish "no" to all claims to finality in this unredeemed world. Still others will understand the term as a tribute to Jesus' extraordinary accomplishments, since under the impact of his model, a major fraction of humanity has been brought closer to God and to redemption.

Is calling Jesus a failed messiah a form of damning with faint praise? No. Such failures are the key to success of the divine strategy of redemption. If one understands covenantally that human life does not end in one lifetime, then the meaning of failure is even more ambiguous—and in this case, positive.

Christianity has held a supersessionist view of history. The Christian interpretation of the destruction of the Second Temple saw it as the divine refutation of Judaism. Little did Christians realize that even in this ugly interpretation of Jewish history, one designed to obliterate the Jews, they were pursuing a deeply Jewish hermeneutic by interpreting history as the carrier of a divine message. To interpret the destruction of the Temple as in some way a divine call is a recognizably Jewish form of reaction to historical events. By fixing on an outward, triumphalist, and hateful interpretation, Christianity missed a deeper alternative whereby God was calling Jews to a higher level of service in the covenant by ending the Temple sacrifices.

Blinding themselves to the vitality and growth of Jewish tradition, Christians were led to overemphasize the miraculous and the sacramental within Christianity. By distorting Judaism's image and presenting it as a fossil, Christians failed to see the truly innovative form of Rabbinic Judaism—its affirmation of covenantal continuity through humans taking more responsibility for the covenant. In Rabbi Joseph B. Soloveitchik's words, through Rabbinic response and the development of *halakhah*, humans become co-creators of Torah, the divine word.

By dismissing Judaism as legalism, Christians are tempted not to hear the divine calling that they become more active in the unfolding of the covenantal way. A less triumphalist, more humble Christianity might have interpreted the continuation of Judaism as the divine summons to Jews to build on the Hebrew Scripture and grow into a new level of participation in the covenant. At the same time, Christianity may have been elected to uphold the sacramental dimension of biblical tradition more powerfully.

The Rabbis grasped that the destruction of the Temple was not the end of Judaism. They understood it as the outgrowth of another divine covenantal move, of a self-limiting God acting to call humans to greater participation in the covenant. Some Christians interpreted the destruction of the Temple as divine rejection of Israel. Such an interpretation takes the infinite divine love—whose grace all humans need—and reduces it to the point where it is not adequate to deal with the flaws of the original people of God. If the divine love could not encompass flawed, fallible Jewry even as it reached out to embrace humanity, then how can it be adequate to the task of healing and redeeming all of humankind? And if the original covenant is so fragile and liable to forfeit, then how flimsy is the rock on which the church is built?

It would have been a more charitable and loving interpretation of God's actions to explain it as a call to the people of Israel to enter exile and to develop an ethic of powerlessness. That ethic preserved the dignity of Jews over the centuries and provided a model for survival in a world of oppression and exile. Inspired by this call, Judaism developed models of *halakhah* that sanctified all of life, not just the holy Temple. *Halakhah* pointed to God in the everyday and in the natural process of history and not just in overt miracles and sacramental incarnations that overwhelmed humans.

Rabbinic tradition accomplished all this not because it failed to recognize "the time of its visitation," but because it was prepared to hear new divine instruction even as it was faithful to the old. Thus Rabbinic tradition is profoundly continuous with the Bible, while at the same time teaching and concretizing a transformation of the human roles in the covenant. It is not too late for Christianity to learn these models from Jews, even as it is not too

179

late for Jews to focus again on grace and the sacramental and the universal in Christianity. Jews, too, need a corrective lest they lose the richness of the divine will and covenantal dialectic.

AN ORGANIC MODEL FOR JEWISH-CHRISTIAN RELATIONS

Judaism denied the occurrence of divine incarnation; it needed to be authentic to its own religious life. This tempted it to overlook the genuinely Jewish dimension of this Christian attempt to close the gap between the human and the Divine. Even while rejecting the model, should Jews not recognize that it grows out of the tormenting persistence of a great distance between the divine-sought perfection and the human condition? One can conceive of a divine pathos that sent not only words across the gap, but life and body itself. I say this not as a Jew who accepts this claim, but as one who has come to see that it is not for me to prescribe to God how God communicates to others. Our task is to find ways for humans to hear God. We should measure religions by the criterion of how people act after they hear the word in community. If Incarnation and Resurrection of Jesus lead to Christian triumphalism, persecution, and idolatry, then Christianity proves itself to be false. If Christianity leads to deeper compassion and understanding and a grasp of the human realities, human needs, and motivated covenantal action, then it validates itself as a channel of the Divine.

Both communities are challenged now to see the other without the filters of stereotype and defensiveness. Since we do not own God, we should be grateful for our own religious experiences—and for the experiences of others. One can go beyond this not only to an acknowledgment of pluralism, but also to an affirmation of the organic nature of the relationship between the two faiths. How else could multiple models be created except in communities that must have their own inner élan, their own procedures, their own hierarchy, and their own standard symbols of participation?

One essential implication of the covenant is that there has to be a plurality of legitimate symbols if the divine intention is to raise humans to the fullest capacities of life. The alternative is that there will be only one religion, one's own. It should be the prayer of believers in this time at least, given the power that humans now have, that one's own group not be the only religion. If indeed we believe that our exclusivity is what God wants, we should be praying that that cup pass from our lips. Perhaps all humans should be praying for the courage and strength to argue with God, and to convince God that humanity will arrive at perfection faster if God follows through on the pluralist implications of the covenantal model.

 A PERSONAL WITNESS

In my teaching, I personally continue to affirm the covenant of Israel and the role of the Jewish community as central to God's plans. I proudly assert the remarkable balance of family, tradition, life, and vision in Judaism. In the past, I would use as a counterpoint in such presentations the image of Christianity as making unreasonable, otherworldly demands. As a rabbi who has had the chance to have a family, I all too often used celibacy as a counter-model, an example of the lack of humanness in Christianity. Or, I would hold up the image of the cross as a symptom of Christianity's excessive demands. It took years in the Jewish-Christian dialogue before I came to see the extraordinary power of those very models that I was patronizing and dismissing.

I was in Sri Lanka in 1974 for a world dialogue of religions. During the conference, we were taken to visit a local village. There I discovered a group of Christians who had left affluent, successful lives in Scandinavia to dwell in the interior of Sri Lanka to set up a little village for brain-damaged children. Typically, such children were abandoned by their parents to death because in the midst of that poverty, parents could not even take care of healthy children. How moved I was. Here were people who left a life of ease and affluence to go 7,000 miles away to live in poverty and to take care of brain-damaged children. They had to take care of them totally; much of the time they wiped them and changed them. The children could do very little. The caretaker's only reward was to watch the children lie there and moan and look at them. Few children could adequately respond to those that treated them.

Suddenly I was struck by the fact that this unreasonable religion with its incredible demands elicits that kind of response. As a rabbi, I rarely elicited such kinds of behavior—precisely because I did not make "unreasonable" demands. As a rabbi I expected—and accepted—a touch of holiness in everyday activities; I did not anticipate such sacrificial, heroic levels of behavior. In that moment of insight, I realized that my stereotyping dismissals of Christianity had blinded me to one of its greatest religious strengths. Simultaneously, I was tempted into being too reasonable in my expectations of myself and my own community.

To be fair to the Jewish position, it can be argued that perhaps it is more difficult to be a spiritual hero every day in a bourgeois existence than it is to go off and make that kind of lifetime commitment. It may be easier to make self-renouncing moves such as accepting monastic celibacy than to take the daily responsibility and frustration of having to love a wife, or raise a child, or meet a payroll. Having said that, it strikes me that my own Jewishness could grow so much more by taking seriously the sacrificial models offered by Christianity instead of trying to score points at Christians' expense. Christians similarly are tempted to glorify their faith's power and to ignore the fact that Judaism's "normal mysticism," with its strengthening of human models, is both profoundly human and deeply religious. Christians have consistently underestimated one of Judaism's greatest triumphs, the *halakhah*, which has hallowed every aspect of life in such brilliant fashion. Typically Christians have dismissed it as tribalism, legalism, or as a lower level of spirituality. The price Christianity paid for this was a persistent loss of worldly spirituality and excessive quietism and asceticism.

Once the triumphalism stops, one discovers that the very themes one dismissed in the other are present in one's own repertoire. Heroic self-sacrifices and spiritual renunciation are profound, if less-stressed, themes in Judaism, just as the motifs of going into exile or the peoplehood of those who believe in God are present in Christianity. This is not to say that the two faiths are identical. There are fundamental differences in priorities, method, and form as well as in beliefs and history. Yet if one looks carefully, even the differences are nuanced. Major themes in Judaism show up as minor themes in Christianity. Major themes in Christianity, including themes that Jews try to dismiss (such as the kingdom of God as a primary spiritual phenomenon, which is found in the Kabbalah) are in fact important minor themes in Judaism. A much more integral approach would have been to admit from the outset that each group has these tendencies and to deal with them in their natural development. A humbler assessment of our own capacity (coming out of a commitment not to distort or use the covenant for our own purposes) would lead to a more positive attitude toward the other community and willingness to use the other faith as a benchmark to check our own excesses and to learn from the other. Each faith should welcome the other as the spiritual and moral check and balance for the sake of the kingdom that we all seek to create.

THE TASKS BEFORE US

Both religions have a major task at hand in the generation after the Holocaust. Both religions need to take up the charge of correcting their own deviations from the covenantal way. They need to overcome the denials of the image of God in the other, which erode the religious power of each faith tradition. Both have to take up the challenge of developing a liturgical community that can nurture the image of God and thus help humankind avoid being swept into idolatry of secular power. Both communities need the humility of learning from secularism and from each other.

Paradoxically, giving up the stereotypes and hatred and giving up the negative otherness of the other opens up the risk of assimilation and of losing ourselves. But we gain the possibility of richness in our own understanding and of an identity that is not dependent on the denial of the other. We act out of weakness in retaining the otherness of others because we are afraid we cannot withstand the temptations growing out of choice. Is not the ultimate message of the covenant that God wants us to exercise choice?

Models of faith are what we have to gain from each other. Those models evoke our own deepest possibilities. Thanks to the openness and respectfulness of American society, those models reach across religious lines. A Christian's self-sacrifice or prophetic self-criticism or a Buddhist's willingness to incinerate himself (while avoiding inflicting casualties on others) in defiance of evil can inspire a Jew or a Muslim whose experience is totally different. These models bring out possibilities that I never before saw in myself. Thus, as each religion struggles with its own corrupt tendencies, it can turn not just inward for help but to other groups for external guidance and inspiration. As David Hartman has suggested, perhaps now that Jews have returned to Israel they will have enough power and enough self-assurance to face Christians as equals with respect and with deeper understanding (in the process, giving up the defensiveness and fear of past relationships).

What will we accomplish by doing this? Both religions can show the world a model of service. Both groups would show that we understand that, as believers, we are channels and vehicles of the Divine, not the imperialist owners of God. In a world that kills en masse for that which it believes in but is religiously tolerant because people do not care about religion, in a world where the secular authorities have now slaughtered on a scale to match and surpass the old religious wars, perhaps we can start over again by checking all the stereotypes. Those who glorify the secular and those who glorify the religious can admit that humans own neither God nor other humans. Let the various religious and ethical models shine forth; let us challenge each other to grow and deepen and hear the call of God to advance redemption and to renew the covenant in this generation.

This is a special part of the mission of this generation: to renew revelation, to continue the covenantal way, and to discover each other. At least let these two religions model the truth that the love of God leads to the total discovery of the image of God in the other, not to its distortion or elimination. If committed and believing Christians and Jews can discover the image of God in each other, if they can uncover and affirm each one's proper role in the overall divine strategy of redemption, surely the inspiration of this example would bring the kingdom of God that much closer for everyone.

Covenantal Pluralism

"You are my witnesses, says the LORD" (Isa. 43:10). The people of Israel are God's servants called—yes, chosen—to witness to their loving God and the divine plan for humanity and the cosmos. In my usage here, "the people of Israel" refers not to Israelis alone or to Jews only but to all who affirm that God has made a valid covenant with Abraham and his descendants and all who take up the covenantal task of world redemption so the covenant can be fulfilled, for that is the purpose of making the covenant. That is to say, Christians also—and, indeed, Muslims too—are recognized as Abraham's cherished children, at least when they purge themselves of supersessionist claims and hatred of Jews.

To be true to its witness, the people of Israel tell three stories to the world, i.e., the rest of humanity, in the presence of God and in the presence of their fellow human beings. Drawing from their many experiences and traditions, they tell (1) the story of Creation, the divine vision of an intended perfect world; we stake our existence, both as Jews and as Christians, that this world will come to be; (2) the story of covenant, that process operating through a Divine-human partnership whereby our imperfect world will be brought to that state of perfection; and (3) the story of redemption, sometimes called the end of days or the Messiah story, which is the culmination and realization of the process. At the end, as our story goes, holistic perfection will be achieved. There will be peace between humans, between humans and all the rest of life, between all of life and nature itself, and between all of the above and God. To put it another way, these three stories add up to one comprehensive story that I believe is best described as the triumph of life.

This master story can be summarized. We (i.e., all living things, sustained and nurtured by God) will fill the world with life. We will reshape the historical reality, the flesh-and-blood world we inhabit, to sustain that life at the highest level. Life will multiply and triumph *quantitatively* over all its enemies, including death and disorder. Life will equally triumph *qualitatively.* All of life's capacities will be developed fully and realized. When life blossoms in its fullest capacity in a world that treats all of life—especially human life, the most developed form—and sustains it with the highest and fullest respect that it deserves, then life will be in harmony with existence and deeply related to God, its source and sustainer. That is our story and our claim.

Telling this story of Creation is our witness. The present facts contradict the narrative fairly substantially. Still, the story of Creation is shared and told, almost as one, by Jews and Christians alike. This story leads humans to see existence—as best we can—from the cosmic perspective, *sub specie aeternitatis.* From that vantage point, what do we see as Jews and Christians? There are three grand movements in the unfolding pattern of this cosmos. First, the world is moving *from chaos to order,* from the moment of the big bang when there was not even a law of nature to the regularity and dependability of the laws of the world we inhabit.

Second, the world is moving from *nonlife to life.* This is the surprising claim of our tradition. Over these billions of years the world has moved from a state in which no life existed to the emergence of life. From that one cell, however many times replicated, life has grown quantitatively and developed qualitatively; it has luxuriated and spread into a vast range of forms over a variety of sustaining conditions. The statement that life is growing and, indeed, that the world is moving from nonlife to life is counterintuitive. How can one account for the ascending current of life when we all encounter death in almost every moment of our lives? We know that all living things die. The answer, of course—the key—is God, the hidden, infinite source of life with limitless goodness, love, and power that sustain life and nurture every possible form of life into being.

This divine source evokes the third grand movement of the cosmos in which we participate. Life is growing ever more to resemble its ground, God. Life moves *from being less to becoming more and more like God.* The highest form of life, the human, represents the high point reached thus far. In human form, life so resembles its Maker that it is called—in the Bible that we share—the "image of God." This emergence of the image of God is the turning point in cosmic history according to our two faiths. Up to that point, life had been sworn to "be fruitful and multiply" (sociobiologists would call it "maximizing reproductive success") through a built-in controlling program, a selfish gene, if you will, that drives the process. The image of God's consciousness is so much like God's that humans are able to grasp this over-all pattern (of which we ourselves are part) and to join voluntarily in its realization. Similarly, the human image of God has a capacity to love that is so much like God's that humans are able to love all their fellow creatures and every aspect of the universe, as well as the Maker of it all and the beauty of the plan. Once humans understand and embrace this understanding, they will lovingly identify with and willingly participate in the process of perfection; at least that is what our religions believe.

So, God has invited us as humans, the image of God, to enter into a covenantal partnership—a partnership of committed love—to join fully in perfecting the universe, *tikun olam*. The people of Israel joyfully acknowledge, or we should joyfully acknowledge, that God's first covenant, the Noahide covenant—never superseded—is made with all of humanity, not with Jews and not with Christians alone. Indeed, it is made with all sentient beings. All are called to recognize and participate in Creation's patterns, to accept limits, to direct their choices and actions to the side of life. We are called upon to join in working for order against chaos. We are chosen to become part of the process of the movement from nonlife to life. We are commanded to increase life and to make it grow ever more like its Maker. The purpose of the religious way of life is to create the nurturing ambience of memory and experience, of relationships and actions that sustain human growth and turn it toward God.

Being in the image of God brings with it more than godlike capacities. It bestows intrinsic dignity, a climactic extension of that respect to which all of life is entitled.

The people of Israel hold these truths to be self-evident: that all humans are created in the image of God and endowed by their Creator with certain inalienable dignities, among which are *infinite value, equality,* and *uniqueness,* the birthright of every son and every daughter of God.

Now we can offer a fuller definition of the triumph of life, the great theme of the Creation narrative. The world will be filled with life, especially life in the image of God. In order to perfect life qualitatively as well as quantitatively, humans must develop their godlike qualities, to become ever more like God. Consciousness (enabling understanding of the greatest mysteries of the universe), relationship (including love of existence and all existent beings), the power of life and death, and the power to shape chaos into order, will, and freedom—these are God's qualities. We are called to develop the analogous human capacities to their limit. *Imitatio Dei* is the central religious path. Humans are to walk in God's ways by acting and becoming more and more like God. In turn, these capacities are to be used to upgrade the world, particularly to increase its capacity to sustain and nurture life at its highest dignity. A world that was restructured to respect human life's infinite value, human life's fundamental equality, and the uniqueness of every person—such a world would have to be a paradise. Poverty, hunger, oppression, all forms of systematized discrimination (e.g., racism, sexism, and anti-Semitism), all war, sickness, and even death would have to be overcome. Ultimately, these conditions are incompatible with the intrinsic dignities of the image of God, with the infinite value and uniqueness of each person.

The prophetic vision that Jews and Christians share teaches us that in the end the human-Divine partnership will voluntarily and jointly re-create Earth as paradise, as the Garden of Eden that was the originally intended venue for human existence in the bosom of God. A Garden of Eden created—not bestowed by a Father, however generously that Parent may give or play favorites in so doing—becomes the Garden we have created all of us together, which will be shared equally by all human and all living creatures together.

As Jews and Christians, we are called to witness to Creation. We urge all humans to join in this process with one elemental commitment: to choose life and not death in all that we do. We urge that, no matter how long inequity, deprivation, and powerlessness exist, humans not surrender this universal vision of improvement. As members of covenanted religions, we are committed to take up the task of perfecting the world, resisting the temptation to betray the goal by abandoning the deprived to their fate in order to live with our own advantage.

To show the way toward that perfect world, we tell the second story of the process of perfection, the story of covenant. The main point of this shared covenant story is that God has summoned humans to partnership in this process of perfecting the world. The divine respect and love for humans eventually leads to a full and equal partnership. (The term "eventually" refers to the maturation of the covenant, which we are living through in our time.) Initially, the covenant is hardly an equal partnership; still, out of divine respect, God calls all humans to participate in our own liberation. As the biblical stories of the Garden of Eden and the Flood indicate, God is often tempted to bestow perfection or to force humans to be free. But God must resist that temptation, and, indeed, we must also.

Giving or living the covenant represents a choice not to follow the main alternative historical policies that have been followed to perfect the world. To choose covenant as the vehicle of redemption represents a decision not to bestow perfection by divine grant or miracle. Similarly, the process of covenant is in tension with the dream of perfection through apocalyptic action. The affirmation of this worldly covenant represents a rejection of the idea that redemption will occur through spiritual enlightenment only. If covenant is the way to perfection, then release from this world (seeing through existence and finding it an illusion) is not the answer. This latter way is the path of Kabbalah and of pietistic salvation, as of most Eastern religions, but it is not what covenant is about. Covenant rules out escape to another world, not even to a world to come, where perfection exists now. Finally, the Divine-human joint venture is a methodological alternative to a purely human revolution, in which humans take full charge, releasing themselves from God in order to achieve revolutionary transformation in their lifetime. Let it be noted that the path of smashing the old regime and perfecting the world now has been the main competitor with Jewish-Christian-Muslim loyalty over the last two centuries.

Each of these alternative methods includes elements of the covenantal mechanism. Each is an outcome of the breakdown of the dialectical tensions held together in covenant. Each of these alternatives makes its appearance in Jewish and Christian traditions also. Ultimately the method of covenant negates those alternatives in favor of the continuous, this-worldly, permanent process of perfection carried out by humans responsible to (and sustained by) the divine partner.

Covenant is in service of the fulfillment of Creation. It tells each one of us, addressing us collectively as organized in communities, that there is a cosmic struggle (reflected in each of us personally as well) between the force of life and the force of death. As humans we are asked to direct all our actions to the side of life. No action is neutral in this struggle. Since the goal of covenant is the triumph of life, its primary commandment is "Choose life" (Deut. 30:19).

"Behold I place before you today life and good, death and evil" (Deut. 30:15). The apposition is intentional. In every good act is the choice of life. That is the definition of good. There is in every evil act a choice of death. That is the definition of evil. Since we live in an imperfect world and humans are finite and flawed, not every action is a pure choice of life or death. Hence, we have guiding principles in our covenantal codes. In all situations, given what cannot be changed, there is still an ideal way to behave: to maximize the choice of life.

The covenant proceeds on certain assumptions. First, "I, God, am with [you] in trouble" (Ps. 91:15). The process of upgrading starts where humans are, in the suffering, evil-stained, broken reality where we live. God reaches out, often initiates, and often helps, but humans must respond and take full responsibility.

Second, human models are needed and chosen to serve as pacesetters. That is what Israel, the covenant people, is about; therefore, that is what being a Jew or a Christian is about. Chosenness is not some inner charisma that I possess; nor is it some benefit bestowed arbitrarily. Even when unmerited grace is given, Scripture never loses sight of the greater vision that it serves. Election is predicated upon the redemption of humanity and is intended to advance that process. The inscrutable mystery is by what right anybody plays this role. In any event, the Torah does not start with the mystery of election, with the "beloved son," but with Creation itself. This paradigm people, the people of Israel, is meant to serve the advancement of the perfection of Creation. Election is not an end in itself; that would be idolatry. The people of Israel are human, of course, all too human. They frequently fail to live up to their mission. The avant-garde often substitutes sovereignty for service, self-glorification for servanthood, and corporate advantage and interest for priesthood. Those weaknesses (I do not mean to be cynical) only make the human pacesetting model more attainable by other human beings, for who is capable of totally selfless existence in God's presence?

Third, human emotions ought to be respected and built on. People have distinctive roots, languages, memories, and relationships. People do not grow in vacuums or in a "generic" humanity. They grow in communities, and communities have their own needs, their own lives, and their own distinctive patterns. The covenantal process starts with the affirmation that God loves us in our particularity, in our distinctiveness, in our body odor, in our pettiness, in our greatness, and, of course, in our historical existence as Jews or Christians or Muslims or Buddhists or whatever we are. First, we understand and affirm that truth; then we widen our own community and embrace the whole world eventually. To deny particularity and attachment, to engage in rejection of family and parent-child obligations for the sake of humanity's perfection, runs a real risk of undercutting love and turning people inhumane. This is the subtext of the Genesis stories.

To love a child is to play favorites. However, if one is not capable of loving a child or a parent particularly closely, then one is less than human. The challenge of covenant is to grow, to expand that consciousness and that sympathy for my own family until I come to the deepest truth: that everybody is my brother and sister. We are all children of Adam and Eve. Jews and Christians have differed sharply in the relative weight and risks in this balance of particular and universal, but, wherever the emphasis is placed, there are no guarantees of achieving the perfect equilibrium. Judaism sought to uphold family, but this ideal easily sinks into tribalism. Christianity sought to break through to all of humanity, but this idea often ends up as the imperialist agenda of an all-conquering missionary party, pushing for its own interests.

Fourth, the human pace is the true rate of perfecting the world. One must learn to live with a process that takes so long. Since the covenantal goal cannot be achieved in one lifetime, the vision and the mission must be passed on from generation to generation, or the cause will die unfinished along the way. To pass on the covenant, one must create a partnership between the generations, not just between God and Israel. That means one must have children or adopt them. One must create a community to transmit values and memory. In order to achieve transmission, the community needs institutions and boundary practices and leadership characters and distinctive rituals that nurture and express its humanity. But these very mechanisms often create barriers and burdens; they generate enmities and hostilities. They often misdirect the community's energy. However, there is no other way of carrying out the mission—if one wants to work with humans.

The elected people of Israel play three classic roles as an avant-garde. First and foremost, they are teachers of humanity. They spread the vision, telling of God's wondrous ways. They educate us not to settle, not to sell out, and not to lose patience. Second, they serve as a model community, the living exemplification of the values and the path to perfection. They inspire by example, which means sanctification of God's name *(kiddush ha-Shem)*, or they offer a model of failure that degrades the divine reputation *(hillul ha-Shem)*. Last but not least, they are also coworkers with other humans in the process of perfection, because the divine covenantal love is not exhausted with any one people. After all, the Philistines were brought out of Caphtor and the Aramaians from Kir just as much as Israel was brought out of Egypt. Others can give their witness and their model as well. That also is the genius of covenant; it enables us to affirm the particularity of each group, to make room for other groups to give their witness and exemplify their particular way, as well.

Judaism and Christianity share the conviction that the covenant with Abraham, Sarah, and their descendants is foundational. It is the starting point of our journey. Both affirm the authenticity and authority of the Sinaitic covenant that transformed Abraham's way of God into the way of life of a people. However, we know that in the first century, in the midst of Judaism's encounter with Hellenism and in the course of a wracking political struggle, Jewish Christianity was born within the body of the Jewish people. This occurred shortly before the Jews experienced catastrophic destruction, exile, and powerlessness. For Judaism, over the course of the next centuries, this exile became a moment of covenant renewal, the flowering of Rabbinic Judaism. The Rabbis understood that God had self-limited to enable greater play for human decisions to shape the outcomes of history. In contrast to God's treatment of the Egyptians, God had not stopped the Romans. In allowing the destruction of the Temple, God had become more hidden in order to call Israel to a fuller, more responsible partnership in the covenant. The hidden God was more present. The *Shekhinah* was everywhere—but had to be discovered. So the Rabbis educated the people as to how they could experience and practice holiness everywhere. They developed an ethic of powerlessness that gave dignity and meaning to Jewish life in the worst of exilic circumstances.

The Christians—attracted by Jesus' charisma, and moved by the retelling of his story—became convinced that the Messiah, the fulfiller of messianic promises, had come among them. Therefore, salvation was available right now. The mainstream of Christianity also became convinced, or at least affirmed in its faith, that God had become flesh, had become human, in order to achieve the goals of the covenant. Faith in Jesus, rather than Jewish observance, now opened the covenant to all of humanity. Ironically, this last accomplishment, i.e., universalization of the covenant, was a longtime dream that remained a highly sought conclusion of the covenant in Jewish understanding as well. When Judaism said no to the messianic claim, it pointed to the continuing evil in the world. Christians, rather than admit the contradiction in the presence of the evil, found it easier to respond by dismissing Judaism as "carnal," using Christian power to silence Jewish competition and to make Jews pay for their recalcitrance.

To the second Christian claim of Incarnation, i.e., that God had become flesh in their midst in order to deliver humanity from evil, Jews responded, "Absolutely not." Sometimes Jews charged Christianity with idolatry for speaking of incarnation. Such divine action is not necessary, argued the Jews. The covenantal divide between God and humans can be crossed in other ways. Jews were convinced that this was an age of Divine Presence through hiddenness. The Temple-like visibility of Jesus was unnecessary and inappropriate. Christianity responded that God intervened decisively to prove Christianity is right, i.e., through Resurrection. Since the history of the covenant is preparation for this moment, only Jewish obduracy and spiritual blindness could account for their resistance. Therefore, Judaism was labeled a blind fossil religion and was dismissed as superseded. Jewry was cast out from God's presence. He who is first shall be last.

Since Christianity based its authority on the foundations of Judaism, the ongoing existence of Jewry became a problem, a living contradiction to the faith. This inexorably led to the policy of eliminating the contradiction by explaining away (through stereotyping and theological degradation), converting, or killing Jews. Jews, feeling that their own vital signs were strong and that God's presence was closer than ever, became convinced that Christianity was an idolatrous, heretical cult following a false messiah and practicing a murderous ethic (as experienced in the Jews' own body).

Thus, both Christians in their contempt for Jews and Judaism and Jews in their rejection of Christianity and Christian power were pushed down the path of writing off this world and this life. Christianity and Judaism taught their followers to choose life; however, in their relationship to each other, intentionally or not, they chose death. I speak not just of death, killing, or murder. Hatred is also the death of life, the killing of life's capacity for love. When the gospel of love spread hatred of fellow human beings, it led to tragedy. When the religion of the image of God in every human being saw Christians as *"goyim,"* it deviated from its best values.

How can Judaism and Christianity reassert the responsibilities of the covenant and take their proper role in the partnership of perfection of the world? One can start by saying that the moral and cultural credibility of Judaism and Christianity depends on overcoming the legacy and the image of their interactive hatefulness, and on their ability to set a standard of mutual respect that minimally equals the best standard of modern culture. Second, both religions face a common threat of being swamped by secularization and modernity that neither is strong enough to handle alone. For that matter, modern culture itself desperately needs religious and spiritual reinforcement that neither religion alone can give. Third, we live after the *Shoah,* which has made it clear that if we still believe in *tikun olam,* we need all the help we can get from every possible partner.

The Holocaust has unleashed a paroxysm of Christian self-critique and theological determination to overcome the "teaching of contempt" tradition. This is a healing sign of life and of remarkable spiritual and religious renewal that Jews still do not fully grasp. Any religion that can self-critique so powerfully shows incredible vitality. A faith that shows such a deep capacity for repentance demonstrates its capacity to be a vehicle of love and its fitness to help lead the world toward the perfection that God wants. This incredible renewal, this choosing of life, enables us to say that someday this period will be looked at as one of the great ages of Christianity's service to humanity. Of course, the *Shoah* has also dramatized the moral outrageousness of any tradition's—and that includes Judaism's—carrying on unrevised, negative stereotypes or contemptuous judgments that degrade the other. Contempt breeds apathy to others' fate, if not the will to participate in assault upon them. "Never again" demands the end of *all* contempt traditions wherever located, at all cost and as swiftly as possible.

I speak from the perspective of postmodernity and in the aftermath of the Holocaust when I offer an alternative reading of the birth of Christianity and the covenantal relationship between Judaism and Christianity. It was always God's plan to bring the vision of redemption and the covenantal way to a wider group of humanity. That is the purpose of an avant-garde, to bring the whole army to its destination by scouting the dangers, by opening up and testing trails, by pushing ahead and pulling everybody else after them. Therefore, it was in the fullness of time that Christianity was born. After thousands of years the people Israel—in the narrower definition, the Jewish people—had sufficiently internalized the covenant to be able to take on new levels of responsibility. They were capable of shifting to a more hidden holiness without losing their connection to the Divine. It was the same fullness of time, in an era of the death of the gods—the Hellenistic gods—and the encounter of cultures, that there was remarkably high receptivity to the spiritual/ethical messages of the covenant, especially if they could be articulated in Hellenistic terms, to and for gentiles.

To reverse a classic image, it was God's purpose, then, that the shoot of the stalk of Abraham be grafted onto the root of the gentiles. Thus, they could be rooted in God and bear covenantal fruit on their tree of life. The group that would do it naturally—who else?—would have to grow out of the family and covenantal community of Israel. This is neither replacement nor repudiation but an offshoot, a reaching out to new masses. To be heard and followed, this religion must swim in the sea of the gentile people and their culture. It dare not be excessively culturally or literally Jewish. Therefore, although it grows in the bosom of Judaism and is profoundly marked by Jewish interpretation, it can and must and will take on the coloration of the people that it reaches. This very development would have to become independent, or it would erode Jewish distinctiveness and undermine the capacity of the Jewish covenant to continue as distinctively Jewish.

My argument is quite simple: Christianity had to start within Judaism, but it had to grow into its own independent existence if justice was to be done to the particularity of the covenant. The signal that triggered this growth, I would argue, would have to be discernible to the minimum number it would take to start a new religion. It would have to go unheard by the bulk of Jewry, not because of deafness or spiritual blindness, but because the signal was not intended for them. The Jewish majority would shortly be called to its renewed covenant, to its Rabbinic flowering. It was most inappropriate that a sacramental, more temple-oriented model be offered them. By contrast, gentiles entering the covenant needed such an approach. Did God then become incarnate to cross the covenantal divide in order to rescue humankind? Far be it from me as a Jew to prescribe to Christians or to God what happened in that religious experience. I can only suggest that the resurrection signal had to be so marginal, so subject to alternate interpretations, and the incarnation sign so subtle, as to be able to be heard in dramatically opposing fashions— one way by the band elected to start the new faith and another way by the majority of Jews called to continue the classical covenantal mission.

Such a resurrection, such an incarnation, no Jew need fear or fight. We need no monopoly of divine revelation or presence. I pray that the Holy Spirit will be present in all Christian activity, as I pray that it will be present in all Jewish activity. I am convinced equally that God would be far from intervening decisively to endorse the new covenant or supposedly to refute or supersede the old. What would such behavior say about the dependability of God's promises? Why should the original covenant, the older of the two covenants, be refuted by the birth of a new avant-garde any more than the first Noahide covenant was terminated by the election of Abraham? Far more likely, far more covenantal, and far more loving is the possibility that this was the divine resort to covenantal pluralism, so as to reach more human beings in human fashion through human communities.

The triumphalism, the rejectionism, the cruelty, and the mutual defamation all came out of the human need for reassurance that "indeed, I am the favorite child." The favoritism would make the travail of the faithful worthwhile. Somehow, if I suffered, it was not so bad, as long as I was assured that I had the right religion and the others had nothing. These deviations reflected the self-aggrandizement of communities that forgot that the ultimate prayer is that God's will be done, not that my agenda win out. Fratricide reflects the failure of imagination to conceive that the parent—in this case, the infinite Divine love—is not exhausted by one people's redemption. There is enough love in God to choose again and again. It is truly a case of a divine parent's loving each child infinitely without loving the first- or second-born any less.

The saddest part is that within the gospel of love there developed a permanent kernel of hate that only weakened its redemptive capacity. The saddest outcome is that the ongoing crucifixion of Jesus' family and loved ones, the Jewish people, climaxed in an act of genocide so horrendous that it can truly be described as a crime wrapped in purported divine instruction, "which I never commanded . . . and which never entered my mind," yet for which responsibility must be taken (Jer. 19:5). The saddest fact is that Jewry's counter-self-definition to Christianity pushed Judaism toward its own breakdown forms: tribalism, legalism, asceticism, and denial of this world. While the Jewish teaching of contempt was less acted upon, at least part of that restraint was because of Jewish powerlessness. Today, we live in an age of Jewish power restored; the continuation of such a self-centered tradition could turn lethal. Jewish people are as human as members of every other group; Jews need the same warning against the corruptions of power. It is time for repentance, for reconfiguring the relationship, for overcoming the internal degradation of the other, and for a new alliance of the people of God for the sake of witnessing to humanity and perfecting the world.

We know that actions evoke like reactions in all human endeavors. The power of love, the divine inspiration, and the ethical purity needed to overcome these millennia of hatred and conflict would itself give enormous new credibility to the joint and distinctive witness of each community. It would pave the way for the reassertion of religious leadership across the spectrum of the modern world's issues.

We have not yet grasped the richness of God's covenantal pluralism. Pluralism means more than accepting or even affirming the other. It entails recognizing the blessing in the other's existence, because it balances one's own position and brings all of us closer to the ultimate goal. Even when we are right in our position, the other who contradicts our position may be our corrective or our check against going to excess. After all, we are dealing with matters of enormous import and stake. I feel a great empathy for the Roman Catholic Church as it struggles between its conscience that tells it that women are equal, its insight that tells it that women and men must have distinctive roles, and its faithfulness that whispers to it that it dare not change gender roles lest it betray the tradition or undermine its own authority. My own Orthodox Jewish community is in about the same place. I must say I sleep better at night knowing that other religions are struggling with the same questions or that any decision I make that is one-sided will be corrected by other denominations in my own tradition or by other religions.

Pluralism offers us a better model than approval or disapproval. Let different denominations and groups stake out different positions. Let this be our chance to experience situations where those who are opposed strengthen and learn from each other. In the matter of abortion, the either/or position dominates. But (whichever position is right) the anti-abortion position has been a moral check against a potential devaluation of life, which would be the result of turning abortion into a casual practice. In turn, the pro-abortion position has upheld the priority of the mother's life and thus operated to balance the moral scales. When we enter new moral ground, let pluralism be our insurance. As the patriarch Jacob said, if one camp is badly beaten, then let the other camp be able to flee (Gen. 32:9). One of the best ways to traverse a slippery slope safely is to hold hands with each other along the continuum of positions so that each is held back from sliding and no one falls off the cliff. Pluralism also bespeaks God's love of variety and uniqueness. In pluralism we do not filter out the differences or turn everything gray. We encounter the full intensity of distinctive positions, witnessing in our uniqueness without distorting in our passion. By this token, pluralism is not relativism, for we hold on to our absolutes; however, we make room for others' as well.

This essay was originally presented in Tulsa, in the heartland of Evangelical Christianity. I know it is difficult to ask Evangelicals to consider the possibility that their own absolute faith in Jesus Christ can make room for the ongoing fullness of revelation, authenticity, and fulfillment in the Jewish covenant as an independent religion. Yet, the deepest truth is that unless we hold on to our absolutes in pluralist fashion, they turn pathological and tend to destroy others. We can avoid this pathology only if we get to know the limits of our position. My truth cannot or does not cover all people, all possibilities, or all times, because God wants others to contribute. We need the checks and balances to prevent the spinning out of control of our individual positions. This is why our dialogue is so vital and so necessary. We are embarked on one of the great moral adventures of all time: to give up triumphalism, to accept that it is God's will that will be done, to accept the fact that we are only servants and agents, and to know that we have not been the sole vehicles of God's love or the redemption that is coming. It is this generation's calling to undertake this task for the sake of redeeming suffering humanity.

Let us side-by-side, then, bring the Messiah instead of arguing whether it is the first or second coming. Instead of the fighting and the belittling and the denying that delays the coming, let there be mutual activity and love that hastens it. If we understand this alternative, then we will truly be worthy of our calling. We are the generation called to explore freedom, power, and affluence, which lie within the grasp of all humanity. There is sufficient food now to feed everybody. It is the distribution system that is broken. There is sufficient technological and economic power to create affluence for everybody. What is lacking is the focus on productivity and the will to exercise it. Let us undertake these tasks of repairing the world.

We are challenged to decide life-and-death questions that others did not live long enough to face. Fifty-five years ago during the Holocaust, my cousins in Europe could only decide how to die. My ancestors 500 years ago could only decide how to hunker down and maintain their dignity, despite being a battered people. The choices of poverty are fewer; of martyrdom and slavery, starker; of involuntary status as a Jew or Christian, simpler. But, what a privilege for us that our choices must be subtler and less obvious, that we must choose how to live rather than how to die, how to serve God in our strength rather than our incapacities, how to serve God as a favorite child, one of many favorite children! What parent will not welcome the opportunity to validate this deepest religious truth: I love each of my children as my favorite, and my love is not exhausted by that fact.

Pluralism and Partnership

In his book *Yemei Zikaron*, master theologian Rabbi Joseph B. Soloveitchik points out a central implication of the core concept of Judaism that the human being is created in the image of God. He builds on the halakhic principle of *shlucho shel adam k'moto*—that in order to serve as someone's messenger/agent, the agent must be like the sender, i.e., the agent must share the values, attitudes, and goals of the sender in order to fulfill the delegated role.

Soloveitchik reorients the metaphor and plays it backwards. The fact that the human is so like God as to be in the image of God is a sign that the individual (every human being) is God's messenger or agent. The human dignity/capacity and godlike qualities that constitute "being in the image of God" are a faithful sign that the human being is appointed by God to serve as God's agent in the world.

The key question that each person must ask is: What *is* my appointed mission?

Since today there are no instant oracles, no priests with direct lines to God, and no prophets available to give the answer, the individual must reflect deeply. One must read the sources, pray, listen to instruction and the community, and ponder the events of one's life to detect the mission and try to carry it out. (It may take a lifetime to discover.) While there is no easy answer, says Rabbi Soloveitchik, there is one powerful signal that everyone is given. The time, the place, the circumstances, and the community into which one is born is the hint. The mission is rooted in the time and the place.

If I am a Jew born in America in the second half of the twentieth century, I can guess that my mission is less likely to be a model of how to live as a pariah people, treated as outcasts clinging to a purportedly superseded religion and trying to maintain dignity and identity in the face of persecution and vulnerability. My task is less likely to be how to keep hope of restoration of Israel alive at a time when one cannot act on this hope and the way to Israel is barred. Yet this was the essence of the mission of most Jews (or their leaders) between the years 70 and 1900 C.E.

The mission of a twentieth-century Jew in the free world (including Israel) is more likely connected to serving God and working for *tikun olam*, to preserving Jewish identity and applying those values under circumstance of freedom, access to power, and affluence. After all, these are the circumstances, the challenges, and the temptations of this time and place. There is where the search for personal mission should focus.

In the spirit of Soloveitchik, let us explore: What is the mission (or a mission) of Jews and Christians (and for that matter, Muslims and other religionists who share their values) in the free world on the cusp of the twenty-first century and the third millennium?

We are living through one of the great cultural transformations of all time. Simultaneously, this is a moment of extraordinary religious breakthrough: the arrival of a society so free and open that it enables us to discover/experience the image of God in the other human beings. The Talmud tells us that being born in the image of God brings with it three fundamental, intrinsic, and irrevocable dignities: *infinite value, equality*, and *uniqueness*. One might say that if I encounter the other human being as he or she really is (viz., an image of God), then I am struck by his or her infinite value, equality, and uniqueness. This evokes awe, respect, and love from me. Then my treatment of the other person changes. If I experience this person's equality then I cannot enslave him or her. I cannot abandon a human being in poverty or hunger if I experience that person's infinite value. Then much of religion's task is to first identify and teach that the other human being is in the image of God. Religions must work to restructure the world to respect the image of God. This is the meaning of the messianic vision of Judaism in which humanity overcomes poverty, hunger, oppression, and war. Even sickness and death are to be defeated, for they are incompatible with the value and uniqueness of the individual. They will be overthrown in the Messianic Age, the goal of the Jewish and Christian covenant.

Unfortunately, for most of history, the human being's dignity as image of God was obscured by the poverty and deprivation that pitted people against each other in a struggle for survival. Furthermore, the internal culture, for

199

the most part, hid the truth by presenting outside group members as less than the image of God. Throughout human history, dominant cultural groups (indeed almost all groups) created a moral/cultural world in which their own people/faith/culture constituted the illuminated foreground (= The Children of Light) and the rest of humanity made up the shadowed background (= The Children of Darkness).

In an insulated, ethnocentric world, one's own value, beliefs, and heroes were presented positively. The other was "not present" or was presented in a "skewed" version, frequently stereotyped and manifestly inferior to the in-group and its values. The other was rated from the scale of my group; in general, such people were less worthy or unworthy of the ethical/religious treatment that the in-group morality demanded in the treatment of my own group's members. In this world, only some people, mostly in my group, were encountered or treated like a true image of God. Similarly, my/our truth—the nurturing ground of the human—was divinely revealed, absolute, and correct. The other truth of the other culture was, at best, a paler reflection, typically inferior, if not evil or beyond the pale.

Now modernity has brought into being a society so open, mobile, and increasingly free that one encounters the others directly and in their full dignity. Note: this model is idealized. Many people in the West and whole societies elsewhere are mired in poverty and hierarchy and do not experience this improvement. Yet it may be said that thanks to communications, many deprived people become aware of this new phenomenon with its concomitant gift of dignity (of which they are deprived). Many then experience this deprivation with greater cognitive dissonance; it evokes greater resistance and protest and generates guilt in the privileged to the extent that communication makes them aware of the oppression of others. Thus the encounter has effects even when it does not yet reshape the society. In those societies that are being reshaped, this new encounter in turn evokes more sense of the other's right to be free, to be treated with justice, etc. This paves the way for more transformation. This cycle leads to more freedom, more openness, and more discovery of the image of God of the other.

In this process, inherited fixed categories and hierarchies are undermined and the sense of fixity, permanence, and givenness gradually disintegrates. For this reason, modern culture is marked by the growth of liberalism but also relativism. Cumulatively, the proliferation of experiencing the equality of the other leads to paralysis of the capacity to judge them (for judgment classically is embedded in hierarchy). Similarly, as each religion/culture loses its capacity to "other" the other and to skew and stereotype the alternate cultures, it loses its monopoly on being right, as well as on its givenness. Therefore, modernity is often experienced as a culture that undermines faith. Our task is to reverse that effect, i.e., to assure that upgrading the dignity of the other does not erode the legitimate claims and teachings of religion.

What then is our mission? I submit that it is to explore and establish a principled pluralism. When culture and values are no longer embedded in structures that are fixed, '"genetic,"' or absolute, and when the spirit of choice and freedom is strong, then the sense of absolute claims, which typically undergirded classic religions, is lost. For many, if not most people, the result that emerges is relativism, which is the loss of capacity to affirm any standards. But the deepest religious response is pluralism—the recognition that there are plural absolute standards that can live and function together even when they conflict. The deepest insight of pluralism is that dignity, truth, and power function best when they are pluralized, e.g., divided and distributed, rather then centralized or absolutized.

In this chapter, I will try to describe the sociology, phenomenology, and theology of pluralism. Then I would like to argue that our calling is to move even beyond pluralism to partnership between the faiths. To affirm the partnership is to take a further step away from viewing the world and the other from the self-centered, concentric circle in which I and my faith/truth are at the center toward viewing the world from a "cosmic perspective"; i.e., I and my faith group see ourselves as participants, as one of the organized groups among the divine hosts to be deployed with others together—as God sees fit—to perfect the world.

SOCIOLOGY OF PLURALISM

Modern culture creates large urban concentrations of population with a variety of people and cultures together. The neighbor is frequently someone from a religion or culture hitherto treated as stranger and presented through stereotypes and filters. Modern culture also is saturated with media and communication. For the first time in history, there is no shelter or "in-group" environment. Often the other culture/faith is presented through the media in all its strength and particularity; thus there is no "protective tariff" of favoritism or self-presentation for my culture. The community also loses the time period (such as childhood) when it had a monopoly over the information fed to its own constituents. Finally, the combination of mobility, affluence, and freedom leads to frequent direct and positive encounters with the other and the other's culture/religion. The net result is that the others are now experienced in their uniqueness, in their value, and in their religion's religious power. Just as I recognize the other no longer as other but as image of God, so is their faith recognized not as a foreign culture but rather as a dignified, spiritually vital religion that raises people in the image of God. Thus technology and communication, which are theoretically neutral, play an important role in bringing the other—person and culture—into my life and into my universe of moral obligation.

Pluralism is the outgrowth of this situation. People recognize the power of the other religion as valued in its own right, yet experience their own religion's power equally. Since they can neither dismiss the other faith nor give up their own, the natural outcome is pluralism.

THE PHENOMENOLOGY OF PLURALISM

In modern society, the encounter with the other, followed by the recognition and then the affirmation of uniqueness and equality of the other, typically occurs in a frame that does not devalue or suppress the (erstwhile) insider faith, or its uniqueness and value. People experience the other faith as valued in that it nurtures other human beings in the image of God. This evokes respect and honor for the other faith. Since one's own faith is not being suppressed, the result is two (or more) religions simultaneously coexisting in the believer's mind whose claims and expressions are experienced as valued. Sometimes the response is "voluntary" and is articulated in the structures and language of the insider faith. Sometimes it is "involuntary"; the respect is expressed behaviorally while it remains dissonant with the official claims of the faith. (This is what tolerance is all about.)

Relativism emerges when the erstwhile insider faith has little or no persuasive power, i.e., once the monopoly is lost. The erstwhile believer does not convert to the new experienced faith, but concludes that there is no monopoly nor any standard of absolute truth anymore. Since the old "absolute" standard has been broken, all standards are judged to be accidental, arbitrary, or notional.

Fundamentalism emerges when people find that the old absolutes have lost their power once they are brought into the presence of the other. The fundamentalist fears (correctly) that this erosion raises the threat of the loss of all values. Therefore, the fundamentalist proposes to bring back the old values the only way he or she knows, i.e., in the absence of alternative voices. The fundamentalist proposes to recreate the old conditions of absolute faith by the political/cultural action of repressing the new voices and reimposing the old in-group/out-group morality and cultural presentation. The problem with this solution is that it also restores all the old stereotypes, negative filters, and concomitant mistreatment and suppression of the other (all for the sake of the "highest good" and the restoration of the absolutes).

One must beware of simply dismissing fundamentalism. It draws its power from a more sophisticated moral calculus than we acknowledge. When people become convinced that all fundamental values—God, family, right and wrong—are being undermined by the new openness and its concomitant relativism, they may conclude that they must sacrifice the lesser good (choice, freedom, and chance for mobility) for the sake of the greater good (fundamental values that guide life). Willingness to make this kind of sacrifice is particularly likely among people left out of the social and economic advantages of the emerging society.

Pluralism is made possible by the ability of a religion or a truth system to maintain its vitality and to continue to move its own adherents, even in the presence of the other. However, for many, the breaking of the old absolute monopoly leads to an unthinking relativism, since they do not experience the ongoing vitality of their faith.

The essential difference between pluralism and relativism is that pluralism is based on the principle that there still is an absolute truth. There still are valid values; we still can and must say no to certain systems and ideas. How then can this view coexist with allowing for alternate views and conflicting values?

The pluralist affirms absolute values but has come to know their limits. The absolute values do not cover all the possibilities. Pluralism is an absolutism that has come to recognize its own limitations.

PLURALISM AND ITS LIMITS

An idea, a faith, or a truth may be absolute but nevertheless be bounded. This makes room for other absolutes that may lie beyond this realm. Most ideas and operative truths in religion are not located at a fixed point of truth or existence. Most ideas and truths are, in fact, *continuum truths*. Take the concept of covenant. Covenant is an alliance, a treaty between God and humans, which in Judaism and Christianity finds expression as a partnership between God and humanity (or, in the more particularist form, between God and the Children of Israel). Note, however, that "Children of Israel" is defined differently in Judaism and Christianity over most of their overlapping histories. The covenant idea ranges along a continuum beginning from one pole when God does just about everything. Indeed one could argue that although Islam does not use the category of a covenant because of its emphasis on submission to God and the human's role as slave/servant of God, its position is the closest to the divine dominant pole and is the equivalent of covenant, albeit unnamed. The continuum of covenant's meaning extends to the condition where divine intervention is frequent and visible through miracle; the meaning continues along the continuum to the concept of a Divine somewhat less manifestly interventionist in day-to-day action but speaking through prophecy and oracle. The continuum moves toward wisdom, in which humans interpret and read more of the divine will—especially in the "book" of Creation, which is less manifestly divine. The balance of covenant then moves along the continuum toward interpretation and human activity accountable to God and acting on behalf of the divine. Finally, the balance moves to the sector where human activity becomes increasingly central, then to the modern schools of the human coming-of-age where the line between the secular and religious is exceedingly thin. Perhaps the cutoff point—where one is off the covenant continuum—is pure secularization where God is declared to be a figment of human imagination. By this definition, the human is fully responsible for all actions and activity and there is no higher authority to which humans are accountable that can guide or forgive humans. Note: The same type of continuum can be laid out for most of the central ideas of religion.

In the past, the centeredness of each group and its sense that the world was organized around it gave rise to the absolute (unlimited) claims of one's own tradition. Now the presentation of the world/faith/truth beyond makes one aware of the limits of one's own position. One comes to recognize that one's own faith occupies an important point or sector along the continuum, but it does not extend over the whole length of the continuum. On a continuum from zero to 100, perhaps my truth extends from 40 to 75; however, before and after it, there are points on the continuum of the very same idea that are left for others to occupy. Perhaps within the range (or part of the range) of my truth, there is absolute truth (which may even contradict others' truth; see below). But there are other parts of the continuum, occupied by legitimate others who may be presenting (absolute) truths that cover other valid aspects of the same ideas/value/truth. Thus, absolutes may coexist sharing the same basic idea/value/truth yet articulating or expressing a different mix of the constituent ideas' polar insights. Compare Islam's fundamental stress on submission and servitude to Christianity's emphasis on the mediating role of Jesus (and, for that matter, his mother) and to Judaism's emphasis (especially since postbiblical times) on the human's direct and active role. Note: Here again, I have simplified. Each tradition has its movements (and periods) that take up other aspects of the continuum and explore and apply it. Furthermore, there are parallelism and overlap among the truths. Still, each dominant tradition seems to be clustered about a different sector of the continuum.

In the past, if one wanted to reject the other, one would abstract the central idea of each from the continuum, emphasize that contradiction between them, and reject the other as if it came from an alien or wrong source rather than being a neighbor on the very same continuum.

Just as there is a continuum of meaning to truths, so there may be a continuum of peoples to whom God reveals and who are chosen to be God's servants. Thus any truth may speak absolutely to me and others, yet it is not intended for others who may be spoken to by other revelations and chosen for another sector of service. If one considers the divine love of human uniqueness and the divine respect for the variety of geography, language, and various forms of human rootedness, then one is particularly drawn to the concept of absolutes that operate over part of the human continuum, leaving room for others' experiences of the absolute that are different. Maybe in some details they are even contradictory to my experience, yet they are still authentic and chosen. Suffice it to cite Isaiah's vision that the day will come when Israel and its two chief enemies/oppressors in biblical times up to his day, i.e., Egypt and Assyria, would all three be recognized as covenantal, chosen people (Isa. 25:19). If these three can be in this same class, then every people and truth can be!

Finally, there is the continuum of cases. My truth can be 100 percent valid over a range of cases, but it may allow room for new cases or other circumstances in which others' truths are allowed or needed to operate. If one adds to this that some people, or even cultures, may constitutionally prefer answers that are balanced toward authority or uniformity while others may gravitate toward individual choice and variety, then the same absolute answer may not be appropriate for the variety of peoples. This leaves ample room for cases, peoples, etc., where truths do overlap and where the contradictions may lead to disagreements or even refutation without leading to delegitimization or conflict.

This brings us to the second principle of pluralism. Pluralism is an absolutism that recognizes that an absolute truth/value need not be absolutely right to be absolute. Absolute, needed truths may incorporate elements that are erroneous or even evil that need to be corrected. All revelation that is communicated to humans, and all truth that is given over to human beings is (like the humans to whom it is given) only true/absolute/divine on balance. A wise absolutism will understand that this limitation (imperfection or incompletion) does not undermine its true authority. On the contrary, denying the weakness/limitation weakens the credibility of the rest of the truth, and may allow some evil to be done in the name of the faith system. This will further undermine the part that is the truth. By contrast, the awareness of limitation leaves room for the other's insights—truths that may exist in those interstices where one's own truth is flawed. Or, the other's wrong element may be contradicted by one's truths without disqualifying the rest of the other's truth (or of mine).

This understanding leaves room for important faith systems/truths to be in conflict or even to contradict each other in part. Yet their bearers may come to see that there is room for both because they are united by some still larger, all-encompassing principle that validates both, whatever their disagreement or whatever the errors or contradictable truth on the other side. In the era of ethnocentric culture/faiths, typically the criterion truth was defined whereby the others forfeited their validity. Today, with an enlarged vision and interactive encounter, one may frame the conflict within the broader principle that contains the disagreement and prevents it from escalating to delegitimization. Thus, in the past, Christians defined belief in God Incarnate, mediating and sacrificing for humanity, as *the* criterion for religious legitimacy. By this standard, Judaism was found wanting (as was Islam), so it was delegitimated and defined as superseded. Judaism in turn made this very Christian criterion the definition of idolatry, which meant that anyone coming to this view must leave the community. Anyone who accepted that belief was delegitimated.

Today, one would define the broader principle as God in our midst as we seek to respond by engaging in the task of *tikun olam*. Within this broader rubric, one can continue to disagree and even contradict the other without leaving the same camp. Thus we are disagreeing *l'shem shamayim*—for the sake of heaven—without losing our legitimacy and without being pressured into compromising our integrity. With this broader definition sustaining our particular distinctive, even contradictory, views of the Godhead, we avoid being sucked into conflict, or even aggression and cruelty, by the theological argument; in the past, our "contradictions" prevented working together for the greater goal.

This brings us to another theological dimension of pluralism. Today, all truths are spoken by humans to humans, i.e., by an image of God to an image of God. Implicit in this fact is that all truths have a double dimension. In part they are expressing facts or objective correlatives with facts or some insights or illuminations. The other dimension is that they reveal the character of the one speaking or teaching this truth, i.e., that an image of God, a being of infinite value, quality, and uniqueness, is speaking. If the truth assessment is complete and comprehensive, it will take the speaker's nature and existence into account. Already in the halakhic rules of truth, we find that the fact that the one speaking (and/or the listener) is an image of God may tilt the balance of a statement from true to false. A true statement that totally degrades the image of God may thereby become false. A false statement that recognized the image of God of the other may turn true. The Talmud illustrates this principle by declaring that every bride is beautiful and of good character (because in the eyes of her groom, she is). This is the view of the School of Hillel, and it overrules the school of Shammai's objection that it is not true that every bride is beautiful and of good character; see Babylonian Talmud, *Ketubbot* 17a.

One can simplify this principle even more. Pluralism reflects a truth that if a person of such weight (e.g., of infinite value and uniqueness, who is equal to me) speaks, then the source itself gives an idea some putative truth claim. At the least, the principle of pluralism implies that the person speaking has such weight that he or she has the right to be heard even if he or she is in error or totally wrong. Thus my ideas may be propagated by me even if they can be shown/proven to be wrong. By dint of being an image of God, I am entitled to be heard. My ideas (which come from me, an image of God) are weighty enough to be weighed, judged, and criticized, and not dismissed or suppressed. (The only limit would be if my ideas would harm others with no recourse. See below.)

There is another implication in this analysis. The image of God is not raised in a vacuum. The image of God is nurtured by a faith and by a culture. Then, any religion or culture that shows that it can raise people in the image of God, i.e., of value, equality, and uniqueness, cannot be suppressed ethically. A faith that raises people in the image of God can be criticized, corrected, and even rejected, but it deserves the consideration that comes after being heard. To suppress a faith's view is to claim that it is so unworthy and so evil that if it is heard, it will create subhuman monsters. (This claim is contradicted by the quality of the people that it is raising.) This also explains why Christian anti-Judaism could not stop with the religious contradiction. If a religion is hateful, legalistic, spiritually blind, and God-killing, then why are its practitioners clinging to it? The only answer can be that they, the believers, are as monstrous as the religion that they are practicing. This leads inevitably to anti-Semitism. This application fits all religions, including Judaism, when they demonize other religions. Such demonization leads in a straight line to the evils committed in religion's name in so many places in so many cultures.

Having articulated all the limitations on absolutism implicit in pluralism, one must reemphasize nevertheless that pluralism does *not* give up absolute claims or standards of right and wrong—when they are in their proper place and boundaries. In principled pluralism, practitioners of absolute faiths do not give up their obligation to criticize that which is wrong (or what they believe to be wrong) or that which leads to less than full realization of truth, found in the other faiths. The critique is made within the rubric of a broader shared truth and does not deny the legitimacy of the other faith. In the argument between truths, the truth might be further clarified or the balance of support for truth improved. And, because the other is not being demolished, one may listen and learn from the other or one may be persuaded to modify one's own views or to illuminate them with the insights of the other.

There is yet another absolute dimension to the pluralistic view. Another faith/system/truth may indeed, upon analysis, be discovered to be totally wrong. Indeed it may be so evil as to be denied the right to be preached or propagated. After all, even images of God may turn to evil and use their free will to become murderers or child molesters or totally evil people. This raises the possibility that the faith/culture/truth by which they are being nurtured is evil and does not deserve to exist. (It may be that they are only misapplying or disturbing a valid system; that problem should be dealt with in some way other than suppression.) But one can say of Nazism or of a religion that would teach child sacrifice or glorify killing, immorality, or injustice that it is not only wrong, it is illegitimate. Pluralism allows for this possibility, albeit it operates on the presumption that this case is unlikely. Also, given past abuses, pluralists will prefer to defeat illegitimate ideas without suppression. Pluralists prefer to give free speech and leeway to others—especially since unleashing this tendency to suppression may give free rein to the worst tendencies in one's own religion. Use of force could bring forth behavior in my own system that could lead it to forfeit its own legitimate values. Still, in the end, pluralism demonstrates that it has not relativized truth and has not given up the standard of right and wrong by its continuing ability to say no to that which demands a no, and not just by its ability to say yes to that which was hitherto (unjustly) denied.

FOR PLURALISM AND COVENANT

The other fundamental theological ground of pluralism is the concept of covenant. In this concept, the main goal of the faith, of the Divine-human partnership, is to create a human being in the image of God and to reshape the world so that it will sustain the image of God in its fullest dignity. For this reason, one must work to overcome poverty, hunger, oppression, war, sickness, and death—all of which contract the intrinsic dignities of the image of God.

Covenant teaches us that God's main intention is to create a human being in the image of God, i.e., a creature of infinite value, equality, and uniqueness. The goal is *not* to create an obedient servant for the greater glory of God. For if that were the goal then God could create a human who is programmed to obey or God could bring repeated floods/destructions until humans surrender and obey. Instead, God affirmed free will and the primacy of choice. God imposed limits on God's self and allowed humans to exercise their freedom, even to the point of committing sin. In entering into covenant, God accepts that stopping evil and ending suffering will not happen at God's preferred pace but only as fast as humans are able to change and grow into full acceptance of truth and consistent good behavior. This concession extends the infinite divine suffering indefinitely, yet God so loves humans as to accept that delay. Clearly, the motivation is that God wants an infinitely valuable, equal, and unique—hence free—human being to come out of the covenantal process.

One cannot separate the ends and the means. Humans cannot grow into value and equality by being dragooned. They can only learn to be free by being allowed to act freely even if they sin or misapply their freedom. Thus, they learn by trial and error to be responsible and free. This is the validation of pluralism that allows people freedom to err, to sin, and to grow in order to arrive at a mature and free set of truths, beliefs, and positions. Only such values can be lived in the full presence of the other.

This points to the deeper level of truths in the divine realm that undergirds covenant and in turn is the infrastructure of pluralism. The Infinite God creates and sustains reality and is the ground and nurturer of life. God loves life; God's infinite power and love generate and stimulate life in all its varieties. But God's infinity is so overwhelming and so all-encompassing that it leaves no room for any other existence. In order to make room for existence, God's full Presence, which occupies all space and time, must limit itself (*tzimtzum,* in kabbalistic language), i.e., take on restraint and limitations, in order to make room for the others' existence. Direct, unmediated contact with God would consume and demolish humans. "For the human cannot see Me and live" (Exod. 33:20).

In the same way, the divine truth is so sweeping that it cannot be contained/absorbed by humans; again, God must impose self-limits and dress revelation in human language and metaphor in order to make it graspable by humans. Similarly, out of love, God limits the word of God so that it can give life and sustain it. Thus we learn a deep truth. The Divine Infinite supports the infinite variety of life and the infinite value of the human being. But it does so by accepting limitations on its self in order to make room for the existence and dignity of the other. God turns these limits into dependable structures by entering into relationships, especially covenantal relationships, with humans. The Divine establishes reliable limits on which humans can depend and to which they can appeal. This gives humans room to grow and to flourish in freedom.

The human being's highest calling—being already born in the image of God—is to develop this resemblance even more by a process of *imitatio Dei*. If the Divine Infinite, who is capable of perfect modulation, nevertheless exercises power by self-limitation, then we learn that all power, love, and wisdom must limit itself to enable the full dignity and value of the other to grow. Pluralism is a profound form of *imitatio Dei*.

We can extend this principle one step further. Only the Divine Infinite that is self-limited can sustain life and not destroy the other. Thus, the covenantal God, the God of revelation, is the God of Life, and God's word is the Tree of Life. By contrast, human systems—even divinely revealed ones—are constantly being extended without limit by their believers—unless they stop out of respect for others. But humans, by definition, cannot enclose the infinity of God, either in its expression or by their comprehension. There is a real danger that the human version/understanding, which is by definition finite, will be extended by believers into an infinite claim that allows no room for the other. This human extension ends up with a pseudo-infinite; *this is the definition of idolatry.* Idolatry is the partial, created or shaped by finite humans, that claims to be infinite. Idolatry mimics the Divine and claims the absolute status of the Divine, yet it is, in fact, finite. This pseudo-infinite cannot sustain the infinity of life (or of human dignity). In fact, we know that idolatry is the god of death and that it creates a realm of death.

Thus, we can generalize. All human systems (even those that are given by divine revelation) that claim to be absolute, exercise no self-limitation, or leave no room for the other turn into idolatry, i.e., into sources of death. It is no accident that Nazism, which sought perfection and eliminated all restraints and limitations (resorting to political dictatorship, economic and social utopianism, *gleichschaltung,* and all-out war on the Jews as the obstacle to perfection), created a realm of total death—the kingdom of night. All political systems and all religions that allow themselves to make unlimited absolute claims are led to idolatrous behaviors. They often generate death-dealing believers, frequently driven by the excess of good rather than by purely evil goals or claims. Similarly, all social systems that "other" the other and absolutize their own host culture/policy turn idolatrous and then degrade or destroy others. That is why pluralism of power and power centers, of truth and truth centers, and of dignity and dignity centers is the best ground for life and for human dignity for all. Since sustaining life is the purpose of the religious systems (at least as implied by covenant), this pluralism is the highest form of religious behavior.

It is a tribute to the twentieth century's sweep that it widened our perspective to appreciate the dignity of the others (and to feel their sheer weight). We also have learned the bitter lesson of the Holocaust, which taught us of the unlimited death-dealing implied in modern totalitarianism.

PLURALISM AND PARTNERSHIP

Having glorified pluralism and held it up as the model of true religious service, let me conclude by arguing that we must go one step beyond it—to partnership. Pluralism moves beyond tolerance in that it not only accepts the existence of the other, but also seeks to recast its own understanding to affirm the ongoing validity and dignity of the other. Partnership goes one step further. The concept of partnership suggests that my truth/faith system alone cannot fulfill God's dreams. Therefore, the world needs the contribution that the other makes for the world's own wholeness and perfection. The partnership perspective suggests that God has assigned different roles and different contributions to different groups, and that the other groups are needed for *tikun olam*. The partnership perspective suggests that many existential truths are dialectical, and that a truth that is deep in one area may not be able to do justice to the antipode—so the other faith is needed to explore that possibility in its fullest depth. Among all of us, we can provide for the fullest scope of human expression. We need each other to represent the full range of the service of God.

Thus, a Jew with a partnership theology would affirm the classic Christian specialization in a religious system that explores faith and ideology as central categories, precisely because so much of Judaism's depth is organized around the significance of biology for faith community and the dialectic of birth and choice, action and attitude. Thus, a follower of Islam marveling at the perfect submission that Islam teaches would affirm the relevance of another path (Christianity), in which God intervenes to suffer with and to lift up humans, and with a Judaism that places tremendous emphasis on human action and responsibility in the world. This would be a particularly valuable widening of the circle of faith in modern times; otherwise, the growth of human power and capability may lead to a situation where the most significant human activity grows beyond religious categories and direction. (This has happened to some extent and has brought terrible abuses and great secularization in its course.)

This approach leads Jews and Christians to learn and incorporate the other's insight. Listening to Islam's emphasis on the importance of human humility and submission to God would strengthen the Jewish and Christian critique of human excesses. This is a needed reaffirmation in an age when human power is at such a peak that it turns arrogant and threatens to spin out of control, endangering environment and culture alike.

One can point to the partnership role of Buddhism in challenging this-worldliness through its negation of existence, or to Christianity's role in offering a dialectic of this world and the world to come, or to modern Judaism's attempt to make the secular (this world) holy. All are needed; each when isolated individually becomes ineffective or overwhelmed in the broader worldwide cultural/political situation. All may contribute to filling out each other's insights and correcting one-sidedness in the other or in itself. Each partner can recover main themes from the other, often by recognizing that this has been a minor theme in its own tradition. (Thus, each tradition becomes a resource that can be drawn upon to find the vocabulary and repertoire to incorporate into one's own insight). Each partner can see the other reaching certain people or deeply suffusing certain cultures in a way that it cannot. Together we can bring the whole world closer to God.

Partners seek out and show active interest in each other and draw upon the other's experience. (Neo-Orthodox Protestant scholars and theologians were enormously helpful to me when my own Orthodox tradition had not yet coped with certain modern challenges.) Partners seek to help and strengthen the other, such as Christians have done for Soviet Jews, and such as Jews in the United States have begun to do for persecuted other faiths around the world.

Together as partners we can work to check materialism and to sanctify the material. Together as partners we can work to channel and soften the power of market forces toward a balance with *tzedakah* (help that is righteousness and not just caritas), help that is redistributive and not just ameliorative. Of course, even as religions partner to restrain capitalism, we must maintain humility in the face of the incredible productivity and human liberation successes that the market has accomplished.

If we can move to pluralism and then to partnership, we can see ourselves as servants of God who are content to achieve God's goals even if we ourselves do not turn out to be the center or the exclusive beneficiaries of the redemption. Then we can say that our model of passionate, principled pluralism can overcome both relativism and absolutism and offer a valid third way. We can learn the humility of seeing our limited role in the vast cosmic scheme as a worthy and fulfilling role. We can take satisfaction in knowing that *harbay shluchim lamakom* (God has many agents/messengers). We all should feel grateful that we can be one of them. "Blessed be all that come in the name of the loving God" (Ps. 118:26; my translation).

Covenants of Redemption

 ## GOD'S UNIVERSAL AND PARTICULAR COVENANTS

The religion and the people of Israel came into being to mediate the conflict between bringing the *ideal* world (Creation redeemed and history fulfilled) into existence and living in the *real* world (Creation and history as they are now) in a meaningful way. According to Jewish tradition, God, out of love, imposes self-limits—first to create and sustain existence, then to enable its ultimate perfection. Without yielding the conviction that people should live lives of full dignity, God allows history to go on in a flawed world and in societies full of degradation. Without giving up the desire that humans always act on the side of life and value, God—after the Flood—chooses to respect human freedom and allow people to sin without destroying them.

To reconcile the poles of the ideal and the real, God enters into covenant. The primordial self-limitation is expressed in establishing natural order/law and being bound by it. The regularity and dependability of the natural order gives humans the sense of trust to work and build the world and to feel responsible for their lives. Similarly, God does not continuously interfere with history; nor will the Divine enter into human lives with constant miraculous intervention. Rather, God calls humanity into active partnership. Singly and collectively, human beings are commanded to use their godlike capacities to complete the world. In turn, God promises to be with humans and to work with them all the way, neither to reject them nor to coerce them until all is realized.

All other living forms are genetically programmed to maximize creation of life and to live in the natural order. Humans alone have the fuller consciousness that enables them to understand—and to reject or to willingly join in—the rhythms of creation. For humans to be summoned into covenant, then, is to be singled out in love; the call to do more and to get closer to God is the content of the experience of election.

Only divine self-control and a profound commitment to full human development can motivate God's promise to neither reject nor coerce human beings; only the recognition that coerced righteousness would violate human equality can evoke God's ongoing willingness to bear the pain of an unredeemed world. The covenant is grounded in an infinite divine respect for humanity; it is driven by a loving desire that human beings emerge out of the natural and historical process as fully independent, dignified creatures.

How can God move the world forward toward perfection and still allow humans to be free? God can do this by joining with humanity as it is (with mixed values, contradictory urges, and cross-purposes) and where it is (in a world of shortages, limitations, and conflicting interests), in a partnership to work together for redemption. God joins with humanity in this way by establishing the Noahide covenant—a covenant with humanity that precedes the covenant with Israel. The goal is to fill the earth with life—life in the image of God (Gen. 9:1–2,7).

The concept of partnership implies joint and parallel efforts and mutual obligations. This is one of the revolutionary insights of Israelite religion. The covenant mechanism is intended by its Initiator to give over a sense of stability and dignity to humans and to make them feel that God is deeply and equally involved with them. At the same time, the covenant teaches that humans should not view their power as absolute. Human authority comes into being within a framework of relationship and accountability to God; it is bound by the rules of the Divine-human partnership, biblically called the Noahide covenant.

The Noahide covenant is permanent, but the Torah tells us that God chose Abraham, Sarah, and their children to be the bearers of an additional, particular covenant. Particular group covenants are needed because the emergence of a universal *brit* (covenant) brings with it a great risk implicit in the exercise of human power and freedom. Unified or centralized human power can inflict evil unchecked. Ironically, this danger is exacerbated by the very vision of perfecting the world. All these godlike capacities can be enlisted in the cause of totalitarianism, which, strengthened by good intentions and dreams of perfection, will stop at nothing to realize its goal. The glittering ideal of the perfect world can blind the eye to the cruelty being done in the name of advancing the cause. The music of redemption drowns out the anguished cries of the victims of progress and soothes the conflicts in the breast of killers for kindness. To prevent the possibility of utopian totalitarianism, one must break up the centralization of human culture, power, and institutions.

The particularization of the Noahide covenant and the sharing of the covenantal task between smaller (national) groups restores the human scale of the movement to perfect Creation (*tikun olam*, repairing the world). Small group covenants also open up the possibility of experimental, varied pathways toward perfection. Local successes can be spread around or imitated by other groups; failures or dangerous tendencies can be contained within the limits of the community or locale.

Of course there is a trade-off in adopting such a strategy of redemption. The use of human groups as agents of covenant may lead to the growth of parochial loyalties. The creation of an in-group/out-group mentality often leads to double-standard morality codes and to the reduction of the humanity of the outsider. Conflicts of interest frequently emerge between the group's needs and the cause of *tikun olam*, the very cause for which the group has come into being. This danger of chauvinism can be offset only by engendering a moral universe in which particular human bonds of affection and morality are nurtured but are balanced by being set in an overarching culture of universal love and responsibility. This constant tension (and the inevitable recurring outbursts of tribalism or runaway universalism as one tendency or the other gains strength) will be a prominent aspect of Israel's covenantal history. On the other hand, the particular covenant opens the door to a more richly textured and more human religious experience. Each group can incorporate its own language, its own specific historical experiences and family memories, and its own favorite symbols into the warp and woof of its religion.

Covenanting with smaller groupings of humanity also addresses the question of the pace of perfection. How can human beings be inspired with the vision of *tikun olam* without being overwhelmed by constant pressure from divine revelation? How can humans be moved to change the status quo as quickly as possible? The answer that is most respectful of human dignity is: by calling into being an avant-garde to serve as pacesetter for humanity, a cadre of humans to undertake the task of working toward redemption at so high a level as to inspire others to greater efforts by their example. The vanguard is willing to work in a highly disciplined way and to be held accountable for this effort so as to become lead partners in humanity's covenant with God. The Bible works with one small group; the family of Abraham is elected to be the pacesetters for humanity. This family *brit* neither repeals nor replaces the universal covenant. After all, God's covenantal love, *hesed*, is steadfast; God's calling proves to be irrevocable.

In the development of the particular covenant out of the universal, the partnership with God is intensified. The human partner is further empowered, as evidenced by Abraham's intervention to plead for Sodom (Gen. 18), in contrast with Noah's passive acceptance of the divine decree to wipe out all life on earth (Gen. 6:13–22).

THE ABRAHAMIC COVENANT

The gift of election is given to Abraham and Sarah and their family, and not to an individual. The goal of the mission is to advance the triumph of life. Only the family has the biological capability of creating life and also the bonds of love to nourish and raise it successfully. The family is the womb of humanness; its love confirms and deepens the individual's image of God. Affirming the family makes clear from day one that the natural affection and emotional links that bind the family are not to be thrust aside for the sake of the greater good, namely, the assignment to repair the world.

Covenant incorporates committed love, a love that is willing to be bound to the other. Entering the covenant represents the lover's promise to be steadfast in the face of obstacles and failure; the partner is binding herself to be there even when the emotion of love flags. The singling out is a proclamation of love and divine good purpose for the Abrahamic family and all of humanity (Gen. 12). Abraham's family is singled out to establish the human scale of redemption and to hasten its pace and, thereby, its arrival for all. Thus, when Abraham responded to his call, he changed from being a local notable to becoming a blessing for the other families of the earth. Moreover, the choosing of Abraham and Sarah is designed to pluralize the ways to salvation; by living in harmony with the divine order, their descendants are to release the channels of blessing already inherent in the Creation. When the other peoples walk in Israel's footsteps, they, too, draw forth the divine abundance from the wells of blessing that lie beneath the surface of life. Thus Abraham is a source of blessing for all.

With election comes the promise that Abraham will receive the gift of the land, with the condition that eventually his descendants will inherit it. The future gift makes clear that having been asked to uproot in order to move ahead in the covenant, Abraham's family will obtain a new place to settle. The divine faithfulness to this promise led to the great liberation in the Exodus that is the cornerstone of the Mosaic covenant. And the profound connection of land and calling confirms the dignity of embodiment and the significance of economic life and labor, now and forever.

The commanded sign of the covenant—circumcision—underscores the profound transformation of Abraham's condition as a result of his joining in this pact. The organ of generation is marked with a sign of dedication; in turn, that mark in the flesh constantly evokes God's promise, the assurance of the expansion and victory of life in the world. Moreover, God's blessing is now intimately intertwined with God's human partner. Circumcision reminds both God and Abraham of their sacred undertaking and ultimately sets the children of Abraham inescapably apart in the eyes of their neighbors. Finally, circumcision makes it clear that Israel is of the flesh as well as of the spirit; this again underscores the affirmation of embodiment. The Israelite body sends the message that God-is-in-our-midst, incarnate.

Abraham and, later, the children of Israel, are teachers to humanity everywhere; to many, they are the first to bring the message of the presence of God and the call to walk the way of the Lord through life. So closely is God's name associated with the people Israel that even if some circumcised Israelites do not want to testify, their existence is an involuntary witness.

The link between circumcision and covenant was directly challenged by the Apostle Paul and by Christian hermeneutics during and after the break between the two religions. In Paul's argument, the true Jew is one who is such inwardly, and the true circumcision is of the heart (Rom. 2:29). In defending Judaism, some Jews intensified the stress on the biology and carnality, the very law that Paul and other Christian theologians disputed. A rereading of Abraham's life, especially of the chapters on cutting the covenant (Gen. 15, 17), refutes the easy contrasts that developed out of these early, polemical disputes: Abraham as the icon of pure faith versus Abraham the one who is given specific commandments and who undergoes circumcision in response; Abraham the universalist father of many nations versus Abraham the particularist father of a family that stands alone. Such partisan readings are simplistic; the chosen's function is richly complex. Abraham's call includes acting as all of the above. The covenantal instructions extend across a continuum of meaning.

THE COVENANT OF SINAI

At Sinai, the Abrahamic covenant was renewed, deepened, and extended to a whole people. Abraham's *brit* had all the great strengths of a family covenant; it also had all the limitations of a family covenant. Blood ties make the exercise of mutual responsibility elemental. The frame is too biological, running the risk of excluding others not born into the system.

A nation incorporates people beyond the immediate family. At Sinai, the people of Israel, including absorbed mixed multitudes, were elected to be God's people. The nation's experience of being chosen was spelled out in the later synagogal liturgy, which includes references to being singled out, being loved and desired by God, and being exalted. In grateful response, the Israelites accepted the partnership offered at Sinai. The covenant that came with chosenness included making the nation holy/special through additional commandments that made the people Israel an avant-garde in God's service. The Sinaitic covenant was powerfully shaped by the Exodus. Liberation was the act that singled out the people Israel. The Exodus challenges the reigning status quo and points to a future perfection even as it affirms the meaningfulness of history. Thus the Exodus generates the dialectical tension between the real and the ideal, and the events at Sinai again make the point that a covenant is required to close the gap and to guide living along the way to redemption.

By focusing on the Exodus, the Sinaitic covenant deepens Israel's commitment to the perfection of time (history) and not just space (Creation) or spirit (humans). God's mighty acts of redemption *are* in history and not in some mythic realm. Of course, Israel's religion is not simply the product of the victory of the Exodus; the people of Israel will continue to testify in exile and after defeat.

The mission to testify places an enormous weight on the shoulders of the chosen people. Every day they must witness to infinite value in a world where values are degraded. In their behaviors, they must act responsibly when others "unburdened" by covenant may take advantage. When external events bring crushing forces to bear on them, they must find the internal fortitude to persist in hope and testimony. Given the incredible faithfulness and persistence in the face of suffering that the covenantal people have shown, one is almost convinced that God knew exactly what God was getting in selecting this family. In any event, at every step, covenantal actions summon up distinctive blessing for the covenant people; simultaneously, these blessings operate in exemplary fashion and extend to all humanity.

ISRAEL AND ITS BLESSINGS

God's promise to establish Israel in dignity in its own land is an example of the blessing bestowed upon the covenant people and of the extension of this blessing to the world. The promise implies that the soul of Abraham's children is bound to this land in a special way and that the land is uniquely responsive to them. At the same time, the right to live somewhere is the anchor of self-worth. The covenant model suggests that all peoples should have a homeland where their right to exist is self-evident and unquestioned. Unfortunately, most people tend to slip into the corruptions of being landed—becoming tribal, exploiting or excluding the outsider, or worshiping the gods of this space, however morally outrageous their demands may be. Moreover, people do not necessarily feel an obligation to turn their land into the locus of a moral, humane society. In the act of election, God asks the beloved to step up and lead the way for humanity. The Chosen People are to make the Promised Land a microcosm of perfection, a land in which economic equality, righteousness, justice, and equal treatment before the law will be the lot and right of everyone, citizen and stranger alike.

When the people of Israel did not set an example for the world in this way, they were degraded or exiled, God's Name was profaned, and the covenantal message was damaged. The other nations misread the sight of Israel in exile as proof that there is no profit in living covenantally.

The nations misunderstood the situation in two ways. First, they failed to discern that the expulsion occurred because Israel had not lived up to the convenantal standard that is demanded of God's people. Second, they failed to grasp that since Israel is planted in God, exile cannot make it lose its soul or its way; it can move from one land to another and maintain its values and its being because it is grounded in God. It is also the case that when living in the homeland, this very groundedness in God should prevent Israel from absolutizing land possession and should remind Jews of their part in *tikun olam,* of their role as a blessing to the nations.

To be a blessing to the world, Israel must play three roles. It must be a teacher, a model, and a coworker. As a *teacher,* each living generation must pass on its values to others, starting with its own children. Because the goal of perfection cannot be achieved in one generation, the covenant is, of necessity, a treaty among all the generations, as well as between them and God. If one generation rejects the covenant or fails to pass it on to the next generation, then the efforts and sacrifices of all past (and future) generations are wasted as well. The encounter with God and the experience of cosmic care give Israel insight and gird it with strength to teach covenantal values. As teacher of humanity, Israel becomes God's witness (Isa. 43:10,12). In a flawed world, however, the faithful can only testify to their experience of the Divine Presence and of being saved, and this testimony may fail to convince others. If the messenger suppresses his or her testimony, or if the messenger's behavior contradicts the message, or if the facts of life and the condition of other people are dissonant with the affirmation, then the witness may well bear no fruit.

As a *model* for humanity, Israel must be a community within which covenantal values are maximally lived, at least to the extent realizable now in an imperfect world. By so doing, Israel can create a liberated zone—a land within which equality and all other forms of human dignity are respected. In serving as a model, Israel becomes "a light of nations" (Isa. 42:6). The term "model" must not be idealized. This model people is only human, with all the attendant limitations. At times, Israel looks out only for itself and fails to teach; at times, its behavior contradicts its witness. At such times, Israel is a model of what not to do. When Israel does rise to heights of faithfulness, courage, and responsibility, it is worthy of emulation.

Finally, Israel must be a *coworker* for redemption. One people cannot lift up the whole globe by itself; Israel must work with others. At times, some people have been tempted to dream of an apocalyptic ending that will burn away all the wicked (all the others?) and leave Israel alone, victoriously vindicated. This event would certainly be a morally unsatisfactory outcome of the divine election of Abraham. Throughout the Bible and thereafter, there are echoes of valid revelations to other peoples and traces of mighty redemptive acts bestowed on other nations (Gen. 14,18ff; Num. 22–24; Isa. 19–21,23; Jer. 1:4–10). Suffice it to say that at the end of days when the whole world is redeemed, other nations will have contributed their portion and will share in it fully (Isa. 2:1–4; Mic. 4:1–5; Isa. 57:6–7).

All the world is holy, suffused with divine presence. However, the transcendent is veiled by the evil and failure in the world. Someday perfection (life, peace, and harmony with God and Creation) will be manifest. In the interim, Israel is the holy place/nation/time where God's presence is more visible, and consequently, life is more triumphant there than elsewhere. In accepting the covenant, Israel agrees to become just such a nation of priests (teachers, role models) who offer an intensified model to challenge the nations. If Israel lives up to its full commitment, it becomes the signpost to which all eyes turn to be inspired to work for the final perfection.

THE NEW COVENANT OF CHRISTIANITY

Each stage of the covenant has its own time. Rabbinic tradition counts the 10 generations from Noah to Abraham as a measure of divine patience in the face of disappointment; sin and the power of the status quo go on after the Flood as before. Out of the intensifying divine search for partners in *tikun olam*, God chose Abraham to initiate another experiment and to move the world toward perfection. This is the precedent for further experimentation.

One can speculate on the timing of events in the first century. It was always God's plan to bring the vision of redemption and the covenantal way to more of humanity. After thousands of years, the Jewish people had sufficiently internalized the covenant to be able to take on new levels of responsibility—as they would evidence in the aftermath of the destruction of the Second Temple. Challenged and enriched by Hellenism, the Israelites were capable of relating to a more hidden holiness without losing their connection to the transcendent God.

At the same time, in the Hellenistic world, there was a high receptivity to the spiritual/ethical messages of the covenant, especially if they could be articulated in Hellenistic terms, to and for gentiles. Non-Jews could be made aware that they were rooted in God also. Bringing considerably more people into covenantal relationships with God would be an important fulfillment (albeit not a complete one) of the promise that Abraham's people would be a blessing for the families of the earth.

The group that would bring the message of redemption to the rest of the nations had to grow out of the family and covenanted community of Israel. But the community was not intended to be a replacement for Abraham's family; nor were its achievements the proof of a divine repudiation of Sarah's covenant. The new avant-garde was to secede and connect to new masses of people in their language and images. This new religion should not be too Jewish, behaviorally or culturally, if it were to be absorbed by the gentiles. Therefore, although the new articulation of the faith grew in the soil of Judaism and was profoundly connected to past Jewish symbols and history, it metamorphosed to integrate with the people that it reached. Once one grasps that the emergence of this group was the expression of divine pluralism, i.e., God seeking to expand the number of covenantal channels to humanity without closing any of them, then the next step follows logically. The new development would have to become an independent religion, or it would undermine the continuing, distinctive Jewish lifestyle and witness.

Christianity had to start within Judaism, but it had to grow into its own autonomous existence to preserve the particularity of the original covenantal ways while enabling deeper exploration of the polarities that characterize the covenantal dialectic. Jesus' life, the catalyst that crystallized the new religion, was to be shared with the minimum number sufficient to shape and broadcast a new religion. The new articulation of the classic message was not intended for the Jewish majority, which was shortly to be called to carry out its Rabbinic flowering. Rather, simultaneously with the emergence of Christianity, the bulk of Jewry was swept up into one of the great renewals of Jewish history.

What was that initial signal? Was it a special teacher who gave new vitality and freshness to his followers' religious lives, communicating a sense of special closeness of the presence of God? Was it a revolutionary advocate for the poor and outcasts or against the Romans, proclaiming the kingdom of God, preaching a political, economic, and spiritual transformation out of which the first would be last and the last would be first? Was it some miracle maker whose truest miracle was to channel God's love and, hence, the sense of election to those who followed him? Or was the signal the miraculous, blazing glory proclaimed by many Christians who read the Gospels quite literally today? By contemporary standards of proof, likely we shall never know the answer. In any event, the period of that initial signal was overtaken by the crisis of Jesus' Crucifixion.

Was this shocking, God-mocking, torturous death the end of miracles? The proof that the brutal status quo would always win? The cruel refutation of the teaching of love? The ultimate phenomenology of Godforsakenness? The faithful few, thinking like Jews, concluded that death and destruction do not get the final word. On the contrary, defeat tests faith and opens the door to new and deeper understanding. Then they received another, activating signal: an empty tomb. The fact that Jesus did not even attain the minimal dignity of a final resting place—an undisturbed grave—should have been the final nail in the crucifixion of their faith. Instead, they increased hope and trust in God. Soon they experienced the same (or greater) presence in their midst as before. Once faith supplied the key of understanding, the empty tomb yielded the message of the Resurrection. Whether they received this message within three days, as the Gospel story indicates, or within three decades, as the most probable scholarly account has it, is of secondary importance. Inspired, they redoubled their telling of their redemption story. Inspired, they interpreted every inherited symbol and tradition as foreshadowing their redeemer. Among Jews who were hearing other divine messages loud and clear, their preaching made little headway; among gentiles, as was intended, it spread and spread.

The original people of God soon encountered their own crisis—the destruction of the Holy Temple in Jerusalem and the exile that soon followed. Was this catastrophe the end of the covenant? In light of Jewish religious/national fervor and their revolt against Rome out of loyalty to God, why did God not vanquish the Romans even as God had overwhelmed the Egyptians?

Instead of despairing, most Jews increased their hope and trust in God. The Rabbis emerged to teach of God's self-limitation, of God's "hiddenness," which was designed to call the people of Israel to participate more fully in the covenant. In the Temple, the manifest God showed overwhelming power, speaking through prophet and breastplate, and holiness was "concentrated" in Jerusalem. Now, God was calling on Israel to discern the Divine that was hidden but present everywhere. To see God everywhere requires a special skill; learning and law now became the keys to religious understanding. The Jewish people, in biblical times an ignorant peasantry awed by sacramental, revelatory experiences in the Temple (or elsewhere!), were now trained by the Rabbis to study and speak through prayer to a God who no longer revealed Godself to Israel. The sacramental religion of the Bible was transformed into the internalized, more participatory faith of the Rabbinic period. Even as Christians responded to their great religious experiences by proclaiming a New Covenant, Jews responded to their extraordinary flowering by affirming a *renewal* of the covenant.

In the aftermath of the destruction came the tragedy in the parting of the ways (note: *in* the parting of the ways, not *of* the parting of the ways). As Christianity spread among gentiles, they heard the message in a way that made Jesus more literally godlike. Jews looked away from the shared values, the shared sense of covenant, and the shared memories and focused on the Christian teaching that Jesus was God, which made Christian teaching more unacceptable, indeed inferior, in Jewish eyes. Soon gone from Judaism, or rather muted within, were the themes of grace, love, and the pathos of divine suffering—covenantal all, but now deemed to be too Christian.

At the same time, as Christianity spread among gentiles, it elaborated a theology that eliminated *halakhah* (starting with the practices that separated Jews from non-Jews). Furthermore, to the constant Jewish critique that the world was manifestly unredeemed (therefore, Jesus could be no true redeemer), Christianity responded by spiritualizing redemption (and dismissing Judaism as a "carnal" religion). The conjunction of anti-halakhic thinking and the dismissal of biology (Christians are children of Abraham in the spirit) encouraged an otherworldly focus and reinforced a dualism that often pitted the soul against the body and the flesh against the spirit. Rootedness in the land also was spiritualized away; no land was sacred, and only the heavenly Jerusalem really mattered. Christianity preserved the covenantal dialectic between the ideal and the real. However, in its main thrust it leaned to one side of this dialectic, a skewing that was reinforced by its increasing perception of Judaism as the devil's advocate, rather than as God's balancing voice.

Experiencing their own real sense of God's love as election, Christians assumed that the Jews must have lost theirs. Then Christians became convinced that their interpretation of the common symbols was the only one. As Christians saw it, the destruction of the Temple and the subsequent exile of the Jews was decisive proof of Christian interpretation of God's intentions. Precisely because of the Jewish origins of Jesus and shared patrimony with the Jews, the Christians were driven to insist that Judaism was superseded. The final confirmation of Christian supersessionism came with the success of Christianity in the Roman Empire. A triumph of the spirit, i.e., bringing God, love, covenant, redemption, and ethics to countless pagans, turned into a victory for a politically established religion and a license for triumphalism.

In their triumphalism, Christians overlooked the extent to which theirs was a one-sided and partial reading of the biblical tradition in the light of their redemptive experience; they ignored the possibility that God had supplied the Jews with a different interpretive key. Instead, Christians concluded that the Jews had to be spiritually deaf and dumb or willfully devilish to resist Christian understandings. From this conclusion it was not a big jump to medieval Christianity's demonizing and dehumanizing of the Jews and, from there, to the Holocaust. Thus a gospel of love—which often acted that way among gentiles—turned into a sermon of hatred of the original people of Israel, especially as election became self-centered and the experience of chosenness turned into a claim to hold a monopoly on God's love.

The narrowing of its messages that grew out of its unconditional rejection of Judaism penalized Christianity itself in no small measure. The focus on crucifixion privileged suffering as the ultimate form of service to the Lord. This religious norm strengthened ascetic tendencies in the religion and devalued the spiritual significance of pleasure. The model of self-abnegating sacrifice as the key relationship to God generated fideism, sometimes at the expense of reason; it also nurtured the self-image of a powerless human, dependent on a mediator, unable to help himself or play a fully dignified role in the covenant. Sometimes, such attitudes spread to other cultural disciplines.

For their part, the Rabbis could only envision a covenantal pluralism inside Judaism. They understood the Christian claim that if Christianity was right, Judaism was wrong. Since Jews experienced religious vitality and the presence of Holy Spirit in their community, they concluded that Christianity was an imposter faith and that Jesus was a false messiah. Precisely because of a shared Bible and because of the Jewish origins of Christianity, Jews were driven to insist that Christianity was idolatrous, i.e., it advocated the worship of a man. Just as the Christian rejection of Judaism penalized and distorted Christianity, so, too, Judaism was skewed by Jewry's inability to admit the vitality of Christian religion and its contribution to meaning and ethics around the world. To reduce the impact of Christianity's triumph among gentiles, Jewry dismissed the significance of this world and of politics and military power. Law and learning were stressed in counterpoint to the grace and love of the gospel, to the extent that tendencies to legalism or underrating the spirit were stimulated. Also, a certain narrowing of Jewish concern from all of humanity to the tribe of Israel took place.

COVENANT AFTER THE *SHOAH*

The *Shoah* was the reductio ad demonic absurdum of interethnic, inter-religious hatred. The Nazi demonizing of the Jews drew upon the subculture of degradation and hostility that grew out of past Christian teachings of contempt. After the *Shoah,* the burden of this past teaching was insufferable to repentant Christians. The *Shoah* made clear the overriding need to end all circles of hatred that surrounded and isolated groups of others. The isolation not only made Jews vulnerable, but also tempted bystanders into indifference and silence. Jews had to ask themselves if they would not be guilty of similar failures were the people and religions that they disrespected at risk. Responding to the Holocaust created an overwhelming moral need to restore the image of God to the other. This restoration required recovering the uniqueness of the other by throwing off the lenses of stereotype and of caricature. The Nazi absolute—a combination of centralized power and unrestrained ideology—made the Holocaust possible. The commitment to "never again" allow such mass murder and degradation demanded the breakup of all concentrated power and absolutisms—even cultural and religious ones. Pluralism—the setting of healthy limits on absolutes, valid or otherwise—emerged as a key corrective to the abusive tendencies built into all traditions of ultimate meaning. The more people of faith were committed to restore God and the image of God in a devastated post-*Shoah* world, the more they were driven to recognize God's intended pluralism.

Jews, too, must understand that theological contempt cannot be separated from human responsibility. As Hillel said, in summary of the whole Torah, "What is hateful to you, do not do to others." Jews must recognize the full implications of the truth that "God has many messengers." It is not enough to speak of the tradition that there is salvation for individuals outside of Judaism. This generality does not do justice to the full spiritual dignity of others who live their lives in religious communities, and not just as individuals.

In this spirit, one can make the following declaration about Christianity from a Jewish perspective. Both religions grow out of Abraham's covenant and out of the Exodus. The Exodus, as understood by the Hebrew prophets, is an event that points beyond itself to future, expanded redemptions. The messianic impulse is a fundamental expression of Judaism's ongoing vitality. In that sense, Christianity is not a mere deviation or misunderstanding; it is an organic outgrowth of Judaism itself. As I have argued above, Christianity is a divinely inspired attempt to bring the covenant of *tikun olam* to a wider circle of gentiles. God intended that Judaism and Christianity both work for the perfection of the world (the kingdom of God). The logic of such a move is that, together, both religions do greater justice to the dialectical tensions of covenant than either religion can do alone.

Judaism's focus on family as the context for *brit* is constructive; pursued one-sidedly it can lead to tribalism and amoral familism. The religion needs to be balanced by a faith that breaks out of the family model and explores the power of a universal, faith-defined belief group. Rabbinic Judaism brings humans more powerfully into participation in the covenant, but it needs a counterpart religion to explore the element of grace and transcendence in a more central way. In this perspective, Jewish covenant peoplehood and Christian faith community are both validated. Both models are a necessary expression of the plenitude of divine love and of the comprehensiveness and range of human roles in the covenant. By the same token, it is not too late for Christians to enrich their own revelation by learning from interpretation and the development of *halakhah* how humans become (in Joseph Soloveitchik's words) co-creators of Torah, the divine word. Nor is it too late for Jews to enrich their own way by focusing again on grace and the sacramental and universal motifs played out in Christianity.

What if we use the same approach to the method of redemption? What if we assume that God is using both religions in tandem because together the full possibilities in messianism as the mode of redemption are better realized? What illumination does this approach provide on the dispute between the faiths as to the nature of the Messiah and whether the Messiah has come or not?

Posing the question this way opens intriguing new vistas on the issue that has so divided Jews and Christians all these years. In particular, Maimonides (Rambam) can be read anew to shed light in our current encounter. In his great code, *Mishneh Torah* (*Yad HaChazakah*), Maimonides starts by indicating that the title "Messiah" is used both for King David, who as ruler saved the people Israel from the hands of its enemies, and for "the later Messiah, a descendant of David, who will achieve the final salvation of Israel."[1]

Maimonides suggests that every ruler (by implication, leader) who arises and seeks to achieve the messianic goals—and achieves some of them—may be presumed to be the Messiah. By Maimonides' definition: A credible candidate should engage in (= study and teach) Torah (the written and the oral) and practice its commandments; prevail on Israel to walk in its ways and repair its breaches; and fight the battles of the Lord.[2] If the would-be redeemer fully succeeds, he will restore the Temple (i.e., the manifest Presence of the Lord) and gather the dispersed of Israel (i.e., make whole the people). Such accomplishments would prove that "he is for sure the Messiah."[3]

The climax of the final step includes that he "will repair the whole world to serve the Lord together."[4] In other words, the Messiah is known by the fruits of the Messiah's labors. The title must be earned the old-fashioned way: by redeeming Israel—and the world. Presumably the messianic redemption will include perfecting both the socio-political-economic as well as the spiritual condition of the world—at least that is how the Hebrew Scripture described the final perfection and how Jews continued to define it.

In the uncensored edition of his classic, Rambam spells out the further implications of this pragmatic criterion to establish the identity of the redeemer: ". . . if he [= the presumed Messiah] does not meet with full success, or is slain, it is obvious that he is not the Messiah promised in the Torah."[5] But failure in the effort does not make a ruler into a false messiah; not if, like Hezekiah and (according to Maimonides in a different context) like Bar Kochba, the would-be redeemer tried to accomplish the right goals and taught the right values.[6] Then the failed candidate "is to be regarded like all the other wholehearted and worthy kings of the House of David who died . . . [without achieving the messianic goals—IG]." Maimonides adds that failed redeemers are raised up by "The Holy One, The Blessed" to "test the multitude."[7] Presumably the test is of the people's capacity to rally to a presumptive Messiah (proving that the messianic hope is still alive), to distance from a failed redeemer (proving that the people are not detached from reality), and to still remain open to future candidates (= never give up the messianic vision).

Rambam's view opens the door to the argument (articulated in the essay earlier, "Toward an Organic Model of the Relationship") that if Christianity repents of its assault on Judaism, then Jesus should not be viewed as a "false messiah," but as a "failed messiah." Strikingly, Maimonides makes one side of this point in the continuation of his uncensored argument. He writes of Jesus of Nazareth as an example of the prophecy in Daniel that a group of people "shall lift themselves up to establish the vision [in Maimonides' interpretation, a reference to the messianic vision—IG] but they shall stumble" (Daniel 11:16). Says Rambam: "For has there ever been a greater stumbling than this? All the prophets affirmed that the Messiah would redeem Israel, save them, gather their dispersed, and confirm the commandments. But he [Jesus] caused Israel to be destroyed by the sword, their remnant to be dispersed and humiliated."[8] In other words, in Maimonides' view, Christian destructive behavior vis-à-vis Jewry, which really means the persecution and degradation of others by Christianity, constitutes the proof that Jesus is a false messiah. From which one may argue that the cessation of such behavior—better still, the initiation of respect for Jewish dignity and loving, protective actions for Jewish security—open the door to reclassify Jesus into an honorable category.*

True, in the uncensored text Rambam also adds another reason for judging Jesus to be a false messiah: "He was instrumental in changing the Torah and causing the world to err and serve another beside God.[9] I would argue that this judgment holds true when Christianity presents itself as the religion that replaces Judaism and abolishes it. Then indeed in Jesus' name, the Torah is being illegitimately changed and Jews are being led to serve another beside God (assuming that Jesus is being served as a divine being by Jews whose erstwhile religion led them to serve God directly and alone). However, if we now are dealing with a Christianity that is pluralist and fully affirms the ongoing validity of the Sinaitic covenant and of Judaism as a religion, then the above strictures arguably do not apply. In this view, to Jews the Torah is valid and binding as before. One is reminded of the teaching attributed to Jesus in the Sermon on the Mount: "Do not suppose that I have come to abolish the Law and the prophets—I tell you this: so long as heaven and earth endure, not a letter, not a stroke [a probable reference to the Rabbinic Oral Law tradition, which derived laws from the strokes/jots/tittles that are part of the calligraphy of the Torah's letters—IG] will disappear. If any man, therefore, sets aside even the least of the Law's demands, and teaches others to do the same, he will have the lowest place in the Kingdom of Heaven, whereas anyone who keeps the Law, and teaches others so, will stand high in the Kingdom of Heaven" (Matt. 5:17–19).[10] Admittedly there

---

* In 1906, Rabbi Abraham Isaac HaCohen Kook, the visionary, mystical giant of modern religious Zionism, wrote an historical essay in which he referred to the alternating waves of movements focusing on learning/reason as against spirituality/charisma in Judaism's history. Kook suggested that the constant alternation rescued Judaism from periodic regression and routine and moved the faith toward renaissance. Although he expressed deep criticism of Christianity, Kook made a positive statement about Jesus possessing "wonderful personal power, his soulful current was great...." (reprinted in *When God Becomes History: Historical Essays of Rabbi Abraham Isaac HaCohen Kook,* trans. Bezalel Naor, p. 50). The remark shocked the traditional community in which Christianity was anathema and which objected even to pronouncing Jesus' actual name. Kook was forced to play down and explain away what he said. His comments continued to draw criticism for decades. Nevertheless, years later, in a letter to Elhanan Kalmanson, he wrote a private justification hinting that he was only guilty of being ahead of his time. Kook wrote, " ...Being as the new paganism [= Christianity—IG] made a man into an idol, *and we suffered so much as a result,* we stand resolute in our eternal opposition to this idolatry, We will not substitute our cry of Shakez teshakzenu (Abomination!) with any other concept until which time as this segment of humanity will nullify this idolatry *and publicly acknowledge our great truth. Only then at that fortunate time will our writers be able to say something positive* concerning this personality—but only then" (text dated to Tebeth 5685 [= January 16, 1925—IG], in Naor, op. cit., p. 59—my italics). In another passage, Kook points to the self-contradictory way in which Christianity, as a religion seeking to be a religion of love, nevertheless shed blood and spread hatred (especially of Jews). *Igrot ha-Rayah* (Jerusalem, 1923), Letter 11. I thank Fred Gorsetman for this reference.

are antinomian passages in Jesus' name in the Gospels also. But, in any event, a repentant Christianity would not apply such teachings to Jews. A pluralist Christianity reaching out to pagan gentiles is leading them to serve the God of Israel as they never have before; arguably this statement is true even though Jewish religion objects to the interposition of Jesus and the Trinitarian claim that he is part of God.*

From this pluralist perspective, Jesus is no false messiah who teaches evil values. Rather, when Christianity, in Jesus' name, claims absolute authority and denigrates the right of Judaism or of Jews to exist, then it makes him into a false messiah. Short of such claims, however, Jews should recognize Jesus as a would-be redeemer for the nations. This recognition would allow Jews to acknowledge the historical fact that for hundreds of millions of people, Christianity has been and continues to be a religion of love, consolation, and redemption.

Let us then return to the earlier question: what possible advantage could there be to the realization of messianism in having a would-be redeemer appear in a second religion? In his uncensored text, Maimonides goes on to say: "But it is beyond the human mind to fathom the designs of the Creator; for our ways are not His ways, neither are our thoughts His thoughts."[11] Here is a tacit hint that there is a possible "theocentric," positive perspective on the development out of Judaism of another religion making messianic claims. Maimonides is saying that I/we Jews would not have done it this way, but God's thoughts outstrip our present categories. (I translate that the divine pluralism eluded the medieval absolutist mindset.)

Rambam continues: "All these matters relating to Jesus of Nazareth and the Ishmaelite (Mohammed) who came after him, *only serve to clear the way for King Messiah, to prepare the whole world to worship God with one accord* . . . [italics supplied—IG]. Thus the messianic hope, the Torah, and the commandments have become familiar topics—topics of conversation (among the inhabitants) of the far isles and many peoples, uncircumcised of heart and flesh."[12]

Maimonides has pointed to the advantages of a two-front (possibly multi-front!) religious outreach. For millions, nay billions of people, the ideas of God and a promise of a messianic final redemption, hitherto utterly foreign to their pagan or other religions, have become credible alternative beliefs. For billions of people who would have accepted the status quo of poverty, slavery, hierarchy, war, sickness, and nasty, brutish, short lives as the given, inescapable human fate, a vision of intrinsic value, equality, and entitlement to a dignified life has been revealed. As the rain and snow drops from heaven

---

* Elsewhere, specifically in his "Epistle to Yemen" in *Igrot HaRambam,* ed. Yitzhak Shilat, vol. 1, pp. 120–121 [Jerusalem: Ma'aliyot, 1981], Maimonides speaks far more harshly of Jesus, blaming him for being deeply antinomian.

and returns not there but soaks the earth and brings forth vegetation, yielding seed for sowing and bread for eating, so does the divine vision and word not come back unfulfilled.

This vision has set in motion wave after wave of liberation, of human dreams of a world perfected. This word has undermined the status quo by softening the hard-baked crust of fatalism and allowing the upwelling forces of human need and desire for dignity. The iron laws of necessity have been melted, paving the way for cultural transformation after transformation. The positive impact has been extended by the secularized versions of these religious insights, including science building on the concept of Creation to analyze and exploit natural laws; liberation-oriented, social, and economic philosophies that disseminate egalitarian practices and principles of social responsibility and solidarity; democracy spreading the principles and practices of human dignity; and capitalism distributing affluence and improvements in standards of living.

Even though Jesus was not able to complete the perfection of the world through Christianity, he has created an appetite for the final redemption that is planted in the hearts of multitudes. There it remains dormant, but like tinder brush these hearts are more ready to be set on fire by further intervention. This brings us to another advantage of this two-pronged approach. The Christian "yes"—the Messiah has come—illustrates the extent to which God is present in the world, that the vision communicated powerfully is already half the battle won for its realization, that reality is a challenge and not a fixed fact, that the spiritual component is an important part of the final perfection. The Jewish "no"—the Messiah has not come and accomplished the goals yet—illustrates the extent to which God is present in the world, that no aspect of the vision should be yielded by spiritualization or disembodiment, that vision must not blind us to reality, that the earthly, bodily, human component is an important part of the final perfection. Since no religion can keep these tensions in perfect balance, the dual differing emphasis in the witness of Judaism and Christianity, properly (not destructively) pursued, can better keep humanity on track as we work for the perfection of the world.

Despite their past polemics, the two religions are not as totally contradictory on this issue as is the popular impression. For one, Christianity has tacitly recognized that the world is not yet redeemed by promising a Second Coming and by various Christian movements in history proclaiming that imminent arrival. Moreover, despite the spiritualization of messianism, Christianity—especially modern Christianity—ultimately has come down on the side that upholds that the final redemption will include political, economic, social, and earthly perfection.

For its part, Judaism has acknowledged that although the world is, at best, only partially redeemed, the messianic reality is presently alive in our midst—especially in the form of the Sabbath, a day with the flavor of the Messianic Era, here and now. Judaism also seeks to instill a covenantal consciousness in all humans. Covenantal consciousness sees everyone's life as part of an unbroken chain of life from the first cell to the first human to those who will live in the future generation that will see full redemption in their lives. For this reason, resurrection is a moral necessity so that all who participated along the way in the covenantal process of *tikun olam* will be there to share in its bliss. By this same covenantal consciousness, no one's life is finished with that person's death. The covenantal person identifies with the lives of those who have gone before and brought us to this point. That is why Abraham; Sarah; Moses; Miriam; David; Rabbi Akiva and his wife, Rachel; down to contemporary role models, are living models whom one addresses familiarly, whom one imitates, whom one learns from and studies as a dialogue partner. By the same token, nobody's past failures are final, for one's children and grandchildren take up the covenantal task, and one's work will yet be completed. Those with covenantal consciousness experience the future generation's accomplishments as their own. That feeling is what enables the covenanted to sacrifice, to deny themselves the pleasure, to defy present illegitimate authority, to persist, to do the right thing by the standard of the final perfection. Therefore, Christians have the right—instead of oppressing or demeaning those who say that Jesus is not the Messiah—to work all out to perfect the world, to achieve universal love and life. By acting this way, Christians would turn Jesus into not a failed messiah but an unfinished messiah, one whose career continues and whose name—like the Jewish teaching about God's name—can be sanctified, i.e., made credible or can be desecrated, i.e., made incredible, by the witness and behavior of the believers.

But what of the fact that Christianity went much beyond classic Jewish teachings about the Messiah as redeemer and taught that he is God Incarnate? Is this not a fatal obstacle to a Jewish affirmation of Christianity as an independent, dignified, covenantal parallel partner? Maimonides makes clear that whatever erroneous doctrines Christianity (or Islam) may teach does not undercut their fundamental contribution "to prepare the whole world to worship God with one accord."[13] Says Rambam: "They [the peoples of the world reached by the other Abrahamic faiths—IG] are discussing these matters [= God, messianic hope, the Torah teachings] and the commandments of the Torah. Some say, 'Those commandments were true, but have lost their validity and are no longer binding;' others declare that they had an esoteric meaning and were not intended to be taken literally, that the Messiah has already come and revealed their occult significance."

Maimonides makes clear that, from a Jewish perspective, these wrong teachings do not take away the accomplishments of these religions—by God's inscrutable will—in preparing the world for God. In other words, Christian (and Muslim) teachings prepare the world for a more perfect truth even where they may be presently mistaken. In part, Maimonides says so because he believes that as soon as the true King Messiah appears, the gentiles will recant and accept the true redeemer's teachings. In a more pluralist spirit, we might apply this idea in three ways. One is that the world will be perfected for all of humanity; "they shall do no evil nor cause any harm throughout My Holy Mountain [= Earth]" (Isa. 11:9) [my translation]. Second, the final "worship of God with one accord" will make room for pluralist religious conceptions and practices that will be recognized by all as being directed to the same God. Thirdly, as the dialogue unfolds and as contemporary thinking interpenetrates Christianity, the dimension of monotheism will be strengthened over the dimension of Trinitarianism. In this model, Jesus need play no less central a role for Christians in bringing God to people and people to God. It is just the interpretation of the category or status he is in that will be clarified. If you will, he will be the paradigmatic image of God that lifts up humans and brings them closer to God—rather than God's self. Here I feel a need to fall silent, for these are matters of such centrality to Christianity that they should be discussed and resolved within the circle of faithful believers and not determined by the views of believers of a different faith, no matter how well-intentioned or loving their concerns.

From a Jewish perspective, one hopes that the growing Christian emphasis on Jesus as the path to God rather than on Jesus as God Incarnate may yet win out as a more proper understanding. If it does not, then Jews and other non-Christians may argue that Christianity is wrong in this understanding. But a single error, even on a major point, does not destroy the overall legitimacy of Christianity's covenantal way. Implicit in pluralism is the recognition that there are limits in my truth that leave room for others. Such limits may include the acknowledgment that erroneous doctrines do not necessarily delegitimize the faith that incorporates them.

If the Christian insistence that Jesus is literally God or part of God wins out, then many Jews will argue that closing the biblically portrayed gap between the human and the Divine, between the real and the ideal, by incarnation is idolatrous or at least against the grain of the biblical way. But even if incarnation is contradictory to some biblical principles, the model itself is operating out of classic biblical modes—the need to achieve redemption, the desire to close the gap between the human and the Divine, the role of divine initiatives in redemption, and so on. Thus one can argue that incarnation is improbable and violates other given biblical principles, or that it is unnecessary in light of the continuing career of the Jewish people. But one can hardly rule out the option totally, particularly if it was intended for gentiles and not for Jews. Leave it to God what religious messages should be given, and to other faith communities how signals should be heard in those communities—unless they have evil consequences for others.

Both Judaism and Christianity share the totality of their dreams and the flawed finiteness of their methods; nonetheless, they differ so fundamentally that the traditional record is dominated by bitter conflict. However, from a pluralistic perspective—from the perspective of a divine strategy of redemption rather than from within the communities embedded in historical experience and needs—both religions have more in common than they have been able to admit to themselves. Both Jews and Christians have a revolutionary dream of total transformation and yet remain willing to accept the finitude and limitations of humans and to proceed one step at a time. Both groups persist in preaching their messages despite the difficulties they have encountered along the way; they press ahead in the face of their historical suffering. And despite the terrible history of their relationship, each has witnessed to God and the human covenantal mission in its own way. For what often seems an eternity, both have hoped and waited, and both have transmitted the message and worked for the final redemption. Both need each other's work (and that of others) to realize their deepest hopes.

I conclude, therefore, as a faithful Jew nevertheless, that the Christian experience of election is valid; they have experienced God's love that singles out the beloved and transforms and revivifies life. They must understand, however, that God's love is capable of singling out again and again; they are not the sole beneficiaries of chosenness.

There remains one question to be asked. When Christians carry on their covenanted mission, are they members of the house of Israel? Are they in a parallel covenant or part of a single covenant alongside Jewry? Personally, I believe that world religions such as Islam and noncovenantal faiths such as Buddhism and forms of Hinduism should be recognized as movements legitimately striving to fulfill the universal divine covenant with humanity. However, only Christians (although possibly also Muslims) may be deemed to be members of the people Israel, even as they practice different religions than Jewry does. To articulate and defend this thesis would require another essay as long as this one. I adjure you, who love Jerusalem, by gazelles or by hinds of the field, let me not wake that love or rouse that enmity until the time please!

Notes

1. *Mishneh Torah*, Book of Judges, Laws of Kings, ch. 11, h. 1.
2. *Mishneh Torah*, ch. 11, h. 4.
3. Ibid.
4. Ibid.
5. *Mishneh Torah*, text translated in Isadore Twersky, editor, *A Maimonides Reader* (New York: Behrman House, 1972), p. 226).
6. *Mishneh Torah*, ch. 11, h. 3.
7. Ibid.
8. Ibid.
9. Ibid.
10. Translation from *New English Bible*, Oxford University Press: 1970, The New Testament, p. 7.
11. *Mishneh Torah*, ch. 11, h. 3.
12. Ibid.
13. Ibid.

Index

REFLECTIONS

In Appreciation of Irving Greenberg

James Carroll

I am among that legion of Christians who have been brought to new levels of awareness about Jewish experience and belief, as well as about my own Christian faith, through the life's work of Rabbi Irving Greenberg. I first encountered him in the early 1970s when, as a young Catholic priest, I was in the audience to hear him speak of the Holocaust at a major Jewish-Christian symposium in New York. I had already begun the journey toward a fuller Christian reckoning with the relationship between that historic crime and the Christian failure to effectively oppose it, but Rabbi Greenberg helped me confront the deeper question—how the sorry tradition of Christian contempt for Jews set the groundwork for the *Shoah*.

This volume is replete with essays that put on full display what has made Rabbi Greenberg one of the most effective dialogue partners the Christian community could ever hope to have. His conviction that God acts in history led him early on to the profoundly brave decision to pursue his own reckoning with the Holocaust, in partnership with Christians. That, in turn, led him to develop a stinging critique of Christian theology and tradition— one that included a firm acknowledgment that the Christian "teaching of contempt" has its origins in the church's own most sacred Scripture. But his partnership with Christians also resulted in his prophetic appreciation of the sacred values enshrined in the tradition that calls Jesus "Lord." Rabbi Greenberg set out to do nothing less than develop a Jewish theology of Christianity, an impulse that, whatever it has meant within the Jewish community (and it is not for me, as a Christian, to say), has had a profound impact on the thinking of Christians.

One of Rabbi Greenberg's most distinctive proposals, and one of his bravest, is that Jesus might properly be considered a "failed" messiah, or, as more recently articulated, an "unfinished" messiah. As his reflections on the history of this idea make clear in this book, the notion has been received with reservations or outright rejection by both Jews and Christians. Yet, speaking for myself, the invitation to think of Jesus in this way has been formative. Christian triumphalism—the conviction that the Church is *the* locus of God's full and complete revelation—is based on a grave act of forgetfulness. We Christians believe that the Messiah has come in Jesus Christ, but a less emphasized tenet of the faith holds that God's Kingdom is not full and complete until the Messiah comes *again*. The neglected idea of the Second Coming suggests that the work of Jesus—the revelation entrusted to the church—remains radically incomplete. Because that is so, the church must stand humbly before all that it is not yet, all that it does not know, all that remains hidden in the mystery of God's purpose for creation. The church is not in *possession* of the truth, but is on pilgrimage *toward* it. The humility that comes from such knowledge is the precondition of authentic Christian respect for Judaism, and for other religions. Rabbi Greenberg's provocative use of the word "failed," or "unfinished," is offensive only if his contrasting of both notions with "false" is ignored. Here is one small instance of his creative challenge to Jews and Christians alike, as I take it, that the time has come to think in new ways, for the sake of what he calls "a new encounter."

And the break in time that makes this challenge so, of course, is the Holocaust. Holocaust deniers have it that the horror did not take place; but Holocaust minimizers strike a more dangerous note, because to many, theirs is a more acceptable argument. They want the Holocaust removed from the consciousness of the West as a primal point of moral reflection, as if the *Shoah* were just one of many equivalent catastrophes. It takes nothing away from the suffering undergone by other peoples at various times and places to understand what was particularly evil about the Holocaust. Rabbi Greenberg's great contribution has been to insist, and insist again, that the genocidal Nazi assault on the Jewish people, *as* the Jewish people, stands as a defining epiphany. Speaking as a Christian, that has been especially so in my tradition. The slow, uneven confrontation with the facts of the Holocaust, and what led to it in the heart of Christian Europe, has been the foundation of the post–World War II renewal of Christian theology and practice. In my own Roman Catholic tradition, this renewal has at its core the Second Vatican Council and the church's subsequent efforts to rid itself of all forms of contempt for Jews and Judaism. That precious process—well begun, but far from complete—would not be occurring without the steadfast and brave witness of numerous Jewish figures. One thinks of the histo-

rian Jules Isaacs and Rabbis Abraham Joshua Heschel, Marc H. Tanenbaum—and Irving Greenberg.

It is not for me to define what the Jewish-Christian dialogue has meant
for Judaism, but, speaking as one whose faith has been transformed by it,
this encounter has meant everything to the Christian Church. We see the
main elements of this transformation boldly laid out in the preoccupations of
Rabbi Greenberg's work. What does it mean to say that God suffers, and how
is this notion Jewish as well as Christian? Can divine election involve, in
Rabbi Greenberg's ingenious phrase, "multiple choice?" How to move beyond tolerance to a mutual affirmation of the other's self-understanding?
How to move beyond pluralism, as he puts it, to partnership?

Rabbi Greenberg's unwavering devotion to the State of Israel, and his
readiness to see its establishment—and its security—as a profound marker
in history, puts a clear challenge to the old Christian need to imagine Jews
offering witness through statelessness. The State of Israel, too, is a crucial
subject of this interfaith encounter, but that presupposes the full Christian
affirmation, at last, of Jews at home in Israel. Rabbi Greenberg embodies a
proper insistence on this, as a witness and teacher.

This book is a record of, and a testimony to, the Jewish-Christian dialogue.
It gives the world the compelling voice of one of its pioneers, whose testimony shows that criticism and self-criticism can work together, enabling the
growth, even in ancient rivals, of trust and, perhaps, love. That this project of
mutual study, learning, respect, and finally partnership came after—or even
out of—the Holocaust is an unprecedented sign of hope, pointing not just to
an ongoing reconciliation of Christians and Jews, but—as Rabbi Greenberg,
with the usual reach of his large heart and open mind, insists—"to better future understanding between the nations and religions of the earth as well."

James Carroll is the author of ten novels; the memoir An American Requiem, *which
won the National Book Awar;, and of* Constantine's Sword, *which won the National Jewish Book Award in history. His latest book,* Crusade, *is drawn from his
antiwar columns in the* Boston Globe.

Response to *For the Sake Heaven and Earth*

David Novak

For the Sake Heaven and Earth shows why Irving Greenberg is such an important Jewish theologian. His importance is well deserved because of his courage—both moral and intellectual—especially in his positive assertions about Christians and Christianity. His moral courage is evidenced by how much he has been willing to risk being vilified because of these assertions in the Orthodox Jewish community of his birth and upbringing, a community where he has served as a rabbi and in whose synagogues he still worships. His intellectual courage is evidenced by his insistence that Jews radically rethink Judaism's view of Christianity after the Holocaust. Even though Greenberg constantly reaches out to all Jews, this rethinking can best be done by Orthodox Jews, as they are most secure and intense in their Jewish belief and practice. (Whether Greenberg still considers himself "Orthodox" in the political sense, even though he continues to live according to the normative Jewish tradition, is a question his readers should ask him themselves, especially after reading his quite personal first essay. With God's help, though, this book will have one or more sequels.)

Greenberg avoids the label "Holocaust theologian" (probably to distance himself from some of the Jewish Holocaust theologians who conclude that Judaism—indeed, the God of Israel Himself—died in the Holocaust along with many of the most faithful Jews), yet there is no doubt that his confrontation with the aftermath of the Holocaust in the early 1960s (when the fact of the Holocaust was only about 16 years in the past) led to his theological awakening. What is most significant, and again courageous, is that this theological awakening was coupled with his discovery of Christian thinkers (most significantly Reinhold Niebuhr's disciple, the late Roy Eckardt), both in person and in their writings, who were also asserting that Christianity's view of Judaism had to be radically rethought after the Holocaust. And, just as Eckardt realized that this Christian rethinking could not be done without dialogue with living Jews, so Greenberg recognized that this Jewish rethinking could not be done without dialogue with living Christians. Jews and Christians clearly need to discover new ways of living together with peace and understanding.

Readers of this book need to appreciate the courage of Greenberg's positive theological engagement with Christianity. Indeed, the usual, and I submit easier, route (both morally and intellectually) taken by Jewish scholars as diverse as the late theologian Eliezer Berkovits and the contemporary Jewish historian Daniel Jonah Goldhagen, has been to lay the full responsibility of the Holocaust upon Christianity, thus making contemporary Christians inescapably guilty for the greatest agony of the Jewish people. Their overt message has been that Jews should avoid Christians and any engagement with Christianity. Their covert message has been that after the Holocaust, Christianity has lost any moral warrant, even for its own survival.

Greenberg's approach to Christianity, which can only be carried on through and with living Christians, has had to overcome traditional Jewish "Christophobia" that thinks Christianity can do nothing but denigrate Judaism and proselytize Jews, and assumes that this usual manifestation of pre-Holocaust European Christianity is still wholly with us. It has had to overcome the widespread Jewish view (recently exacerbated by the controversy over Mel Gibson's film, *The Passion of the Christ*) that anti-Judaism is so essential to Christianity that Christians cannot live their Christianity without it. But because Jewish theologians, like my late revered teacher Abraham Joshua Heschel and Irving Greenberg, have been willing to engage in deep and patient dialogue with Christian thinkers, the vast majority of Christian theology today has been able to rethink Christianity in such a way that contempt of Judaism and overt proselytizing of Jews have been eschewed. Moreover, many of the Christians thinkers who have learned so much from Greenberg, especially from his theological concern with the Holocaust, do not believe they have compromised their Christianity because of him but, rather, their Christianity has been deepened for them by him.

Finally, Greenberg's courage compels him to tell Jews that we need to rethink and revise some of our own negative views of Christianity, views which, to be sure, might very well have been hastily expressed in reaction to earlier Christian persecution of Jews. If Jews are to have something like a covenantal relationship with Christians (a point Greenberg needs to explicate more precisely in the future), then Jews are going to have to recognize that both communities worship the same God, even though we cannot worship God together as one community. Yet, there is a strong strand of Jewish theology that asserts Christians do not worship "our" God. If that is true, then we must conclude that Christians worship a false god (since "our" God is the One God, the Infinite Creator of the universe). To be sure, Greenberg has some support in the tradition for the rejection of this anti-Christian Jewish charge, although it has been deeply debated. So, it would seem that if we are to continue the great benefits the new relationship has brought both the Jewish and the Christian communities, then Greenberg, and those of us who agree with his overall dialogical agenda, will have to be even better prepared to argue this positive commonality, one that eschews triumphalism ("We have all the truth, therefore everything you have is false") and relativism ("Since there is no truth anyway, therefore there is no point in maintaining any differences"). Irving Greenberg has defined the dialogical agenda for many Jews. That is what makes him and this book so important.

David Novak is the J. Richard and Dorothy Shiff Professor of Jewish Studies at the University of Toronto.

# Everlastingly Linked

Michael Novak

The long introductory essay of this book is, alone, worth the book's price; it is one of the most dramatic intellectual autobiographies by a theologian in more than 50 years. How could it not be, when its central subject matter is the *Shoah*, and swirling up from that searing question, another one: How ought Judaism now and into the future regard Christianity? As a description of intellectual passion, "white-hot" is an expression Irving Greenberg uses more than once to describe some of the rare prophetic voices he has encountered during his intense life. At moments, "white-hot" describes his own thoughts as well.

That he has so constantly—after however much struggle, however much pain—turned from hatred to love, from death to life, from despair to energetic action, is a testimony to the rabbi's own great spirit and to the religious depths of the vision that animates him. That is to say, it is a tribute to Judaism itself, for its abundant, life-giving energies. Rabbi Greenberg has asked me to add my own brief reflections to his, even though I have by no means passed through the fires he has. In the flesh, we have barely known one another, but in our writings, we have long shared a certain implicit kinship. I consider his project of reconceiving Christianity from a Jewish point of view of enormous importance to Christians and to the world. None of us has a full view of our own identity until we take account of how we appear in the eyes of others. In the end, we define ourselves from inside out; but what our friends have to tell us, in friendship and in truth, is vital to our own integrity.

I do not share Greenberg's judgment on the Christian Gospels themselves or on the essence of Christianity's vision of Judaism (in the beginning, through the Middle Ages, and today), but I am fortified and invigorated by his views. They give me something to react against, which I very much have wanted—a challenge from a friend who is a serious Jew. Just a few years ago, I suggested tentatively to two or three friends that we should sponsor a book in which Jewish writers put down just what they think of Christianity, now that we have had so much history, pain, and sometimes warm friendship together. They, in turn, suggested that just such a project was already underway (at least one of Irving Greenberg's chapters appeared in the collection).

At a later date, a closer engagement with Greenberg's long arguments in this book will, I know, prove very fruitful for me; but, first, I have to do a lot of study. At present, exigencies of my own schedule allow me only to sketch the outlines of a response. The most useful way to do this is probably to simply set forth my own view of the relation between Judaism and Christianity in a sort of telegraphic form—much too abbreviated, but at least with simplicity and directness.

It seems to me that the relationship is asymmetrical in this sense: Christians, in order to make sense of Christianity, must affirm the truth of Judaism, without whose teachings Christianity is not wholly intelligible. Meanwhile, Jews can be fully faithful Jews without accepting the truth of Christianity at all. I would say that the dependency runs entirely one way, except for one (as it were) external fact: By its dynamic missionary energy, Christianity, today numbering two billion adherents (one-third of the world's population), has brought to the entire world an awareness of the God of Abraham, Isaac, and Jacob that Jews alone (numbering about thirteen million worldwide) could not have spread so far afield. Actually, moreover, the situation for Judaism is weaker than that, since a sizable proportion of these thirteen million Jews say they are not religious.

Still, when Christians meet Jews, even unbelieving Jews, in some special way they meet those to whom Christians are in debt. The Jews brought God to Christians. This is the force behind the thought of Franz Rosenzweig, who held that the mission of Christianity is to bring the God of Judaism to the gentiles. Whatever it is that Christians claim for themselves, including the Christ, they received first from the Jews.

There is another important point. My reading of Jacques Maritain's *The Mystery of Israel* (1941, 1965) brought me to take hold of the fact that God is always faithful to His word, and cannot possibly break a covenant He has entered into. Therefore, His covenant with the Jews remains eternally valid. Furthermore, it is crucial for Christians to understand God's fidelity, for otherwise how could they trust in God themselves? Christians must believe in the continuing validity of the covenant with the Jews if they are to believe in the validity of their own covenant with God.

In one sense of the word, therefore, the Christian faith is not, and cannot be, "supersessionist." It does not, by its own validity, cancel out the earlier validity of God's covenant with his first loved and first chosen people. In another sense, obviously, I believe with all Christians that the second covenant, while not destroying the Jewish law (I avoid here the term "the old law"), "goes beyond" the Jewish law (rather, goes "deeply within" the Jewish law), "adds to" the Jewish law (as in the life of the sacraments), "fulfills" the Jewish law (complementing it with the witness of Christ's life). Jewish friends have told me, kindly, that they think Christianity does this only by becoming unrealistic, open to a kind of perfectionism, or even gnosticism, and the like. They continue to hold to the superiority of the Jewish law over the Christian law. I think they are as wrong in so doing as are we. Rabbi Greenberg has spoken movingly of the depth of a religion that can produce Mother Teresa. He's on the right track. So is the Pontifical Biblical Commission when it writes that Jewish and Christian interpretations of Scripture, even when seeming contradictory, can be, and are, both true in an analogical or parallel sense. It's not an either/or. It is a both/and.

Sometimes, as I say, we learn much about who we are by grasping how others around us regard us and by seeing our place in the world as a whole. In a world two-thirds of which is neither Jewish nor Christian, we who are Jews and Christians are obliged to see—simply by the reactions of others to us—how much we are alike each other, and unlike many around us. We learn of the world outside us that shares little of the vision we Jews and Christians share about the centrality of personal decision, personal freedom vis-a-vis God, and personal responsibility in human history. That world shares little, if at all, of our view of history as a long, wandering, narrative interaction between the Creator and his pilgrim people, and therefore, little of our vision of upward spirals of progress and decline as history moves to its appointed end time. We see that the Creation, put into being by the Creator, is, in His eyes, "good." We see that the history of humanity is meant to see progress. We see that liberty is its central thread and purpose. We see that the Creator has offered us His friendship and called us to walk in the light of His law. We see that human liberty is the bright crimson thread of history, as we sluggish, reasoning creatures come to learn the implications of our own responsibility, little by little.

It can be thought and said—and reflection on our place among all the world's peoples makes this awareness ever more explicit—that Jews and Christians are everlastingly linked in our two covenants with the God of

Abraham, Isaac, Jacob (and, we Christians add, Jesus), and to neither covenant can God be faithless. We are two peoples of one Creator and Father. From another point of view, we might even be thought of as one people of two (complementary but asymmetrical) religions. The distinctness between us must be kept bright and clear, in order to preserve the integrity of each. But the clear links by which destiny—that is, the will and design of God—binds us together must be ever more faithfully and luminously explored.

This is not the place to defend the proposition I mean now to advance, but it needs to be put on the table. Through the ages, Christians have much to repent for in our sins against, and our abuses of, God's first chosen people. Still, it does not seem possible to account for the Holocaust without also factoring in wholly new moral dimensions introduced in modern times by anti-Christian (and anti-Jewish) secularism and modernism. The Enlightenment gave rise to wholly new theories of race and ethnicity, and to primitive doctrines of materialism, genetic reductionism, and the ruthless application of untethered reason to social reconstruction. The "Death of God" that Zarathustra announced, weeping, at the end of the nineteenth century really did mean, for millions of people, that anything is permitted.

The scenes from the death camps that I saw on films as a child in 1944 were burned indelibly into my mind, my emotions, and my memory. As I grew older, I began to collect books on the Holocaust, for it seemed to be, for me, the greatest earthshaking event of the moral-intellectual world of our time. In its light, I felt ashamed for every anti-Semitic act that any Christians, anywhere and at any time, had committed against Jews. But I never believed that Christianity taught or could formally allow any such acts, no matter how badly Christian lay people or churchmen behaved.

I do not in the least blame Jews for learning from their experience with Christians to have a certain spiritual contempt for us. People's beliefs come to be known to others by the actions they take, and bad fruits engender ill judgments; it cannot be otherwise.

But no one can understand the persistent spreading of Christianity, and the continued total commitment of countless young lives to its propagation, at great cost to themselves (often death or imprisonment), without seeing the inner spiritual power of the word of God in such admirable young people. Christians commit themselves to serving life, not death; to building schools and hospitals, universities and clinics, orphanages and homes for the aged, wherever they go.

It must certainly seem to Jews that, in thinking of God as Father, Son, and Holy Spirit—a trinity of persons—we are polytheists, even when we insist that there is only one God. It must certainly seem to Jews that our calling a human being "God" is idolatrous, even gross. It must seem, at least to some

Jews, that our moral code and ways of thinking are not as realistic, not quite as rooted in real things as is Judaism, that they are—far too "spiritual." It must seem to others that our attitude toward those not Christian is tribal, close-ranked, superior, and hostile—for Christians are sometimes observed manifesting such behaviors.

It must also seem to Jews in America, living in a predominantly Christian land, drenched (it must seem) in holidays with Christian feeling and symbolism, that they must always be on guard against the encroachment of Christian ways of putting things, Christian patterns of speech, Christian thoughts—on guard, as a matter of integrity. I can feel, myself, how resistance might become habitual. And suspicion. And a readiness to counterattack.

And yet, and yet, in blessed America, there are wonderful acts of friendship, concelebration, even kinship, mutual admiration, good feeling, trust, and the experience of fighting and dying together on famous battlefields down the years.

In the end, the predicament of Jews and Christians at the beginning of a new century, even a new millennium of the "Common Era," requires each of our communities to try to think well of the other, to work together, to tend ever more assiduously the large, ample, fertile fields in which our intertwined destinies are rooted. Our two communities are not only different, but divided, on radical points. On the whole, though, as this world goes, they have much in common that is precious, deep, and imperishable.

In reading these essays, I have been struck by the great generosity of spirit shown by Irving Greenberg, and the many acts of intellectual courage, in extending a hand of friendship—sometimes with fear and trembling, sometimes with alacrity, sometimes with pain—to the whole Christian community. He has shown bravery in enduring the hostility of his own coreligionists (a common experience in our time, in all communities of belief), even when he thought he was serving the best instincts of that community and its own inner imperatives. He has consistently done his duty, followed the light the Lord has shown him, gone home to think again if he thought he might be wrong, and persisted in the best way he could.

The world needs more faithful Jews like Irving Greenberg and more faithful Christians, not fewer of either. For the faithful ones not only know that they need each other; in one another they often recognize, without knowing how or why, the presence of the same God they both love, and by whom they know themselves to be loved, forevermore.

I thank Irving Greenberg warmly for what he has written, not least for his stern words for Christians, from one who cares to speak to them truly and in friendship. I thank him for being brave and opening up new horizons for both Christians and Jews, separately and together. I share with him the passion of seeing that our destinies are everlastingly linked by God's will, and in God's own mysterious design.

Michael Novak is the George Frederick Jewett Chair in Religion, Philosophy, and Public Policy at the American Enterprise Institute and 1994 winner of the Templeton Prize for Progress in Religion.

The Bold and Gracious Vision of Irving Greenberg

Mary C. Boys

Rabbi Greenberg's essays here represent a major contribution to re-imagining the relationship between Judaism and Christianity and the role each might play in fostering a genuine religious pluralism.

Judaism and Christianity are distinctive in the complexity of their relationship. Amos Funkenstein writes that he knows of "no other two religions tied to each other with such strong mutual bonds of aversion and fascination, attraction and revulsion."[1] For much of their history, aversion and revulsion have dominated. Because from the beginning Christianity had to justify itself vis-à-vis Judaism, much of its self-understanding was by nature "over against" Judaism. Believing Jesus had fulfilled God's promises to Israel, early Christian leaders saw no reason for Judaism's continued existence. Thus, Christianity never developed a theology adequate to explain itself in light of the enduring character of Judaism. Instead, it premised many of its teachings on a caricature of Judaism, and its continuous accusation that Israel had been unfaithful fueled centuries of hostility that were often accompanied by violence.

Only recently have various Christian denominations acknowledged the enduring character of Israel's covenantal relationship with God. This acknowledgment involves, as Greenberg notes, both repentance and regeneration; it also implies an agenda for theology: articulating a self-understanding of Christianity premised on a knowledge of, and deep respect for, Judaism. To argue that Israel's covenantal relationship endures means that everything premised on the previous argument—Christianity has superseded Judaism—

must be rethought. Greenberg recognizes the pioneering work done by Christians such as Roy and Alice Eckardt, Eva Fleischner, Edward Flannery, Franklin Littell, J. Coert Rylersdaam, Paul Van Burern, Ruth Zerner, and John Pawlikowski—friends whose scholarship and commitment to eradicate anti-Judaism have laid the foundation for revising Christian theology.

Readers of Greenberg's essays will learn that he is involved in a similar quest: to contribute, from a Jewish perspective, to "a decisive transformation of both faiths' relationship to each other so that they can never again be a source of hatred toward each other or any other faith community."[2] Making this vision a reality requires educating Jews and Christians in ways that stimulate a deep and learned commitment to their own tradition of faith, while simultaneously inspiring an understanding of the other and participating in the building of a religiously pluralistic society. We might think of this "deep and learned commitment to their own tradition of faith" as "textured particularism," a concept that I have explored in educational settings with Sara S. Lee of Hebrew Union College-Jewish Institute of Religion in Los Angeles. Greenberg's essays illumine our conceptualization.

In our lectures, Lee and I explained that a *textured* particularism is rooted in the rich images, practices, symbols, and stories of one's religious traditions. Such particularism should not, however, be confused with an *impoverished* particularism that is superficial, provincial, and religion-centric, although relatively benign. Likewise, it differs from an *adversarial* particularism that diminishes, caricatures, or even demonizes the other, thereby rightly giving religion a bad name—the sort of particularism that has generally characterized Christianity's relationship to Judaism and other religions of the world.

Greenberg exemplifies the passionate character of a *textured* particularism. His essays reveal the deep, even visceral, connections to his religious tradition and his serious immersion in his community's life, in those symbol-rich moments in which the Divine Presence and the power of the faith community are experienced. They also reveal his capacity to sustain commitment during times when doubt seems to trump faith, particularly when immersion in the horrors of the *Shoah* led him to feel he was "drowning religiously."

At the same time, his profound knowledge of Jewish tradition contributes to a sense of the ways in which his community has fallen short of its vision of God in its hostility (albeit understandable) toward Christianity. The agony of his tensions with the Rabbinical Council of America over his advocacy of an organic relation between Judaism and Christianity is poignant testimony to the personal cost exacted of one whose particularism looks outward and refuses to be restricted by well-worn arguments.

Greenberg's textured particularism does not need to define itself *over against* another tradition—even one too long characterized by a "teaching of contempt" for Judaism. The essay, "Covenantal Partners in a Postmodern World" reconceptutalizes, in detail, how Jews and Christians might understand themselves as partners in the process of redemption, covenanted with a God who, in self-limiting (what the Kabbalah calls *"tzimtzum"*), now asks humans to assume greater responsibility for the world. In reconciling with one another, Jews and Christians serve as models—"two erstwhile antagonists who built their religious claims on the invalidity of the other [and who] now affirm each other's independent dignity as ongoing, legitimate covenantal faiths." Differences are not collapsed; disagreement remains *"l'shem shamayim*—for the sake of heaven—without losing our legitimacy and without being pressured into compromising our integrity." The particularism of both Judaism and Christianity is requisite for a "principled pluralism," lest pluralism be reduced to the lowest common denominator or a naïve relativism.

Religious pluralism flows, in part, from the recognition of the limitations of any given particularism—even of a textured, rich, and passionate particularism such as Greenberg exemplifies. A commitment to religious pluralism flows from the acknowledgment that it is necessary to move beyond the particulars of one's traditions because God alone is infinite and absolute. This is often threatening to one's coreligionists; Roger Haight points to a competitive urge in human beings that spontaneously reckons one's own relationship to God as weakened by the fact that God loves others and deals with them in specific historical ways.

God's infinity implies that the Divine's capacity for relationship with human beings knows no limits. The Infinite God is revealed yet concealed; God is an "elusive presence." Our religious commitments thus always involve the element of mystery. A commitment to religious pluralism, therefore, flows from a desire to expand our understanding of, and relationship to, this God Beyond All Names. Engagement with the religious other is a way to know God's myriad manifestations.

Greenberg writes appreciatively of the ways in which Christianity has brought billions of people to a knowledge of the God of Israel, of the Bible, and of Jewish values, and he expresses the bold hope that we Christians might be considered part of the Family of Israel. My response to his work is one of awe and gratitude: awe at the breadth and depth of his thinking and gratitude for his capacious understanding of Christianity. In his essay "The Respective Roles of the Two Faiths in the Strategy of Redemption," Greenberg defines hope as "a dream that is committed to the discipline of becoming a fact." May the discipline of attentively probing Rabbi Greenberg's eloquent and provocative thinking be a first step in countering the nightmares of our common history. May his readers then respond by committing themselves to partnership in the redemptive process.

Mary C. Boys is a member of the Sisters of the Holy Names of Jesus and Mary, and Skinner and McAlpin Professor of Practical Theology at Union Theological Seminary, New York City. Among the seven books she has authored or edited is Has God Only One Blessing? Judaism as a Source of Christian Self-Understanding.

Notes

1. Amos Funkenstein, *Perceptions of Jewish History* (Berkeley: University of California Press, 1993), p. 170.

2. Roger Haight, *Jesus Symbol of God* (Maryknoll, NY: Orbis, 1999), p. 413.

Response to *For the Sake of Heaven and Earth*

Krister Stendahl

Ever since I first read Irving Greenberg's reflections on the Jewish encounter with Christianity, his grasp and tone, his aims and moves, struck me as gifts and encouragements. I hope it is not presumptious for me to feel a certain congeniality with him across and through our distant traditions. In more recent years, I have come to think that a truly healthy relationship between religions presupposes a capacity to see in the other some things that are beautiful, even and especially things that tell you something about God, but are not part of your own tradition. That is more than tolerance, even more than respect. I call it "holy envy," for it is not yours. It would be cut flowers in your house, so let it stand and grow as you marvel.

Perhaps Greenberg expresses something similar, in a less romantic manner, in his dialectic where Judaism and Christianity *do* need one another as corrective reminders. He describes the role of such a partnership as follows:

> Each partner affirms that its truth/faith/system alone cannot fulfill God's dreams. Each partner recognizes that the world needs the contributions that the other religion can make for the sake of achieving wholeness and perfection for all. A partner affirms (today, I would say: celebrates) that God assigns different roles and contributions to different groups.

Greenberg's "celebration" is akin to my "holy envy." In both cases we let it stand without claiming it in an imperialistic drive to universalism.

There is so much in Greenberg's vision that resonates with me. There is, of course, the way that he takes Christianity seriously, and that at a deeper level of understanding than I have usually encountered in Jewish-Christian dialogue. He does so by a pluralistic vision of the very acts of Redemption and by an understanding of covenants as limiting and limited. Thus, the "other" becomes, by definition, part of God's strategy toward *tikun olam*. He can say about Christianity that it "is not a mere deviation or misunderstanding; it is an organic outgrowth of Judaism itself. . . . Christianity is a divinely inspired attempt to bring the covenant of *tikun olam* to a wider circle of gentiles. God intended that Judaism and Christianity both work for the perfection of the world (the kingdom of God). . . . together, both religions do greater justice to the dialectical tensions of covenant than either religion can do alone."

And what about the Messiah? To Greenberg, Jesus is not a "false messiah," but he is a "failed messiah." Can I leave that without protest, as I say my creed? Or should I take more seriously the point that the kingdom has not come as yet? Is that not why I pray as my Christ taught me: "Thy kingdom come, Thy will be done on earth as it is in heaven . . ."? And I remember that all the words sanctifying our holy meal, the Eucharist, in one way or another "proclaim the Lord's death until He comes." No, to me He is far from a failed messiah, but I still pray with those intense words that my Christian Bible has preserved in the early Jesus-followers' Aramaic: "*Marana tha*—Our Lord come!" (1 Cor. 16: 21), and I do remember that the almost last words in my Bible are: "Amen. Come Lord Jesus!"

Greenberg allows us to follow his thinking as it has evolved over the decades, and it is clear that the response to the *Shoah* is a significant factor in his unmasking of all spiritualizing excuses for action. The rebirth of the State of Israel equally constitutes a quantum leap toward the increased responsibilities that come with independence. But there is more. One of the marks of Rabbinic Judaism has been its trust and joy in the intellectual capacity to interpret the Torah. I am reminded of the passage in the Talmud (B. *Bava Metzi'a* 59b) where Rabbi Joshua quoted Deuteronomy 30:12: "It is not in the heavens!" He did it in order to make clear that interpretation was an intellectual human activity that neither required nor welcomed divine intervention. When the Apostle Paul quotes the same passage, it refers to the word about Christ who has come to earth. The trust in the power of human interpretation is not unique to the rabbis; all holy texts have actually been so treated, but Rabbinic Judaism protected the right of creative interpretations uniquely, as Rabbi Soloveitchik said when he referred to humans as "co-creators of Torah, the divine word." It is this trajectory of human freedom and creativity that Greenberg develops so beautifully. I frequently hear people say that the idea of human rights is not to be found in the Bible—Jewish nor Christian. In a strict sense that is true, but in Greenberg's covenantal perspective, the United Nations' Declaration of Human Rights is, to me, yet another milestone in the drama of redemption, "the infinite Creator's plan to perfect the world for humanity and life." The full dignity implicit in our being created in the image of God is made explicit—at least in words—and with reasonable hopes.

Greenberg's understanding of covenantal freedom and responsibility gives the theological sanction—no, necessity—to keep absolute claims in check. I love his formulation "pluralism—the setting of healthy limits on absolutes, valid or otherwise." Precious is the insight that there must be limits also to *valid* absolute claims. Such limits are implicit in the covenantal structure. There is an analogy between God's limiting his absolute power by respecting human freedom for purpose of a higher perfection and the need for "healthy limits" to even valid absolute claims. It is here that I find the decisive difference between faith and ideology. Greenberg's understanding of covenant also becomes the key to the way God elicits the voluntary cooperation of a humanity that has been given free will. God has limited His absolute power in order to achieve a higher and richer perfection of the relationship. Greenberg's analysis of covenantal freedom and responsibility describes the joint divine human enterprise toward *tikun olam*. Here, he finds a fresh boldness for the acceptance of the increased freedoms that have come with modernity.

Each tradition has its story, its particular way to tell "the story," the story of God and the world. The power of each story is often found in that which is most particular to it. This is one reason why the first rule of religious pluralism is to let each define his or her own tradition. That definition includes how to think about the beliefs of the other. Thus, it is reasonable to anticipate that each religion has an understanding of how it relates to its traditions. For decades, Greenberg has reflected on the encounter between Judaism and Christianity. He now gives us the record which, in the last chapter, intensifies into a call to partnership—and this "for the sake of heaven and earth." I hear the call, including the call to repentance, translated into an urgent duty to unmask and testify against all forms of the Jew-hatred that has disfigured Christianity for centuries, wherever it persists or emerges in new forms and places. There is more. The very vision of the organic and genetic relationship between Judaism and Christianity is historically true and theologically inspired. So deep is the partnership that emerges out of these essays that I feel that I am with him all the way—almost.

When Greenberg comes to speak about "the multibranched people of Israel," I ask myself: Would I say so, or is this his way of telling the story as a Jew tells it? Or when I read "members of the two faith communities remain part of one people, the people of Israel, the people that wrestle with God and humans to bring them closer to each other," I am hauntingly reminded of the way we Christians have claimed to be Israel. To loosen the word "Israel" from its Jewish moorings was the decisive move toward Christian supersessionism, the bane of Jewish-Christian relations. And I wonder if the best way to overcome that invidious construct is by substituting a kind of successionism. Suddenly, I feel it important to be an uncircumcised gentile. An odd solidarity with my fellow gentiles comes over me. As to the gentiles of religions other than my own, a partnership with each of them has its own shape. None is like the other and, to be sure, none like the one with which I began, the partnership of Jews and Christians. It became, and remains, the one to which I feel especially called, by many friendships and 50 years of studies.

Israel's particularism and willingness to accept being a "peculiar people," thus resisting the temptation of universal claims for itself, is what has led me to a biblical understanding of pluralism. This model of religious existence— "to be a light unto the nations"—I found, to my surprise, appears also in the teachings of Jesus in the Sermon on the Mount: "You are the salt of the earth." But who wants the earth to become a salt mine? The only human oneness that fully respects the other is our common humanity in the image of God, prior to any covenant, old or new, Noahide or Abrahamic. Covenants belong to the particular stories. Pluralism is too precious, too hard-won, and as yet too fragile to make any other oneness the overarching one. For my story, the Copernican revolution allows no galaxy to claim the center of the universe, and yet, in our God-willed human limitations, we rejoice in speaking our own language, as when we say that the sun rises and the sun sets. In spite of it all, we do so with full integrity and with feeling. That is what Irving Greenberg has done, beautifully.

Bishop Krister Stendahl is the Andrew W. Mellon Professor of Divinity, Emeritus, The Divinity School, Harvard University and Bishop Emeritus of Stockholm, Sweden.

Notes

1. Amos Funkenstein, *Perceptions of Jewish History* (Berkeley: University of California Press, 1993), p. 170.

2. Roger Haight, *Jesus Symbol of God* (Maryknoll, NY: Orbis, 1999), p. 413.

STUDY GUIDE

INTRODUCTION

The essays in this book were originally published over a period of more than three decades, yet even the earliest ones are remarkably relevant. Indeed, the number of years that have elapsed since the first of these essays appeared presents an intriguing predicament. On the one hand, Rabbi Greenberg's insights—his call for a reimagining of truth, an embrace of the other—seem as needed today as they were when he began exploring them nearly 40 years ago. The essays are prescient, if not prophetic. On the other hand, if the ideas seem novel, it is because we have yet to internalize them. If Rabbi Greenberg's theological solutions are still relevant, then the problems he was addressing four decades ago are still with us.

This study guide was written to help readers delve deeper into Rabbi Greenberg's thinking. It is organized by chapter and includes study questions that facilitate comprehension as well as stimulating personal reflection. With the publication of this volume, we have a new opportunity to heed the calls first put forward by Rabbi Greenberg close to 40 years ago. We have new hope that in the next 40 years we will draw closer to a time when Jews, Christians—indeed, people of all faiths and cultures—will live with dignity and equality: the deserved inheritance of a humanity created in the image of God.

ON THE ROAD TO A NEW ENCOUNTER BETWEEN JUDAISM AND CHRISTIANITY: A PERSONAL JOURNEY

In this introductory essay, Rabbi Greenberg describes how he arrived at his rethinking of Christianity. While these theological innovations may be his most obvious legacy, his methodology is equally instructive. Rabbi Greenberg's life experiences weren't just the *context* for the development of his ideas; they were the *catalysts* of his ideas. His thought references traditional Jewish texts and more recent theological influences, but his real life experience of the world and its citizens are, undoubtedly, his most profound muses.

Study Questions

What experiences led Rabbi Greenberg to consider the Holocaust and the birth of the State of Israel as the touchstones of his theology?

Everyone has a philosophy and/or theology of life, a worldview that orients beliefs, values, and choices. Identify an experience that affected your worldview.

Rabbi Greenberg's realization that Christian anti-Semitism helped establish the conditions for the Holocaust sparked his initial interest in dialogue between Christians and Jews. However, this motive eventually yielded to a genuine appreciation of Christianity. This might be understood as an example of *mitokh she'lo lishmah ba'lishmah*, the Jewish concept that something *not* for the sake of heaven can turn into something *for* the sake of heaven, that a project begun for one reason can eventually take on an even nobler meaning. Identify a situation where you have experienced this process.

COVENANTAL PARTNERS IN A POSTMODERN WORLD

As foreshadowed in its title, this essay is Rabbi Greenberg's most prototypically postmodern work. It is, fundamentally, a historical narrative, but it is more concerned with contributing to a theologically productive future— one in which religious pluralism supports the image of God—than with reconstructing an accurate depiction of the past. This is ideologically motivated history, but it is not bad history. Rather, it recognizes that *all* historical narratives are ideologically biased. Rabbi Greenberg embraces this fact and

268

tries to inject a bias that will help redeem humankind. Theologians and historians are both, first and foremost, storytellers. Rabbi Greenberg is a theologian and a historian, and he is also a master storyteller. This essay is a prescriptive description of Judaism and Christianity's past, a revisionist history that orients us toward a redemptive future.

Study Questions

According to Rabbi Greenberg, what are the three guiding principles of Creation that point us toward ethical behavior?

Rabbi Greenberg suggests that the Resurrection was a real experience, but only for some people. From his theological-historical perspective, the question isn't "Did the resurrection occur?" but "For whom did it occur?" This acknowledges the fact that people experience the world in different ways. Do you think it's better to acknowledge difference and develop a theology accordingly, or look for ways to abolish difference? Is it possible to abolish difference? Is difference good or detrimental?

Rabbi Greenberg suggests that Jews need not consider the theological truth or falsity of Christian doctrines such as the Trinity. Rather, they "need only insist that as open as they were, God did not give them the Christian signal—because God had another mission and purpose for them." Do you agree? Is it ever acceptable to consider the theological truth of another religion's dogmas?

According to Rabbi Greenberg, exile teaches us the importance of being in the world but not totally of the world. What does he mean by this?

THE NEW ENCOUNTER OF JUDAISM AND CHRISTIANITY

According to Rabbi Greenberg, the starting point for the new theological relationship between Judaism and Christianity is the new social relationship between Jews and Christians. With the advent of modernity, insular faith communities gave way to diverse societies. Exposure to people of other faiths undermined many of the negative stereotypes that had encouraged beliefs of theological supremacy, necessitating theological change. This is but another example of Rabbi Greenberg's recognition that ideas have social, cultural, and *experiential* origins.

Study Questions

Even though theologians were not the originators of the new encounter between Jews and Christians, Rabbi Greenberg believes that their contribution is still necessary. Why?

Encounters with people different from oneself—people of other religions, races, sexual orientations—often affect one's beliefs. Identify an instance when your beliefs or worldview was changed after such an encounter.

According to Rabbi Greenberg, our discovery of the Other makes what's precious to other people precious to us. Do you think it should be equally precious? If so, why retain one's own beliefs and values?

What went wrong in the encounter between ancient Jews and the first Christians?

What does Rabbi Greenberg think Christians could learn from Jews? What could Jews learn from Christians? Name two things that you think your faith community can learn from another religion or another denomination within your religion.

NEW REVELATIONS AND NEW PATTERNS

The key to the new relationship between Judaism and Christianity, according to Rabbi Greenberg, is the recognition that the Holocaust and the founding of the State of Israel are "revelational events." This phrase itself points to a new understanding of revelation, one in which divine messages are experienced in historic events. Additionally, whereas revelation is associated with absolutes, revelational events are partial and flawed. Revelation is spiritual; revelational events are infused with secularity. Indeed, one of Rabbi Greenberg's most radical and profound insights is his suggestion that the new revelational events have blurred the lines between the religious and the secular. Rabbi Greenberg's theology challenges religious lines as well. Thus, the Christian interpretation of Jesus' messianic nature is called "Jewish," and the twentieth-century Jewish experience is referred to as "the crucifixion and resurrection . . . of the covenanted people." Rabbi Greenberg's reinterpretation of revelation—the revelational events—reveals a new religious language, one that both subverts and preserves traditional religion.

Study Questions

How would you define revelation?

Rabbi Greenberg suggests that the early Christians acted Jewishly in their interpretation of the Crucifixion and Resurrection. How so?

What did the Holocaust reveal for Christians?

Rabbi Greenberg presents a Christian theological solution *for* Christians when he suggests that recognition of new revelation would be "another case of what the Dogmatic Constitution calls 'clearer understanding ... enjoyed after they had been instructed by the [further] events.' " What do you think of someone outside a religious tradition (in this case a Jew) suggesting theological method for those inside the tradition (in this case Christians)?

TOWARD A NEW ORGANIC MODEL OF THE RELATIONSHIP

Rabbi Greenberg's theology is a conversation with postmodernism. Postmodernism questions the plausibility of truth claims, recognizing that the way people view the world—the way they understand truth—is influenced by their culture and society. Rabbi Greenberg agrees with this presupposition, but does not accept the destructive end to which it is sometimes taken. At once, Rabbi Greenberg rejects all monopolies on truth, embraces all claims to truth, and admits that all truths are at best partial. To have a religiously meaningful life in the postmodern, post-Holocaust age, we must create theological narratives that affirm the religion of others. This is necessary if we are to affirm the life of others, and the affirmation of life is the most profound religious response to the Holocaust.

Study Questions

What, according to Rabbi Greenberg, is the "ultimate test of the validity and the vitality of faith" today? Do you think the measure of a religion's validity can change with time, as this suggests, or is it eternal?

Rabbi Greenberg suggests that Judaism is entering a third stage in its history. What is the primary feature of this stage?

Rabbi Greenberg states that Judaism has never been superseded; yet at the same time he looks for models that accept the faith claims of others. Is this contradictory? Why? Why not?

THE RESPECTIVE ROLES OF THE TWO FAITHS IN THE STRATEGY OF REDEMPTION

"It should be the prayer of believers in this time at least, given the power that humans now have, that one's own group not be the only religion." This sentence is classic Greenberg. It recognizes that different historical moments require different things; it understands the gravity of the current moment—the atomic age; and, while written by a religious person about a religious act, it nonetheless turns religion on its head. By continuing to probe the nature of truth after the Holocaust, Rabbi Greenberg continues formulating a theology that is both deeply traditional and utterly revolutionary.

Study Questions

What, according to Rabbi Greenberg, is the common central message of Judaism and Christianity? What do you think the central message of your religion is?

Rabbi Greenberg defines idolatry as something that makes partial power absolute. Do you agree with this definition? If not, how would you define idolatry? What contemporary phenomena would you classify as idolatry? What can we/you do to check idolatry?

The struggle between universalism and particularism—the pull toward embracing the family of humanity, versus pledging allegiance to a specific community—is a key element of Rabbi Greenberg's thought, just as it is a key element of life in a pluralistic society. Are you more of a universalist or a particularist? To answer this question, it may help to reflect on the January 2004 decision in France to ban religious symbols in public schools. In a sense, the French were pledging allegiance to universalism at the expense of particularism, so your view of this event may reflect your opinion about universalism and particularism.

COVENANTAL PLURALISM

Practicality and reality anchor Rabbi Greenberg's theology, but optimism is its engine. In dreaming of the triumph of life over death, Rabbi Greenberg is at his most messianic. His goal is nothing short of total redemption. Nonetheless, his optimism is controlled. Rabbi Greenberg's own thinking suggests that his theology is but one of many possible truths. The pluralism inherent in Rabbi Greenberg's thought tempers it, making sure that its emotion could never lead to extremism. In addition, Rabbi Greenberg is aware of how his experiences have affected his thought. Rabbi Greenberg acknowledges that the fall of Communism and the prospect of peace in Israel contributed to the extra optimism of "Covenantal Pluralism." This self-consciousness adds a measure of humility that also reins in the potential downsides of extreme optimism. Still, just as his pluralism and pragmatism tame his optimism, his optimism pushes his pluralism and pragmatism to see beyond what is currently practical and true.

Study Questions

What is Rabbi Greenberg's definition of a perfected world? What is yours?

Rabbi Greenberg defines "good" as anything that promotes life and "evil" as anything that promotes death. What is your definition of good and evil?

In an essay published elsewhere, Rabbi Greenberg identifies Rabbi Shimon bar Yohai's dictum, "The best of Gentiles, one should kill," as the "single most terrible text in rabbinic tradition." In light of Rabbi Greenberg's suggestion that " 'Never again' demands the end of *all* contempt traditions," how should Jews treat bar Yohai's statement? Do you think it should be repudiated? Reinterpreted? Deleted from its source? Ignored?

PLURALISM AND PARTNERSHIP

Pluralism is both the cause *and* the effect of the concept of the image of God. The recognition of the image of God in other people brings us to appreciate their humanity and the religion that helped create them, thus leading us to pluralism. At the same time, the concept of the image of God validates pluralism because anything—any religion or culture—that promotes the image of God is, according to Rabbi Greenberg, ethical and valid.

Study Questions

According to Rabbi Greenberg, relativism and fundamentalism are both responses to the modern confrontation with difference. How so?

How would you define the difference between pluralism and relativism?

According to the Rabbinic sage Hillel, a bride should be praised as beautiful and virtuous no matter what she looks like or how she behaves. Rabbi Greenberg cites this is an example of something that may be false but is considered true because it recognizes the image of God. How do you feel about the notion that truths can have false elements?

COVENANTS OF REDEMPTION

Rabbi Greenberg interprets the covenant—the partnership between humans and God—as a model for redemption that stresses both human power and human limitation. This encapsulates the greatness of Rabbi Greenberg's theology: It empowers and contextualizes. Individuals and communities must feel capable of bringing redemption, while recognizing that other individuals and communities are needed to achieve this desired end.

Study Questions

Why is pluralism a necessary response to the Holocaust?

Human cloning and its related research could potentially help cure numerous diseases, yet many politicians and religious leaders object to it. Some believe that the creation of human life should be the domain of God alone. Given Rabbi Greenberg's stress on the balance of human power and human limitation, what do you think he would say about cloning? How do you feel about cloning?

Rabbi Greenberg proposes that Jesus was a failed messiah, not a false one. What's the difference? Do you think Jews can accept this distinction?

In a section added in 2004, Greenberg suggests that, covenantally speaking, Jesus can be seen as an "unfinished messiah." Is this new term more subversive or less subversive of past classifications of Jesus? Is the term "unfinished" a more acceptable or less acceptable description to Jews? To Christians?

Rabbi Greenberg recognizes that non-Abrahamic religions, such as Buddhism, are also "striving to fulfill the universal divine covenant with humanity." Still, he considers only Jews and Christians (and perhaps Muslims)as People of Israel. Do you recognize the validity of all religions? Would you make distinctions between the Judeo-Christian-Islam tradition and others?

Prepared by Daniel Yechiel Septimus